ERRATA

struggles of gods

Papers of the Groningen Work Group for the Study of the History of Religions.
(Edited by H. G. Kippenberg)
Walter de Gruyter & Co., Berlin · New York

---

p. II line 13 from above: instead of **M. Elida** read **M. Eliade**.
p. 17 line 10 from above: instead of **1982** read **1985**.
p. 17 line 15 from above: instead of **them** read **theme**.
p. 17 line 17 from above: instead of **leucidated** read **elucidated**.
p. 23 line 28 from above: after Kuhgewinnung read **:**.
p. 31 line 10 from above: instead of **1983** read **1985**.
p. 31 line 23 from above: instead of **1983** read **1985**.
p. 32 line 21 from above: instead of **1983** read **1985**.
p. 33 line 18 from above: instead of **1983** read **1985**.
p. 34 line 6 from above: instead of **1983** read **1985**.
p. 36 line 6 from above: instead of **1984** read **1985**.
p. 37 line 3 from above: instead of **1983** read **1985**.
p. 54 line 30 from above: instead of **respores** read **restores**.
p. 61 line 36 from above: instead of **1983** read **1985**.
p. 62 line 15 from above: instead of **1984** read **1985**.
p. 156 line 23 from above: instead of **kepe** read **kept**.
p. 156 line 25 from above: instead of **death** read **dead**.

Struggles of Gods

Religion and Reason 31

Method and Theory in the Study and Interpretation of Religion

MOUTON PUBLISHERS · BERLIN · NEW YORK · AMSTERDAM

Struggles of Gods

Papers of the Groningen Work Group for the Study of the History of Religions

Edited by
H. G. Kippenberg
in association with H. J. W. Drijvers
and Y. Kuiper

MOUTON PUBLISHERS · BERLIN · NEW YORK · AMSTERDAM

Library of Congress Cataloging in Publication Data

Main entry under title:

Struggles of gods.

(Religion and Reason; 31)
Includes index.
1. Religion--Addresses, essays, lectures. 2. Religions--Addresses, essays, lectures. 3. Mythology--Addresses, essays, lectures. I. Kippenberg, Hans G. (Hans Gerhard) II. Drijvers, H. J. W. III. Kuiper, Y. IV. Groningen Work Group for the Study of the History of Religions. V. Series: Religion and Reason (Mouton (Firm)) ; 31
BL50.S77 1984 291 84-11501
ISBN 90-279-3460-6

 — Printing: Druckerei Hildebrand, Berlin. — Binding: Dieter Mikolai, Berlin. Printed in Germany.

Table of Contents

Drawing after the impression of an Akkadian cylinder seal of about 2500 B.C., discovered in the town of Eshnunna, the present Tell Asmar, about fifty miles to the north-east of Baghdad. The cylinder was found in the temple consecrated to the god of fertility. It represents two gods with horned caps attacking a seven-headed hydra. Four of the heads hang already limp to death, while three are still raised to strike in defence. From its back long lambent flames arise. In their upraised hand the two gods both hold a spear, pointed at the hydra. Behind the god facing the hydra is a bare headed figure, and another figure, also bareheaded, but smaller. Above this figure is a star. The hydra should be regarded as a monster with evil purposes which was vanquished by the god of fertility who was exposed to the dangerous encounter with the monster. Based on: Frankfort, H., Gods and Myths on Sargonid Seals. Iraq, Vol.1 (1934), p. 2-29.

Introduction: Symbols of Conflicts

H. G. Kippenberg

> "Die Erfahrung von der Irrationalität der Welt war ja die treibende Kraft aller Religionsentwicklung" (M. Weber) (1)

The Groningen Work Group for the Study of Fundamental Problems and Methods in the Science of Religion published in 1973 its first volume 'Religion, Culture and Methodology', edited by Th.P. van Baaren and H.J.W. Drijvers. It dealt especially with the problem of reducing subjectivism in the study of comparative religion. It suggested as a solution that religion should be considered as a cultural phenomenon, that the methods of social anthropology should be applied to it. This program should assure a less biased interpretation of non-Christian religions than phenomenology was able to give. Th. van Baaren criticized this method used by G. van der Leeuw and other historians of religion, as unscientific. He wrote: "Science of religion as a systematic discipline is based on the material collected by history, sociology, anthropology, psychology, etc. and tries to classify these materials systematically, to understand and to explain them. Van der Leeuw and others state, that this discipline only aims at finding relations which can be understood intuitively, but this science of religion is fettered by an intuitive method, the heuristic value of which may be great, but the results of which cannot be verified" (2).

The Groningen Work Group stuck and sticks to this criticism of any intuitive approach. But its members soon had to envisage the no less serious problem of the interpretation of other cultures. How can we compare cultures at all ? We are told that the famous English social anthropologist E.E.Evans-Pritchard said in one of his lectures: "there is only one method in social anthropology, the comparative method - and that is impossible " (3). Ironically, Evans-Pritchard's own work helped to prove the contrary. Nevertheless his remark points to the intricacy of the problem. It is easier to argue that the religion of other cultures cannot be explained merely as the expression of a universal religious experience than to demonstrate positively how other cultures should be described. The translation of cultures is our central problem.

The Groningen Work Group therefore proceeded to this intricate problem of interpreting other cultures. There are roughly speaking two different concepts of cultures: additive and integrative. One can define cultures as "all that is learned". Then religion has to be studied in connection with other functions of culture such as social order, art, economics, law, etc. (So Th. van Baaren in our first volume). Or one can define culture as a model of and for reality. Then religion has to be studied as a concept of order and disorder, structure and anti-structure, legitimacy and illegitimacy. The meetings of the Work Group from 1978 to 1982 discussed especially the second definition and the research strategies related to it. Of course the two main approaches, structuralism (e.g. C.Levi-Strauss) and symbolic anthropology (e.g. C. Geertz) were advocated by members of the group. But they controlled the theories by means of the ethnographical and historical materials provided by the fields in which they are specialists. This led to intense discussion, that influenced the final version of the articles.

In this discussion there also took part several scholars who did not contribute to the published volume: V. Arnoldus-Schröder, H. Bakker, P. Hofstede and K. Jenner.

Th. van Baaren proposed that future discussions should be focussed on the theme 'Struggles (and Alliances) of Gods'. this line of approach turned to be extremely fertile, leading the Group so to say to the borderline of cultural order, where even gods must take pains to maintain order. The gods become necessary because human power fails. Culture apparently can only fulfil its task of integration if the disintegrated elements are explained. One can study culture as a model of reality by studying the disorder out of which it arose. Only superhuman powers can abolish evil and establish order. The Work Group initially also dealt with the alliances of gods, but later restricted itself to the struggles between gods.

The gods' defence of order against threatening chaos reflects a characteristic feature of pre-modern cultures. While modern civilization perceives unexpected events (anomalies) as a challenge to its knowledge and ability, pre-modern cultures accept such anomalies as independent reality. Anomalies are impure, not a refutation of human theories (4). Pre-modern cultures ignore the typical European reasoning that God - if there is one - must be responsible for the world as a whole and therefore must be called to account for its condition. This trial logically results in the passing of the sentence: "God is dead". The world-view of pre-modern civilizations makes anomalies into a separate category of phenomena. Thus an elementary form of 'dualism' is an essential characteristic of traditional culture. It answers people's intellectual needs without relying upon human knowledge and ability.

In his already classical article 'Religion as a Cultural System' C. Geertz described this problem as follows: "The

Problem of Meaning .. is a matter of affirming, or at least recognizing, the inescapability of ignorance, pain and injustice on the human plane while simultaneously denying that these irrationalities are characteristic of the world as a whole" (5). The same idea had already been expressed by M. Weber: the 'explanation' of *irrationalities* was basic to the history of religions. Only if religions succeeded in doing this, could culture function as a model of reality. The Groningen Work Group did not develop any new theories, but simply applied well-known ideas to historical and ethnographical materials and traced its chosen theme in different religious traditions. But we expect the results of this research to affect the theoretical presuppositions. I mention one important repercussion. M. Weber and c. Geertz defined irrationality in terms of general universal threats to human existence. But most of the articles that follow will show the gods struggling against contingent irrationalities arising from specific experiences. This finding may be accidental. But it is also possible that it points to a need to reformulate the theoretical issues. Meaning and its opposite:irrationality are not only anthropological, but also political categories.

Once we leave the general subject of irrationality and proceed to the interpretation of specific religions, we must take into account certain further aspects of the problem. I would describe these as follows:

1) there existed typical images of conflict
2) these images functioned as symbols representing experiences
3) these symbols were sustained by different institutions.

The *images of conflict* are elemental: two men fighting ; the hero combatting the dragon ; the rebellion of a woman against male predominance ; a wicked tyrant attacking a holy man.

Often several of these images are superimposed. Evidently they were intended to generate emotions not sober reasoning. Nevertheless most religions felt the need to elaborate these images systematically, placing the adverse principles in an apocalyptical or cosmological framework. This could result in a dualism (as in Indian religion, Gnosticism, Manichaeism and Catharism). In other cases as for example in Egypt and Mesopotamia, it resulted in an internal opposition within a pantheon, or in angels posing a threat to monotheism (Islam).

These images were used by believers as explanation of irrational events and represented these experiences. The content of these experiences differed basically in different religions. The irrational was not perceived - even by Gnostics - as abstract conditio humana. The wicked adversary remained obvious, identifiable, responsible. He was a representative of evil powers appearing in every day life: the aboriginals resisting conquest (India); persecution of the true believers (Manichees and Shi'ites); sexuality, war and property-rights (Manichees); rival revelations (early Islam); imminent subjection by alien powers (Cathars); class struggle (Nias). World-views related to specific experience were able to recruit believers with specific social interests. If world-views remained vague they lacked such adherents.

The last aspect of our investigation concerns the institutions that embody these symbols of conflict. The symbols could function as ideas of intellectuals (as in Mesopotamia), but they could also be part of an official ritual of reversal (as in Iranian Shi'ism). V. Turner's findings that these rituals often reanimate communitas by emphasizing humility are of great interest for our subject. They elucidate not only the rituals of reversal, but also the symbols of conflict in general. In V. Turner's terms they form an anti-structure. Besides this rituals there existed other forms of performance. The Manichaean and Cathar ascetics wandered about without abode and thus demonstrated the otherness of the divine in this world of darkness and death. In other cases demoniac powers functioned as popular explanations for sickness (in for example Islamic cultures).

The struggles of gods and heros against evil reflect efforts to create culture and to maintain it. The struggles of gods indicate the crisis of cultural orders: that seems to be the formula for our subject.

Finally the whole Work Group expresses its thanks to mrs. Joke Steg, who typed the camera ready copy with care and patience. We also thank Dick Ronner for preparing the index and mrs. Frouke Veenstra for taking care of the illustrations of this volume.

NOTES

1. Soziologie *Weltgeschichtliche Analysen * Politik, Stuttgart, 1968 p. 178.
2. Van Baaren, Th. - Drijvers, H.J.W. (eds.): Religion, culture, and methodology. In: Religion and Reason 8, The Hague/Paris, 1973 p.45.
3. Transmitted by Needham, R.: Polythetic classification: Convergence and consequences. In: Man 10, 1975 p.349-369, on p.365.
4. MacIntyre, A. - Ricoeur, P.: The religious significance of atheism, New York/London, 1969 p.10.
5. In:Banton, M. (ed.), Anthropological approaches to the study of religion, London, 1966 p.1-46, on p.24; for discussion of this article look Talad Asad: Anthropological conceptions of religion: Reflections on Geertz. In: Man 18, 1983 p. 237-259.

A Few Essential Remarks Concerning Positive and Negative Relations between Gods

Th. van Baaren

If religion is a function of culture, then the mutual relations of gods, spirits etc. will also reflect those of men, individually as well as collectively. This subject gains a special interest when we examine in how far the relations between gods are analogous with those between humans in their social and political situation. A further question is how to explain possible divergences between divine and human relationships.

Whether personal relations between gods can exist that do not conform to the rules of the culture in question and that have no parallel in its human relationships is to be doubted, and is a matter I shall not enter into. The same applies to relations of friendship, love and so on and the corresponding conflicts which may also arise among humans, which depend upon a certain measure of personal liberty of choice existing in the culture concerned. This free space may be small, but probably it is nowhere entirely lacking and in a number of cultures it is fairly large. In the first instance then we have three possibilities left:

1. The relations between the gods etc. are analogous with the social reality existing at that moment.
2. The relations reflect a reality that belongs to the past for the society concerned.
3. They form an analogy with relations not (yet) existing in that society, but which are desired or feared as conceptions of the future or possibly as eschatological ideas.

If we consider the nature of the relationships, again

disregarding those that are personal, we can distinguish three groups:

1. Relations of kindredship.
2. Hierarchical relations.
3. Functional relations.

The first two groups of relationships are at once obvious although it remains uncertain in how far the kindred relations should perhaps be subsumed in the hierarchical relation. The functional relations include e.g. the classification of gods in professional groups and divine specialists and the phenomenon of the bureaucratisation of the Chinese pantheon.

The kind of relations existing between phenomena of nature I have not mentioned separately, since in religious thought these are subsumed in the relational forms of the above three schemes.

Whether the mutual relations between the gods etc. are by analogy with those existing among humans in the present or the past is a matter of interest for religious history, but is otherwise irrelevant. If, however, it is a matter of conceptions concerning the future, then it is not actual relationships which are projected upon the world of the gods but imaginary ones.

So far I have made a schematic summary of what is general knowledge, but there is another point of view which in my opinion forms the crux of this complex of problems and which entails a fundamental change in the manner of posing the problem. Not only are actually existing social relations as well as relations only existing in human imagination projected upon the world of the gods, but we can also pose the following question - which will probably have to be answered in the affirmative - : must we not take into account that both the world of the gods and the human world are expressions of a more comprehensive - indeed an all-comprehensive - structural concept of the world ? This introduces an outlook which differs in principle from the former, since this supposed structure would constitute the basis of both worlds.

In the relationships referred to at first men shape the world of the gods after their own world - with or without more or less idealazation - but as religious consciousness experiences the relationship as having come about in the contrary sense men must strain to make their world proceed in obedience to and in harmony with that of the gods.

In the new situation suggested above the cornerstone is formed by the general conception of the constitution of the world, and it is from this conception that both the ordering of the world of the gods and the human world must be derived. Even though we are convinced that the structural concept referred to above is also a result of human thinking, yet the central and fundamental position of this general concept of the structure of the world affords us a new point of view that in a number of cases may perhaps offer a more satisfactory solution than the assumption of a direct parallel between the world of the gods and the world of men.

Perhaps we find a suitable illustration of this matter in the conceptions of the Dogon concerning creation. Although the Dogon work with an extensive system of correspondences between the human world and the cosmos, a more or less orthodox applying of Durkheim does not take us very far. It is really of little moment whether Griaule and his school convey the communis opinio of the Dogon or only the conceptions of a small select group, for in practically every culture we find distinct differences between persons who are well-informed as to the ideational structure of their own religion, and may enrich it, and a majority of persons whose religious knowledge is marginal, as they are passive in this matter and even to some extent ignorant. For our knowledge of the basic world view and the 'theological' notions of a religion we depend in the first place upon the smaller group first referred to.

Especially in the myths of creation and other myths of primeval times structural cosmic conceptions will often play a greater part than social projections, although the latter will probably not be entirely lacking.

The attempts to discover historical reminiscences and social projections in the Egyptian myth of Osiris have not met with much success, and perhaps here too it would be better to start with a definite structure that has undergone a few transformations. The content of the Osirian myth is too well-known to require repetition.

We begin with a harmonic all-sided symmetry:

OSIRIS + ISIS
+ + +
SETH + NEPHTHYS

The murder of Osiris by Seth breaks up the pristine harmony and causes a disharmonic relationship:

Seth ⟷ ISIS + NEPHTHYS
+
HORUS

After the conflict has been ended, harmony is restored in a new form:

HORUS + ISIS
+ + +
SETH + NEPHTHYS

For the present short introduction of general orientation this single example may suffice.

There are various well-known examples of conflict between two groups of gods: the devas and asuras in India, the old and the new gods in Mesopotamia, the titans and the olympic gods in Greece, the aesir and the vanir in Scandinavia. It seems obvious to regard this as the reflection of a conflict between two peoples, two cultures one of which conquered the other. This may very well be so, but I cannot agree to take the historical explanation for granted, though willing to listen to convincing arguments on this point.

I end therefore with the question: might it not be profitable to apply structuralist methods or new developments thereof (for structuralism too is only an intermediate phase) to these problems (as indeed has in part already been done) and might we not then see familiar examples which until now have usually been given an exclusively historical etc. explanation appear in a new light by means of these new methods ?

Tvastar. Some Reflections on the History of an Ancient Indian God

L. P. van den Bosch

1. INTRODUCTION

One of the most important themes in the Vedic mythology is the battle between Indra and Vṛtra. In many stanzas of the ṚV. the poets praise Indra for the greatest of his deeds, the slaying of Vṛtra, the demon of 'obstruction', who threatened the progress of life. In the epithet *vṛtrahan*, 'slayer of Vṛtra', which is most characteristic of Indra (e.g. Macdonell, 1897 p. 60), this exploit is referred to and it constitutes as it were Indra's mythological essence (e.g. Gonda, 1960 p.55). The fact that not a complete version of this myth is found in the RV. is one of the main problems for its interpretation (O'Flaherty, 1975 p.56). In many scattered fragments the bards eulogize the greatness of the god's deeds. The imagery which they use to describe the victory of Indra is coloured by their own experiences. As such it depends on time, place and situation. In many hymns Vṛtra is represented as a serpent or a dragon, who encloses the waters and imprisons them in the mountains. With the thunderbolt forged by Tvaṣṭar Indra shatters the dragon and releases the waters (e.g. Macdonell, 1897 p.54-56).

Some scholars have given a naturalistic interpretation of this myth, because many expressions suggest a close association with natural phenomena (Oldenberg, 1970 p.138 ff.; Hillebrandt, 1965, II p.175 ff. According to them it was originally a 'Gewitter-mythos'. In more recent studies this view is qualified as one-sided (e.g. Gonda, 1978 p.56 with notes). Vṛtra is not a cloud, nor a dragon, nor simply the demon of drought; the mountains in the myth cannot be regarded as the clouds, nor the rivers as streams of rain. In the poetic imagery also many allusions are made to the conquest of the enemies of the Aryans and the renewing of the cosmic order (e.g. Brown, 1942 p. 85 ff.). All these various aspects should be involved in the interpretation. This has led to the opinion that the battle between Indra and Vṛtra should be regarded as a myth which relates how Indra again brought order to a world which was threatened by Vṛtra. With the slaying of this chaos monster heaven and earth are extended and fixed again.

In the ancient Vedic texts no information is found on the origin of Vṛtra, true as it may be that his mother is called Dānu see Nobel, 1957 p.49). In the brāhmaṇas (1), however, the myth is related with more details, although intermingled with many ritualistic motifs. According to these texts, Tvaṣṭar created Vṛtra in order to destroy Indra (e.g. Varenne, 1967 p. 91ff.; Keith, 1914 p. 185 f. and p.188 with note 4; see also Gonda, 1974 p. 381 ff. with references to the varous versions of the myth in the brāhmaṇas). In this version of the myth the god Tvaṣṭar has an important place and he takes action against Indra who has killed Viśvarūpa, i.e. 'he who contains all forms', a son of Tvaṣṭar born from his marriage with a sister of the Asuras, the demons. This Viśvarūpa is described as a creature with three heads and six eyes who consumed with his three mouths respectively soma, surā (2) and all other kinds of foods. According to some versions he is the domestic priest of the gods, but he also maintains secret relations with the Asuras and promises them a share in the sacrifice. Because of this double role Indra is scared of him and he fears that he might lose his royal might. He hurls his thunderbolt at Viśvarūpa and cuts off his three heads. Tvaṣṭar learns of the affair, is angry and excludes Indra from the consumption of the draught of immortality, the _soma._ Without being invited Indra disturbs the sacrifice, seizes the cup with the sacred _soma_ and drinks from it. Tvaṣṭar becomes furious, snatches the cup back and throws the remains of the beverage upon the sacrificial fire. By this act the sacrifice is desecrated. From the remains of the _soma_ thrown upon the sacrificial fire the demon Vṛtra arises and Tvaṣṭar speaks to him the words: 'Grow, having Indra for thy foe'(3). Because the god makes a fault in the pronunciation of his curse, stressing in his fury the wrong term, his proper intention, viz. 'foe of Indra, grow', is not adequately formulated. This is the reason that Indra can gain the victory over Vṛtra. The demon, however, grows and envelops all the worlds and he devours all the food. Indra needs the help of the two main sacrificial deities, Agni and Soma, to kill the chaos monster, but these two, although desecrated, constitute his essence. He succeeds in persuading them to desert Vṛtra and to choose his party. He promises them a reward and they leave Vṛtra to reinforce the party of Indra (cf. also Brown, 1974 p.57 ff.). With the help of these Indra slays Vṛtra.

It cannot be the place here to deal extensively with all the versions of the Indra-Vṛtra battle according to the _brāhmaṇas_, but some observations may be formulated on the basis of the condensed version related above. The ancient myth is placed within a ritualistic context. Viśvarūpa is described as a domestic priest with malevolent characteristics, Indra is excluded by Tvaṣṭar from the sacrifice and the _soma_, Vṛtra is created by Tvaṣṭar by throwing in fury _soma_ upon the sacrificial fire. Indra can gain the victory over Vṛtra, because Tvaṣṭar pronounced his curse with wrong accents. The transition of the sacrificial deities Agni and Soma to Indra is essential for his victory. The great opponent of Indra in the background of these priestly ritualistic versions is virtually the god Tvaṣṭar, who creates the chaos monster. This same Tvaṣṭar however, is in the Ṛ̣V. also described as the god who has forged the thunderbolt (vajra) with which Indra smashed Vṛtra. In many passages he is regarded as the artisan of the gods and this idea is also expressed in his name, an agent noun denoting 'fashioner' or 'artificer'; cf. Mayrhofer, 1956 p.538; 1964 p. 141 ff.; 1976 p.728.

In the ṚV. Tvaṣṭar has only a subordinate role if one chooses statistic criteria. He is mentioned about 65 times in scattered stanzas, but not one hymn is dedicated to him; Macdonell, 1897 p.116. His important place in the brāhmaṇas, therefore, cannot be explained if his role was not much more crucial than these scattered references suggest. The learned authors of the brāhmaṇas must have had their reasons to designate Tvaṣṭar as the adversary of Indra. They mention that Indra has committed brahmicide by killing Viśvarūpa and in consequence of this he is punished by Tvaṣṭar who denies him admittance to the soma sacrifice. Indra violates the sacrifice and steals the cup with soma. According to some versions the sacred beverage does not agree with him and he becomes very sick (4). Mostly, however, Tvaṣṭar interferes without delay and in fury creates Vṛtra from the remainders of the soma. Because he makes some ritual faults he loses his advantage and Indra gains the victory in the end. For this victory the warrior god needs the help of the two sacrificial deities, Agni and Soma. The brāhmaṇas stress the importance of the priestly class and the correct performance of the ritual as essential for the success of the gods.

In this paper an attempt is made to deal with some of the major themes relating to the god Tvaṣṭar in the ṚV. This may also be relevant to explain his place in the Indra-Vṛtra myth according to the brāhmaṇas. In par. 2 the opinions of the most important scholars in the field of Vedic mythology about Tvaṣṭar are summarized. In par. 3 I shall deal with some problems concerning the dating of the various traditions with reference to each other. In the light of these reflections the different view-points will be evaluated in par. 4. Because Tvaṣṭar has the central place in the Āprī hymns I shall investigate in par. 5 his main characteristics in these stanzas which have their origin in a family sacrifice; cf. Van den Bosch, 1981 en 1982; in the following paragraphs I shall deal in outline with the relations between Tvaṣṭar and Savitar (6), Tvaṣṭar and the sacrificial gods, Agni and Soma(7), Tvaṣṭar and Indra (8), Indra and Viśvarūpa (9), Tvaṣṭar and Dadhyañc (10) and Tvaṣṭar and the Ṛbhus (11). In par. 12 I shall discuss the them of Tvaṣṭar as fashioner of Indra's thunderbolt. In the description of these themes the development in the drama with Tvaṣṭar as leading person will be leucidated. In par. 13 I shall deal somewhat more extensively with the ideas of Bergaigne who regards Tvaṣṭar as the main representative of a unitarian conception of the world and constrast him with Indra in whose mythology the dualistic conception becomes manifest. Par. 14 contains concluding remarks.

2. THE VARIOUS INTERPRETATIONS OF TVAṢṬAR IN WESTERN LITERATURE

In his survey of the Vedic mythology Macdonell (1897 p.115-118) deals with the god Tvaṣṭar under the subdivision 'abstract gods'. He reckons him among that category of gods whose name has originally been an agent noun. These nouns were according to the author originally applied as epithets to one or more gods to illustrate a specific aspect of his (their) activities or character. In the course of time some of these epithets attained an independent position and became the names of certain gods. In this context he mentions the name of Tvaṣṭar, who does not have a prominent position as I have mentioned above. Macdonell gives an enumeration of the most important data which are found in the texts. He does not attempt to place these in a plain framework and confines himself to the observation that the name is derived from the rare root tvakṣ-; its meaning, therefore, seems to be 'Fashioner' or 'Artificer'. To excuse his poor treatment he remarks that the god Tvaṣṭar is one of the obscurest members of the Vedic pantheon. This obscurity may be explained by the fact that Tvaṣṭar, like Trita and others, has belonged to an earlier race of gods who were ousted by later ones. Notwithstanding this obscurity he gives an enumeration of the various viewpoints with reference to the original character of this god and he concludes:

> 'It does not indeed seem unlikely that this god, in a period anterior to the Ṛgveda, represented the creative aspect of the sun's nature. If such was the case the Ṛgvedic poets themselves were only dimly conscious of it. The name itself would have encouraged the growth of mythical accreations illustrative of creative skill, the desire to supply the pantheon with a regular divine artificer being natural enough' (p.117).

Macdonell takes with his opinion a position which stands midway between the view of Hillebrandt (1929,II p.372-385) and Oldenberg (1894;1917 p.237-240). Just like Macdonell, Hillebrandt points to the problematic character of Tvaṣṭar and he supposes that the god is derived from a mythical cycle outside the range of the Vedic tribes which did not pay much attention to the mythology concerning of him. The current explanation which is given in imitation of the Indian lexicographers, viz. as 'Werkmeister der Götter' (Hillebrandt, 1929 II p.373), does not satisfy him. He tries to interpret the fragments of this whole complex of myths with the help of the 'naturalistic' theories of his day, but the results are not impressive, as he admits himself.

> 'Das Fazit dieser Untersuchungen ist nicht gross. Es ist möglich dass Tvaṣṭar ein Sonnengott war. Die späteren Texte und Lexicographen haben ihn als solchen betrachtet'. (Hillebrandt, 1929,II p.384).

Oldenberg rejects the opinion of Hillebrandt on Tvaṣṭar, He regards him as a personification of creative activity.

> 'Den Typus eines Gottes, bei dem eine bestimmte, für ihn characteristische Art und Sphäre der Tätigkeit den Rahmen abgibt - einen Rahmen, in dessen vergleichsweise abstracten Umkreis dann natürlich auch andere, vielleicht 'ältere' Materialien, als jener Rahmen selbst ist, sich einfügen können - finde ich auch in dem Gott Tvaṣṭar. Sein Name, von derselben grammatischen Bildung wie Śavitar, scheint etwa wie den 'rührigen Wirker' zu bedeuten. Tvaṣṭar (rūpa), der selbst allgestaltig (viśvarūpa) mit Form alle Wesen geschmückt hat'. (Oldenberg,1917 p.237 f.).

Within this context the various stanzas relating to the god Tvaṣṭar are placed and interpreted.

Keith (1925, p.203-206) gives Tvaṣṭar a place in his chapter on 'Abstract deities and Sondergötter'. He regrets that there is not a term which can be used to describe those gods, who do not rest on the basis of some natural phenomenon or some activity which takes place in external nature, without conveying the false impression which is created by adoption of the current term 'abstract'. He objects to the opinion that in such a case one can speak of hieratical speculation. He points to the fact that these kinds of deification were current in the Indo-Iranian period. When he develops his ideas on these 'abstact' deities, he makes a distinction between those gods who have a well-defined function expressed in their names, and those gods who have surmounted the level of their specialization and have become creator gods and universal gods. Of this last group he remarks:

'In the Veda all of them seem to be traceable to epithets

> of other gods regarded as creators and universal lords, which have been chosen to be the designation of the supreme lord, to the concept of whom the religious and philosophic impulses of the Vedic poets inclined'. (Keith,1925 p.204).

The god Tvaṣṭar, however, is not reckoned among this last group, but he considers him to be an agent god, who has come into separate existence from being first and merely an epithet of a more concrete deity. It is not mentioned who this last god might be. Keith shares the opinion of Oldenberg that Tvaṣṭar is the personification of creative activity.

The authors I have mentioned above do not make a clear stand in their publications against the view of Bergaigne (1878,I p.XIX f.;1883,III p.38-65) concerning Tvaṣṭar in his impressive study on the religion of the Ṛgveda. Although his exegetic opinions with reference to many stanzas have become obsolete, it should be added immediately that his all-embracing approach is interesting and deserves attention. Bergaigne considers Savitar and Tvaṣṭar as two gods who originally formed a coherent whole. In his introduction to the first volume he reckons Savitar-Tvaṣṭar among the sovereign gods and he contrasts them with Indra.

> 'C'est au contraire une opposition essentielle de nature et d'attributs que nous aurons à révéler entre Indra d'une part, et les dieux tels que Parjanya, Rudra, Savitar-Tvaṣṭar, les Ādityas de l'autre. Pour marquer cette opposition avec le dieu guerrier, je les appellerai, faute d'une autre terme, dieux souverains, parce qu'ils règnent sans conteste sur ce monde où Indra ne manifest sa puissance que par des victoires qu'il doit renouveler sans cesse'. (Bergaigne, 1878, I p. XIX).

Among the sovereign gods the father gods form a subcategory. All those gods who are connected with fatherhood are assigned to this subcategory. In this respect they differ from gods like Indra who has no children and who is only called a father in a metaphorical sense. These father gods are conceived as owners of the heavenly treasures. Bergaigne observes that they have ambivalent characteristics. As producers of the fire and the soma, the sacred intoxicant, as 'fathers' of Agni and Soma, they can be benevolent and give the heavenly treasures to mankind, but they also can claim these goods for themselves. Śavitar-Tvaṣṭar belongs to this subcategory. Bergaigne connects the sovereign gods with a unitarian conception of the world:

> 'Toutes ces divinités appartiennent à une conception unitaire de l'ordre du monde dans laquelle le bien et le mal, c'est à dire le jour et la nuit, la pluie et la sécheresse, sont rapportés à un seul et même personnage ou à une seule et même catégorie de personnages célestes. Il en résulte qu'elles ont un double aspect, propice et sévère, un caractère equivoque qui, par opposition au caractère exclusivement bienveillant d'Indra, peut s'accuser dans le sens malveillant jusqu'à les assimiler, dans une certaine mesure, aux démons de la conception dualiste'. (Bergaigne,1878,I p.XIX).

He connects the warrior god Indra fighting against the demons with a dualist conception of the world.

> 'Cette conception est dualiste. Le bien, c'est à dire dans l'ordre physique, la lumière et la pluie, et le mal, c'est à dire les ténèbres et la sécheresse, y sont rapportés à deux ordres de puissances opposés. D'Indra, du dieu,les hommes n'attendent que le bien. Le mal est tout entier l'oeuvre des démons, c'est à dire des Paṇis, de Śuṣṇa, de Vala et du plus célèbre de tous, Vṛtra, consideré surtout comme le voleur des eaux....;par sa victoire, il (i.e. Indra) délivre les aurores et les eaux, il rend aux hommes la lumière et la pluie'. (Bergaigne, 1878,I p.XVII).

Because the sovereign gods do not have the demons as their opponents, they themselves incorporate demonic characteristics. They are responsible for the evil in this world and this evil is identified with darkness and drought in the order of natural phenomena. It is not possible for Bergaigne to give an answer to the question how Indra as an exponent of the dualist conception of the world is related to the sovereign gods, who are exponents of the unitarian conception.

'Nous verrons bien le dieu geurrier Indra entrer en lutte avec les dieux souverains, dont il est d'ailleurs quelquefois nommé le fils ainsi que Agni et Soma, les vaincre, et se substituer à eux dans le gouvernement du monde. Mais ce mythe qui s'explique naturellement par l'assimilation partielle et passagère des dieux souverains aux démons, s'il consacre l'antériorité mythique de ces même dieux sur Indra, ne saurait passer pour une preuve de leur antériorité historique, je veux dire d'une antiquité plus haute de la conception réligieuse à laquelle ils appartiennent'. (Bergaigne, 1883,III p.4).

After these general observations on 'les dieux souverains et les dieux pères' now more about Tvaṣṭar. Bergaigne connects Tvaṣṭar with Savitar on account of the fact that there are three stanzas in which the term savitar is used as an apposition to Tvaṣṭar (5). He is of the opinion that this Savitar-Tvaṣṭar is one of the manifestations of the father god. From this original unity two gods developed in the course of time, Savitar and Tvaṣṭar. The original ambivalence of the father god, i.e. his malevolent and benevolent characteristics, have been preserved in Tvaṣṭar. He has the role of the jealous father, while Savitar is known in the Vedic texts as a congenial god, who grants well-being to the people. In the conflict between Indra and Tvaṣṭar, about which I shall speak below, this ambivalence in the father god is stressed. Tvaṣṭar is not a sheer demon, but an ambivalent figure. His role is conceived sometimes as malevolent, then again as benevolent. As an explanation for this fact he brings forward:

'Mais son caractère équivoque pouvait aisement s'accuser dans le sens de la malveillance par opposition au caractère exclusivement bienveillant d'Indra. Quand la conception unitaire et la conception dualiste de l'ordre du monde en viennent, quoique contradictoire, à ce juxtaposer dans la première les attributs que la seconde répartit entre le démon et le dieu guerrier, sont exposés, en présence de ce dernier, à une assimilation d'ailleurs plus ou moins complète et plus ou moins durable avec son ennemi, avec le démon lui-même'. (Bergaigne,1883,III p.62).

This demonization of some specific aspects of Tvaṣṭar takes a clear shape in some passages of the Ṛ̣V.; see also Bradke, 1885 p.92 ff.; Brown, 1974 p.57 ff.

Just like Hillebrandt, Ammer (1949, p.68 ff.) attributes the problematic character of the god Tvaṣṭar to the fact that he only occurs in the margin of the Vedic mythology. Nevertheless, he is of the opinion that one can find a number of fixed data in the various stanzas which occur again and again. This gives him a solid basis for further research. In the first place he mentions the fact that Tvaṣṭar has forged the thunderbolt (vajra) for Indra. Moreover, he has fashioned the secret soma cup, which is made fourfold by the Ṛbhus who in this respect compete with him. As second feature he names the fact that Tvaṣṭar sometimes behaves benevolently to Indra, sometimes malevolently. Finally Ammer calls attention to the close relation between Tvaṣṭar and man and animal in the field of procreation.

He is of the opinion that Tvastar has the characteristics of a genius of fertility. He disagrees with the views of Hillebrandt and Oldenberg, because these interpretations do not offer an explanation for the conflict between Tvaṣṭar and Indra. Ammer says in this connection:

> 'Ich glaube,dass ein Kernpunkt seines Wesens gerade in der Rivalität zu Indra liegt, die wohl in dem Sinne auszudeuten ist, dass er, der 'grosse Vater', von seinem Sohn Indra überflügelt und aus wichtigen Funktionen verdrängt worden ist. Dafür spricht der Mythos von der Ermordung des Vaters, der Somaraub, durch den sich Indra in den Besitz seiner grossen Kraft setzt, und die Kuhgewinnung die beiden letzteren Fakten, die Indras Macht im vedischen Pantheon begründen, zeigen Indra als den Eindringling, den Eroberer, der andere Religionsformen verdrängt und fremde Funktionen an sich resst. Diese gewaltige Umschichtung hat wenigstens auch bei Viśvarūpa, Tvaṣṭars Sohn, dessen Dämonisierung zur Folge'. (Ammer, 1949 p.73).

Ammer traces Tvaṣṭar as a god who has created the world (Schöpfergott), a demiurg, who has fashioned all living beings and has vivified them. He thinks that this creator god, who may have been a manifestation of the father in heaven, was pushed aside by Indra who became the creator of the world in Tvaṣṭar's place. In the course of time Tvaṣṭar became a genius of fertility and the divine artificer. Bereft of his soma he loses the cows which were fashioned by him. Finally he has to forge the thunderbolt for Indra in the battle against the dragon Vṛtra. According to Ammer, the fight has its parallel in the struggle between Indra and Viśvarūpa. In the light of these opinions the author examines the etymology of the name and concludes that originally it must have had the meaning of 'fashioner' (Bildner). With this interpretation of the name a concrete trait of his character is elucidated. Mayrhofer (1964 p.41 ff.) has examined the etymology of the name in more detail and he concludes that the term tvā̆ṣṭar- originally must have been identical with the Avestic word thwōrəštar- i.e. 'shaper' or 'fashioner', derived from the root thwarəs- i.e. 'to carve' or 'to fashion'.

Gonda (1978, p.27 and 180) discusses the god Tvaṣṭar in the section on 'die Mächte'. He is of the opinion that the agent nouns, to which the name Tvaṣṭar belongs as well, may have been used as function names for one or more gods, but he also claims that some of the 'Sondergötter' denoted by these names may have their origin in the speculative theories of the priests. He conceives Tvaṣṭar as a 'power' denoted by an agent noun which has become more important in the course of time. He is the fashioner, who has made everything.

> 'Kurz er ist der Zubereiter der Formen und hat als solcher sogar Tiere - z.B. das wichtige Pferd - und Götter, Agni und Bṛhaspati, geschaffen. Er wird deshalb um Reichtum und Söhne oder Nachwuchs angerufen: denn auch der Embryo muss einen Bildner haben.(..) Es ist also kein Wunder, dass er auch als Schöpfer (..) und Vorfahr des Menschengeschlechts erscheint: seine Tochter war die Mutter Yamas, des ersten

Menschen'. (Gonda, 1978 p.27).

3. SOME METHODOLOGICAL REFLECTIONS CONCERNING THE DATING OF VEDIC TRADITION

In the preceding survey I have enumerated the views of a number of scholars who have written about the god Tvaṣṭar, but completeness has not been pursued. In paragraph four I shall evaluate these opinions, but first I want to deal with some methodological problems which are connected with the study of Vedic texts. These problems also play a part in the interpretation of the various traditions concerning Tvaṣṭar. In the first place this concerns the dating of the various traditions with reference to each other. The lack of valid criteria to place the various traditions in a historical perspective explains why many of the surveys restrict themselves to an enumeration of the collected traditions in a rather arbitrary manner without tracing their cohesion and development in the course of time. If one restricts oneself to the figure of Tvaṣṭar one can observe that a part of these traditions are conflicting with each other. They cannot be explained if one does not keep in mind the perspective of time. I mention in this context the tradition that Tvaṣṭar forged the weapon of his son Indra, the thunderbolt (vajra). Indra kills the dragon Vṛtra with this vajra after having imbibed courage and strength with the help of soma. This tradition cannot be combined very well with his 'birth-story', reconstructed with the help of RV. 3.48 and 4.18. In this story it is mentioned that Indra after his birth went to the house of his father Tvaṣṭar, stole the soma, fuddled himself with it and killed his father.

Besides this, Ammer (1949 p.73) points to the fact that the occurrence of Tvaṣṭar as 'Schöpfergott' does not tally very well with the tumultuous appearance of Indra in his role of creator who restores the cosmic order in the universe after his victory over the dragon Vṛtra. It is obvious, therefore, that these incompatible traditions have not originated simultaneously in the same milieu. There has been a development in which ancient traditions were amplified by later ones, or even changed. In these ancient traditions the conceptions of man and society are reflected in the same way as in the later ones, which show the transformations. All these multifarious traditions have been compiled in the Vedic texts. Gonda (1975 p.26) makes mention of the fact that in the ṚV. relatively ancient and young traditions occur next to each other, sometimes in one and the same hymn. The main problem, however, is to develop valid criteria to date these traditions with reference to each other. It should be added in this connection that the dating of texts, or even parts of them, in itself does not supply us with valid tools to date the traditions mentioned in them. It is conceivable that relatively young compilations with reference to the Veda, such as e.g. the Mahābhārata, contain very old traditions. Nevertheless, these textual sources supply us with a fixed point if they can be dated: the terminus ad quem. Moreover, the occurrence of similar traditions in different textual sources of related peoples which have passed through a divided development for a long period, may help us with a criterium to get more clarity as to their antiquity. The fact, for instance, that the god Tvaṣṭar is also mentioned in the Avesta as a fashioner of animals pleads for a high antiquity of this tradition; cf. Boyce, 1975 p.81 f.

A third criterium to place a tradition in a chronological framework may be furnished by the recording of certain specific things, which may be placed in a perspective of time construed by other investigators. The tradition which connects Tvaṣṭar with a knife made of bronze (ayas; cf.Mayrhofer, 1976 p. 631 f.) presupposes familiarity with bronze and the ability to hammer this metal. This datum furnishes us roughly with the terminus a quo of this tradition.

Closely connected with the problem of dating traditions is that of their geographical and social origin. Data about flora and fauna may provide us with more concrete information with respect to the geographical situation. Moreover, the range and 'Sitz im Leben' of certain traditions should be mentioned. A relevant example in this connection are the traditions with respect to the Ṛbhus, the deified 'artisans'. In the ṚV. about ten hymns are dedicated to them, (6) but these occur only in a few family books (maṇḍalas). In the other maṇḍalas their names are mentioned, but concrete traditions do not occur. The AV. mentions their names eight times in seven hymns without adding any new characteristics. Keith (1925 p.175) deduces from this that they were not very popular in the Vedic folk religion. Ryder (1901 p.10) reduces the various poets of these hymns to one priestly family and he explains their predilection for the Ṛbhu tradition by referring to the fact that they regarded themselves as their kinsfolk. In the epic the Ṛbhus are hardly mentioned. On account of all these facts one can deduce that the traditions concerning the Ṛbhus were only vivid in a small group of people. It is in this connection important to determine the characteristics of this circle, since a good appreciation of these traditions can then be obtained. One of these traditions, about which I shall come to speak later, alludes to their problems with Tvaṣṭar, who is well-known as the fashioner of the soma cup. The Ṛbhus outrival him in skilfulness by carving four new soma cups. This activity of the Ṛbhus, who are also mentioned in connection with the soma sacrifice in another context, seems to point to an innovation in the soma ritual, in which the one cup of Tvaṣṭar is replaced by four other ones; cf. also Potdar, 1952 p.28. That this innovation was not introduced without a struggle is reflected in the tradition that Tvaṣṭar wishes to kill the Ṛbhus when he has seen the new cups. The fact that this tradition has been handed down in a small circle justifies the conclusion that the innovation must have taken place there.

4. EVALUATION OF THE WESTERN OPINIONS ON TVAṢṬAR

As has been observed above most authors on Vedic mythology confine themselves to an enumeration of the various traditions with respect to Tvaṣṭar without a detailed analysis and without placing these traditions in a clear perspective . When an interpretation is offered the etymology of his name is an important clue. The agent noun tvaṣṭar- seems to have been used as an epithet for one or more gods, but in many cases no answer is given as to the identity of this god or these gods. Besides this, one can ask oneself if the etymology of a name can offer an adequate answer with reference to the 'original' character of a god. The accentuation of one aspect of a god by means of a word which functions as epithet does not typify that god completely. By using other epithets for that same god other aspects are emphasized. Even if an epithet has become the name of a god, it is not inconceivable that this god has many characteristics which are not expressed in the name. It seems, therefore, a precarious enterprise to determine the original character of a god by means of the etymology of his name. The opinions of Keith and Oldenberg that Tvaṣṭar is a personification of creative activity expressed in his name, is therefore inadequate. The same holds good for the view of Gonda. These authors do not give an explanation of the conflicts in which Tvaṣṭar is involved.

Hillebrandt uses for the interpretation of Vedic myths theories in which natural phenomena as e.g. sun and moon take an important place. He supposes that Tvaṣṭar is a god of the sun, but he does not base himself on the data of the Vedic texts, because they in no way refer to him as a god of the sun. The opinion of Hillebrandt that Tvaṣṭar would have belonged to a mythical circle outside the sphere of thought of the Vedic tribes on account of a supposed aboriginal origin of his name has been refuted with arguments by Mayrhofer (1964 p. 141ff.) and Ammer (1949 p.41).

Bergaigne and Ammer do not confine themselves to an enumeration, but they try to put the material in some relief by using the conflict between Tvaṣṭar and Indra as a clue for the interpretation. Bergaigne regards Tvaṣṭar as a manifestation of the 'dieu père' who is representative for a unitarian world-conception. Against this god he places the warrior god Indra. The mythical traditions concerning both parties represent different conceptions of the world, the unitarian and the dualistic, which clash with each other. In the myth of Indra's murder of his father Tvaṣṭar this conflict is expressed. Bergaigne refrains from dating the two world conceptions with reference to each other, because the Ṛ̣V., to which he restricts himself, does not contain enough data for this according to his opinion. A careful reading and comparing of the texts furnishes us with some fixed points, which make a rough reconstruction possible of the two conceptions in a historical perspective. Later I shall come back to these problems.

Besides the dating questions, Bergaigne does not explain why Tvaṣṭar is the main representative of the unitarian conception in this conflict, since he has only a relatively subordinate position in the Ṛ̣V. His claim that Savitar and Tvaṣṭar originally must have been a unity has not drawn the attention of the other authors and asks for further investigation (7).

Ammer regards Indra as an intruder who expels the old creator god Tvaṣṭar from important functions. Gradually he would have been reduced to a fertility spirit and the artisan of the gods. His view is not without interest because he tries to explain the various traditions in the perspective of time, but he does not explain why Indra ousted Tvaṣṭar. Moreover, he does not corroborate his opinion that the traditions referring to Tvaṣṭar as creator of the world are old one, while the other ones should be regarded as younger.

Surveying all these opinions it seems useful to me to start with a new investigation concerning Tvaṣṭar, in which the problems mentioned above will be taken into consideration as well. Within that framework I shall try to date the various traditions with reference to each other, so that one gains an insight into the development of the god and an explanation of the conflict between him and Indra.

5. THE POSITION OF TVAṢṬAR IN THE ĀPRĪ HYMNS.

An important group of hymns which can help us to trace a number of ancient characteristics of Tvaṣṭar are the so-called Āprī hymns of the Ṛ̣V. These nine hymns are characterized by a scheme expressing itself by fixed keywords in corresponding stanzas; Gonda, 1975 p.104. The usual number of stanzas is eleven, and the ninth stanza is dedicated to Tvaṣṭar. In the preceding stanza three female deities are always mentioned, Bhāratī (or Mahī), Iḷā and Sarasvatī, and in the stanza after the one dedicated to Tvaṣṭar, the sacrificial post called Vanaspati has the central place. The fact that this scheme returns in all the Āprī hymns of the various priestly families shows that it must have had 'canonical' authority. It seems, therefore, reasonable to suppose that is must have been older than the text of these hymns themselves and vital for their understanding; cf. Bergaigne, 1889 p.19 f. The various priestly poets were bound to this fixed scheme. A detailed analysis of these texts has shown that these hymns originally had reference to a family sacrifice, which must have been rather popular considering its wide diffusion; cf. Potdar, 1945 p.26-42; 1946 p.29-57 and Van den Bosch, 1981 and 1983. During this sacrifice a sacrificial victim is offered by the pater familias with the help of an officiating priest (hotar). Agni, the god of the sacrificial fire and the divine counterpart of the officiating priest, has an important supporting task in this ritual, because he helps to prepare the oblations. The Āprī hymns contain the liturgical formulations of the various priestly families for this sacrifice. Because the poets of the liturgical stanzas were bound to this sacrifice it is natural to suppose that many ancient notions have been preserved in their texts, which may contain additional information about the nature of the sacrifice. In another paper I have discussed these hymns and the sacrifice underlying it (Van den Bosch, 1983); therefore I shall confine myself to some observations. In the first place one should make a distinction between the deities who have a fixed place in the scheme itself, and the deities who are only occasionally mentioned. The deities who have a fixed place in it have a functional place in the sacrifice at the basis of the Āprī hymns and as such they belong to another level than the varying data. This means that they should have priority in the explanation. Considering the conservative character of the liturgy, as well as its high antiquity, it is obvious that many data concerning Tvaṣṭar must have been very ancient and may go back to at least the Indo-Iranian period, to which I shall return later. In the course of time the brahminical theologians have incorporated the _āprī_ stanzas in the liturgy of the complex _paśubandha_ sacrifice. The stanzas came to be applied as liturgical formulations accompanying the preliminary offerings of this animal sacrifice, although in that context they make an artificial impression. On account of the fact that these stanzas once belonged to the liturgy of an ancient family sacrifice and have been incorporated without alterations, the conclusion is justified that they were so popular that a further acommodation to the new context was not tolerated. One can say, therefore, that the _āprī_ stanzas form as it were a fossilized layer in the complex _paśubandha_ sacrifice. Hereby their conservative character is stressed.

In the family sacrifice underlying the Āprī hymns Tvaṣṭar has the central place together with the three goddesses who have an important supporting task in the realization of the desired purposes. Immediately after the invocation of the god the sacrificial victim is slaughtered and offered to him and the other gods; cf. Van den Bosch, 1983. The reason why Tvaṣṭar is addressed is explicitly mentioned in most of the stanzas. It is for progeny, for manly and healthy sons, for the increase of cattle, for movable property (_draviṇa_), i.e. children and cattle, for prosperity and well-being. The god is invited to come to the place of sacrifice in the house of the _pater familias_ and to grant all these goods. The householder, representing in this sacrifice his family as a socio-economic unit whose material and spiritual well-being should be furthered, offers a sacrificial victim to the god with the help of an officiating priest and he asks the god to sacrifice his goods.

> 'Tvaṣṭar, the eminent (god), has shaped all forms indeed, all cattle. Do thou, (O god), by sacrifice bring forth their greasy abundance'. (ṚV. 1.188.9).

> 'O god Tvaṣṭar, because thou hast brought about the beauty (of the forms), because thou hast become the companion of the Aṅgiras, this (sacrificial victim) should come within the abode of the gods, O sage. Thou shouldst eagerly sacrifice , O bestower of wealth (draviṇoda) and owner of treasures'. (ṚV.10.70.9).

In his capacity of shaper of forms Tvaṣṭar is invited to sacrifice wealth, i.e. to grant children and cattle, because by means of these things wealth is expressed.

The idea of Tvaṣṭar as a bestower of wealth is in the āprī stanzas connected with two conceptions. The first one is that of Tvaṣṭar as the fashioner of the living beings. He is the god who shapes the living beings by 'carving' and 'combining' them until they get their specific forms; cf. Van den Bosch, 1983 ch.4.9. This idea is also applied to the shaping of heaven and earth.

> '(To Tvaṣṭar) who has shaped Heaven and Earth, the two progenitors, by carving them with forms, (and who has shaped) all other beings, to this god Tvaṣṭar thou should perform today at this place sacrificial worship, O hotar with knowledge'. (ṚV.10.110.9).

The idea that the god shapes the forms of man and beast by carving and combining them returns in other texts of the ṚV. (8). Sometimes, however, it is intermingled with the second conception of Tvaṣṭar, viz. as the god who 'unties' or releases the seminal fluid.

> 'May Tvaṣṭar, inclined towards us, 'untie' for us in our navel the stream of sperm, abundant in treasures, abundant by itself, for the sake of prosperity and wealth'. (ṚV. 1.142.10).

> 'Through the hearing (of our prayer by the god Tvaṣṭar) a healthy son is born (to us), bronze coloured and strong, seething in vitality, loving the gods. Tvaṣṭar should untie

> for us the navel, (that is to say) progeny. And may he (viz. the sacrificial victim) enter the abode of the gods.'(Ṛ̣V.2.3.9.).

Also in this conception the god has an active share in furthering the progeny of man and animal. He does this by 'untying' the seminal fluid in the navel; cf. also Van den Bosch, 1983 ch.4.9. This untying implies an ejaculation during which the sperm is sent forth within the womb of the female. The man is conceived here as the placer of the embryo, the begetter, and the woman is the receptacle in which the seed is placed and fed. When the embryo is placed the god helps to shape it with his skilful hands cf.e.g. ṚV.7.34.20 f.

In the Āprī hymns of the ṚV. Tvaṣṭar is not only conceived as the fashioner and the 'untier' of the sperm, but he is also described as the shaper of heaven and earth; see above. Moreover, he is qualified as <u>viśvarūpa,</u> i.e. 'he who contains all forms', and <u>agriya</u>, i.e. 'the oldest' or 'the first born'; see ṚV.1.13.10 ; cf. also 9.5.9. In the widest sense Tvaṣṭar can be conceived, therefore, as a creator god, who bestows material well-being, that is in the eyes of the predominantly Aryan cattle breeding tribes children, esp. sons, and cattle. All these ideas return in ṚV.3.55.19 f.:

> 'The god Tvaṣṭar, the impeller (<u>savitar</u>), containing all forms (<u>viśvarūpa</u>), has multiplied progeny and he has brought it forth in abundance, and these are all his creatures;... He has joined together the two combined vessels (i.e. heaven and earth) and these are filled with his goods; he is renowned as the hero who finds the beneficial goods;...

It cannot be the place here to deal with the various creation myths of the ṚV. in which Tvaṣṭar, or Savitar-Tvaṣṭar, plays an important role; cf. Brown, 1942 p.23 ff. It is, however, an established fact that Tvaṣṭar is a creator god, who for a long time past has been associated with procreation. This important aspect of him has been preserved in the later Vedic traditions. He is qualified there as e.g. sperm-bestowing (*retodhā*) and abounding in sperm (*bhuriretas*); cf. Hillebrandt, 1929,II p.381 f. Accordingly as this fertility aspect became more accentuated in the later traditions, the conception that Tvaṣṭar was a creator god was lost. His skilfulness as a creator became narrowed to the fashioning of embryos and the forging of the thunderbolt.

In the Āprī hymns Tvaṣṭar is closely associated with the three goddesses Bhāratī (or Mahī), Iḷā and Sarasvatī. The stanza preceding that to Tvaṣṭar is dedicated to them. They are implored for prosperity and well-being; moreover, they are called skilful (*svapas*), a qualification which is characteristic of Tvaṣṭar.Some expressions refer to their life-promoting activities. Of these three goddesses Sarasvatī is most frequently mentioned in the ṚV. She is regarded as a personification of the river of the same name and as such she is frequently invoked together with the waters and the other rivers. Her name denotes in all probability 'she who is connected with lakes'. She is especially implored in connection with fertility and procreation. She is called a mother and requested to bestow offspring. Sometimes she is addressed together with other goddesses who are concerned with procreation and a good birth. Compared with Sarasvatī the two other goddesses have a very weak personification. Because Sarasvatī is dominant in this triad, characteristics belonging to her became applied to all three of them. In the Āprī hymns the three goddesses seem to be complementary to Tvaṣṭar.

In later times the conception of the three goddesses being engaged in the process of procreation has been replaced by that of the wives of the gods (*devapatnī*), also shortly called the wives (*gnās*). These wives are requested to help at procreation and child-birth, and they remain in close connection with the waters. Moreover, they are connected with Tvaṣṭar who is said to be the lord of the wives and who is also described as fond of wives. In some expressions of the ṚV. and also in the later ritual texts this combination of Tvaṣṭar with the wives of the gods is a fixed datum. The god and these wives receive together in one offering their sacrificial share in the later Vedic rituals; cf. Van den Bosch, 1984 ch. 4.8 with notes. All these data seem to indicate that Tvaṣṭar gradually degenerated as a creator god to a god who was closely connected with the fertility of female beings. The fact that the devapatnī are willing to share their sacrificial portion with him points to his possible incorporation within the more marginal cult of women; see below par. 11. In certain procreation rites of the official Vedic cult, which are centered upon the wife of the institutor of the sacrifice (yajamāna), the neṣṭar plays an important role. This priest is closely connected with Tvaṣṭar. In RV.1.15.3 the god is indicated by the term neṣṭar; cf. also Hillebrandt, 1929,II p.380 f.; Caland, 1924 notes on ĀpSS. XII.15.9-10.

As mentioned before, the most ancient data concerning Tvaṣṭar go back to the Indo-Iranian period. This is confirmed by the Avesta where Tvaṣṭar is also conceived as the 'Carver' or the 'Fashioner'. In Y.29.6 Ahura Mazdā speaks to the cow which protests against the crude sacrifices in which animals are slaughtered:

> 'The Fashioner (thwōrəšta-) has fashioned (tatašā) thee for the cattlebreeder and the herdsman.'

This Fashioner is also described as gəuš tašan, i.e. 'the shaper of the cow', and sometimes he is identified with Spentā Mainyū, who is sometimes conceived as the hypostatized creative aspect of Ahura Mazdā; cf. Gershevitch, 1959 p.55-57. All these data suggest that Tvaṣṭar was regarded as the shaper of living beings. As such he may have been originally identical with the creator Ahura Mazdā, but this hypothesis requires further investigation.

It cannot be the place here to make a detailed analysis of all data in the Āprī hymns and their possible counterparts in the Avesta (cf. Van den Bosch, 1983), but the important parallel between the āprī stanzas and the āfrīnagān rituals should be mentioned in this context; cf. also Haug, 1890 p.224 f; Boyce, 1975 p.168, 281; 1977, index sub Āfrīnagān. These āfrīnagān rituals of Zoroastrianism, in which Ahura Mazdā often has an important place (Boyce, 1975 p.259 f.), must have had a popular origin, because it is not required that they should be performed within a secluded sacred area with the help of a sacrificial specialist. They are regarded as 'outer' rituals which can be performed at home, near a river or also in the fields.

In the preceding pages it was stated that Tvaṣṭar was the main deity in a popular family sacrifice which was performed by the householder with the help of an officiating priest for the sake of prosperity and well-being of his family. This sacrifice was reconstructed with the help of the āprī stanzas, the liturgical texts for this sacrifice. In some other passages of the ṚV. allusions seem to be made to this sacrifice. In ṚV.6.49.9, for instance, it is said:

> 'Agni, the radiant officiating priest, should perform sacrificial worship for Tvaṣṭar, to whom the first share is due, the glorious god, who bestows strength and who has beautiful hands and arms, the skilful god, who is worthy of worship among the households (pastyā) and who is easily invoked.'

This text clearly refers to a sacrifice which is performed for Tvaṣṭar in the households of the 'Aryan' cattlebreeders. The god has the first right to the offerings. Although the qualification suhava, i.e. 'who is easily invoked' or 'who listens willingly', is not specific for Tvaṣṭar, it is clear that he is not an 'abstract' god. He must have been an object of worship in the homestead of the Aryan people. In ṚV.5.41.8 Tvaṣṭar is further qualified as the lord of the homestead (Vāstoṣpati), who brings prosperity to the people. In some texts, however, this Vāstoṣpati is a distinctive god; cf. ṚV.7.41.1 ff.; 55.1 The epithet _viśvarūpa_, with which this god is qualified in the last mentioned text seems to be an indication of his connection with Tvaṣṭar, who is designated by this term; cf. ṚV.1.13.10; 3.55.19.

On account of the preceding observations the following conclusions can be drawn:

1. Tvaṣṭar had a central place in a popular family sacrifice of the Indo-Aryan tribes which purpose was to further the fertility of men and animals.
2. He is described in that ritual context as a god who releases the seminal fluid and shapes man and animal. His connections with the fertility of them are an ancient characteristic feature.
3. The conception of Tvaṣṭar as an 'abstract' deity or a 'power' denoted by an agent noun which has become more important in the course of time is inadequate. It does not explain at all the occurrence of the god in this popular family sacrifice.

6. SAVITAR AND TVAṢṬAR

As we have seen in par. 2, Bergaigne regarded Savitar-Tvaṣṭar as a manifestation of the father god, who represented a unitarian conception of the world. For this original unity he drew attention to three texts in the ṚV. in which Tvaṣṭar is qualified as _savitar_, i.e. 'impeller'; cf. note 5. In the course of time this aspect of him would have been hypostatized; cf. also Griswold, 1971 p. 276. The benevolent aspects of the father god would have been incorporated in him, while the ambivalent characteristics were preserved in Tvaṣṭar. For this original identification more arguments can be advanced, because Savitar is also described as a creator god, who fixes the earth with bonds and makes firm the sky in the rafterless space; cf. ṚV.10.149.1 ff. He is a supporter of the sky and the whole world; cf. RV.4.53.2.; 10.149.4.

Although Tvaṣṭar is not explicitly mentioned by name in the hymns dedicated to heaven and earth (ṚV.1.160.1 ff. and 4.56.1 ff.), it should be observed that the expressions which are used to describe the creator god are characteristic of him. The images used in them for the creation are similar to those in the hymns dedicated to Savitar.

A second argument pointing to the close connections between Savitar and Tvaṣṭar may be found in the term <u>viśvarūpa</u> which is applied to both. In ṚV.1.13.10; 3.55.19 and 10.10.5 it is used for Tvaṣṭar. In the last mentioned text Tvaṣṭar is called a creator (<u>janitar</u>) and an impeller (<u>savitar</u>) who contains all forms (<u>viśvarūpa</u>). In ṚV.10.8.8,9 the three-headed son of Tvaṣṭar is called Viśvarūpa. The term <u>viśvarūpa</u> is, however, also used in connection with Savitar. He is the sage who assumes all forms; see ṚV.5.81.2. In the cosmogonic passage of ṚV.3.38.1 ff. Savitar (st.8) is described as the ancient great creator on whose instigation the sages separated the two cosmogonic regions (st.3). and constructed the heavens (st.2). In the same hymn he is called Viśvarūpa and represented as an androgynous being, viz. as a bull-cow (st.4 and 5). In another hymn (ṚV.3.56) this same bull-cow Viśvarūpa is described as an androgynous being with three bellies, three udders and three heads (st.3) His offspring is said to be numerous. In the following stanzas (4,6-8) he/she is closely connected with Savitar and seems to be identical with him. The poet may, however, also allude metaphorically to the three cosmic regions which are contained by Viśvarūpa. In ṚV.1.160.3 heaven and earth are represented as an androgynous bovine animal and the poet uses in this context the following image:

> 'Out of the variegated cow and the profilic bull he (viz. the sun) has milked every day his milk, that is seed (sperm)'

The sun is in this hymn regarded as the son of heaven and

earth, but he is also conceived of as a symbol of the creator god, when the perspective changes and other associations become relevant. This creator god is described in the next stanza with expressions which are characteristic of Tvaṣṭar and Savitar; cf. Geldner, 1951, I p.219 and Gonda, 1974 p.106 f. In the world of the cattle-breeding 'Aryan' tribes the life-generating and life-feeding androgynous bovine animal must have been an ideal image to express the essential qualities of this creator god and his creation. This same idea returns in AV.9.4.1.ff. The primeval creator god is in that context also represented as the bull-cow Viśvarūpa, who in the beginning became the counterpart of the waters. The fact that the term viśvarūpa is used for Tvaṣṭar as well as for Savitar is an indication of their original identity.

The hypothesis concerning the original identity between Tvaṣṭar and Savitar can be corroborated by additional arguments. In ṚV.4.53.2 Savitar is called Prajāpati; in the brāhmaṇas this identification is also found; Macdonell, 1897 p.33. In Mbh. 5.9.3, 40 and in the purāṇa literature Tvaṣṭar is identified with him.

According to Bergaigne the god Savitar would have been a hypostasis of the ancient creator god which was split off in the course of time. It cannot be the place in this context to deal extensively with Savitar and his development (Oldenberg, 1897 p.473 ff; 1905 p.253 ff.; Hillebrandt, 1929, II p.100 ff.; Dandekar, 1979 p.1 ff.), but the following observations can be made. In the first place Savitar is said to be of Indian origin; his name has no parallel in the ancient Iranian tradition. In the second place very few mythological traditions concerning him are known. In the fragmentary and obscure mythology on the Ṛbhus it is only related that Savitar bestowed immortality on them when they came to his house; ṚV.1.110.2-3. This poor mythology indicates that Savitar was not very popular in broad strata of the population. This view is corroborated by the fact that the AV. hardly pays any attention to him, but in the ṚV., which reflects the more hieratical views, eleven hymns are dedicated to Savitar, while he is mentioned about 170 times; Macdonell, 1897 p.32. This points to the fact that the concept of Savitar as an independent deity must have been developed in hieratical circles. Moreover, it is generally acknowledged that the connections between the god Savitar and the soma sacrifice do not belong to the ancient traditions in the Vedas, because he is not clearly connected with soma in the ṚV.; Oldenberg, 1970 p.455; Hillebrandt, 1929,II p.118. The idea of stimulation expressed in his name is stressed in many texts of the ṚV. He is the god who impels all things in the universe. Therefore he has acquired a place in the inaugural formula of most Vedic rites imitating the great cosmic processes: 'On the impulse of the god Savitar..' In the description of his appearance many allusions to gold, light and the sun are found. Because the sun had a central place in the rhythm of life of the Aryans as impeller of all things in the universe, Savitar is many times eulogized by the priestly poets with expressions referring to the sun, but these do not explain his original character.

Recapitulating, the following conclusions can be drawn. The two Vedic gods Savitar and Tvaṣṭar can be reduced to an ancient creator god Savitar-Tvaṣṭar, who has been the object of worship in a popular family sacrifice in Indo-Iranian times. This god is qualified as viśvarūpa, i.e. 'Omniform', and eulogized sometimes under the image of an androgynous bovine animal. In the course of time when the Indo-Aryans settled down in India one aspect of this god was split off and became hypostatized, viz. the aspect of stimulation. Savitar came to be regarded as the motor in the cosmos. This development had its origin in hieratical circles which accentuated this idea of stimulation at the cost of the other characteristics of the ancient creator god, but some of his ancient traits have been preserved in the texts describing Savitar.

7. TVAṢṬAR AND THE TWO SACRIFICIAL DEITIES AGNI AND SOMA

In the preceding paragraphs it was shown that Tvaṣṭar had clear connections with the sacrificial practices of the Aryan popul-tion. This view can be strengthened when we analyse his relations with Agni and Soma the two sacrificial deities. Agni is some-times called the son of Tvaṣṭar; ṚV.1.95.2,5; 3.7.4; 10.2.7.; 46.9. In ṚV.6.59.1 f. Indra and Agni are represented as two brothers; this implies that they must have the same father, viz. Tvaṣṭar; see par.8. Sometimes, however, heaven and earth are called his parents; Nobel, 1957 p.4. Moreover, mention is made of the fact that Agni was born in the highest heaven; ṚV.1.143.2; 6.8.2; 7.5.7. He is also called sometimes the son of heaven; ṚV.3.25.1; 6.49.2. This implies that heaven is sometimes personified as his father. In ṚV.1.141.4 it is said that Agni was brought from the highest father to this world. According to ṚV.3.29.14 Agni was born from the body of the Asura. Lüders (1959 p.390) is of the opinion that this passage refers to Dyaus and he excludes Tvaṣṭar; cf. also Bradke, 1885 p.50 f. It seems, however, more probable to me that the old creator god is localized in heaven and is therefore sometimes called Dyaus. The poet of ṚV.3.1.9 alludes to the androgynous aspect of this father god, when he uses the paradox of the udder of the father which was discovered by Agni immedia-tely after his birth (9).

Besides Tvaṣṭar the waters are also closely connected

with Agni. He is called the son or the child of the waters; cf.e.g. ṚV.3.1.12-13; see also Macdonell,1897 p.69 f. In ṚV.3.56.5 Agni is called the child of three mothers and these are identified with the three ladies of the waters. These three ladies are identified by Sāyaṇa with Bhāratī, Īḷā and Sarasvatī; cf. also Geldner, 1951,I p.404 note. These three goddesses were also closely connected with Tvaṣṭar in the Āprī hymns. Hence there seems to exist a close relation between the waters as life-promoting powers and the creator god Tvaṣṭar. In ṚV.2.35.5 it is said that three divine women wish to bestow food upon Agni, the son of the waters, for he has stretched forth to the breast in the waters; Macdonell, 1917 p.71; see also Lüders,1959,II p.588 f. According to AV 9.4.1 ff. the androgynous bovine animal who bears all forms in his belly became in the beginning the counterpart of the waters. In st.6 Tvaṣṭar is introduced as the shaper of forms and the generator of cattle.

Agni has a mediating function as the divine officiating priest. As god of the sacrificial fire he conveys the oblations of the people to heaven where the gods reside; sometimes he is represented in the texts as the god who carries the other gods on a car to the place of sacrifice. He is also a representative of the gods on this earth. Sometimes qualities are attributed to him which are in fact characteristic of the gods in whose service he acts. As such he is called draviṇoda i.e. 'the bestower of wealth' (e.g. ṚV. 1.196.1-7; 2.6.3), a term which is also used for Tvaṣṭar; ṚV.10.70.9; 92.11. as son of the old creator god he can represent him, as may appear from ṚV.10.5.7 where he is described as an androgynous bovine animal. In ṚV.1.146.1 he is represented with three heads; cf. also Geldner, 1951, I p.204 note.

Just like Agni, Soma, the personification of the sacred

intoxicant, has close relations with the creator god. Soma is said to dwell in the highest heaven (ṚV.3.32.10; 4.26.6) and he is called the son of heaven (ṚV.9.33.5; 38.5). Heaven is called his ancient father in ṚV.9.86.14. According to ṚV. 6.44.22 Soma steals the weapons of his demonic father Tvaṣṭar; cf. also Geldner, 1851, II p.139 note. From all these texts it becomes clear that Soma originally stayed with his father in heaven; this father is called at one time Dyaus, at another time Tvaṣṭar. Because Soma can represent his father he is sometimes attributed with the same qualities. He is described as a creator god in ṚV.9.70.2; 86.28 (cf. also Nobel, 1957 p. 234ff.) and a bestower of fertility in ṚV.9.60.4; 74.5. The epithet <u>retodhā</u>, 'bestower of sperm', expressing a characteristic feature of Tvaṣṭar, is given to him; ṚV.9.86.39. Moreover, he is qualified as <u>draviṇoda</u>, 'bestower of wealth', in ṚV.9.88.3. According to ṚV.9.10.3 Soma bestows immortality, but in ṚV.4.54.2 (cf. also 1.110.3) Savitar grants immortality; cf. also ṚV.1.196.6 where Agni is said to confer this.

Just like Agni, Soma is said to be the embryo of the waters and the waters are directly called his mothers; cf. Macdonell, 1897 p.71. It seems plausible that the old creator god with the waters as his female counterparts has in the beginning brought forth Soma. Therefore he is the father of Soma and the owner of <u>soma</u>, the sacred intoxicant. With this drink he can bestow immortality upon the other gods, but he can also refuse this. This implies that the other gods are in fact dependent upon him. In the course of time there has been a shift in the accentuation, and Tvaṣṭar came to be regarded as the owner of the 'unique' <u>soma</u> cup; ṚV.1.20.6; 110.4, etc. In these texts it is stressed that the god has shaped this wooden cup by carving. In ṚV.10.53.9 Tvaṣṭar is described as the servant who distributes the cups with which the gods drink the soma. This inferior position of the god is also expressed in the later soma cult where he receives his portion together with the wives of the gods. Tvaṣṭar, once the owner of the soma, has lost his right to a portion of his own, but receives his share in a subordinate place together with the wives; ṚV.1.15.3; 22.9.;2.36.3. The last mentioned text describes the god as 'fond of soma'. In ṚV.9.73.1 the old creator god , the Asura, manifests himself with three heads and with its three mouths he drinks the soma; for the interpretation of this text see Lüders, 1951.I p.234 f.; Gonda, 1976 p.105 f.

Summarizing: the old creator god manifesting himself in the fragmentary traditions of Tvaṣṭar, Dyaus, the Old Asura and living on in part in the god Savitar has close relations with the two sacrificial deities Agni and Soma. He is their father and he is regarded as the owner of the sacred fire and the sacred drink which they personify. Therefore it is likely that he once had the central place in the cult which was performed by means of them; cf. par. 5 for his place in the sacrifice at the basis of the Āprī hymns. In the course of time his position changed and certain functions were split off. This development is also reflected in ṚV.10.124.1 ff. Agni is in that context persuaded by Indra to leave the father Asura and to collaborate with him. Agni says goodbye to his own clan because he now receives a share in the sacrifice. Soma and Varuṇa follow in his tracks; by this change the dominion of the father Asura and his party is lost. The balance of power between the gods is changed and Indra gains the supremacy. This is reflected in the ritual sphere by connecting the two sacrificial deities Agni and Soma with Indra.

8. TVAṢṬAR AND INDRA

Ṛ‌V.3.48 and 4.18 deal with the conflict between Indra and Tvaṣṭar. According to the first hymn Tvaṣṭar is the father of Indra; Geldner, 1951, I p.388. In ṚV.4.17.4 Indra is said to be the son of Dyaus (Heaven) who is qualified in that context as most skilful (svapastama), an expression which is usually characteristic of Tvaṣṭar. This consolidates my hypothesis that the names Tvaṣṭar and Dyaus originally referred to the same god who was localized in heaven.

The following reconstruction can be made of this conflict; see also O'Flaherty, 1981 p.141-146. Indra's mother carries her son for many years in her womb for fear of rivalry between him and his father, but Indra wants to make his entrée into this world because his time has come; he is born from his mother's side; ṚV.4.18.1,2. After his birth he goes to the house of his father Tvaṣṭar, steals the soma and drinks it from his father's cup; ṚV.3.48.1,4. The position of Indra's mother is not very clear. According to ṚV.3.48.2 f. she helps him and pours out the sacred intoxicant, but according to the other hymn the mother did not look after her child. This version describes Indra's victory over Vṛtra and his releasing of the waters (st.7), as well as his murdering his father.

> 'Who has made your mother a widow ? Who wished to kill you when you were laying still or moving ? Which god helped you when you grasped your father by his foot and destroyed him ? '.(ṚV.4.18.2).

By patricide and the seizure of the soma Indra becomes the owner of the sacred intoxicant. By drinking it he is strengthened and destroys all his enemies. He kills Vṛtra who obstructs the continuity of life by the detention of the waters. By releasing these waters the continuity is restored. Indra is eulogized by them for his recreating activities by which the powers of chaos are destroyed. These waters which are compared with women in ṚV.4.18.6 are qualified as wives of the gods (gnās or devapatnī) in ṚV.1.61.8. The waters as female counterpart of Tvaṣṭar are essential in the process of creation because they feed all living beings and are a requisite for the continuity of life. Their captivity by Vṛtra means death and destruction. Indra destroys the chaos monster and restores the balance by seizing the dominion of his father. The wives of the gods praise him for this deed of cosmic importance with the words:

> 'He has encompassed the broad heaven and earth; these two cannot contain his majesty'.

9. INDRA AND VIŚVARŪPA, THE SON OF TVAṢṬAR

The conflict between Indra and Tvaṣṭar resulting in patricide is transformed in the brāhmaṇas and the later literature into a fratricide. Indra kills Viśvarūpa, the son of Tvaṣṭar; cf. also par. 1. For this development some starting-points are found in the RV. Viśvarūpa appears as the guardian of the cows who are equivalent to the life-giving waters. Indra kills him and releases the cows; ṚV.2.11.19; 10.8.8 f. Above we have seen that the term viśvarūpa was used to denote the all-encompassing character of the old creator god who had shaped heaven and earth and all living beings within them. In the last resort he was responsible for the good and bad things in life. This implies that disasters also found their origin in him. According to the brāhmaṇas, Vṛtra, the demon of chaos and destruction, was created by Tvaṣṭar. In the course of time the totalitarian aspect of him was split off, the conflict was transformed and the more restricted functions of Tvaṣṭar became stressed. Indra's aggression turned against this totalitarian aspect which became embodied in the son Viśvarūpa. On account of this the relation between Indra and Tvaṣṭar changed. Instead of the harmless father the totalitarian ambivalent brother was killed. The _brāhmaṇas_ relate that Viśvarūpa not only maintained friendly relations with the gods, but also with the demons. These connections with the demons made Viśvarūpa an unreliable relation and formed the main argument for the fratricide. Indra was released from the guilt of patricide and Tvaṣṭar again made his entrance, but now as the artisan who forged the weapon of his son, the thunderbolt, with which the latter killed the chaos monster Vṛtra. The theme of the struggle between Indra and the three headed monster Viśvarūpa is in some passages of the ṚV. intermingled with a similar motif of more archaic origin which also occurs in the ancient Iranian texts, viz. the battle between Trita Āptya and the dragon; cf. Rönnow, 1927 p.155ff. A detailed study of this motif goes beyond the scope of this article.

10. TVAṢṬAR AND DADHYAÑC, THE SON OF ATHARVAN.

Besides the battle between Tvaṣṭar and Indra, two other conflicts are mentioned, viz. the one between Tvaṣṭar and Dadhyañc and the one between Tvaṣṭar and the Ṛbhus. Only a few fragments are known about the conflict between Dadhyañc and Tvaṣṭar, so that is is difficult to get a good impression of what happened; cf. Geldner, 1951,I p.108 notes; see further O'Flaherty,1975 p.56ff.; 1980 ch.6. When we reconstruct the myth with the help of these fragments in the RV., the following can be said. The Aśvins, also called the Nāsātyas, want to know the secret place of the mead (_madhu_) of Tvaṣṭar.
The two young twin gods therefore pay a visit to Dadhyañc who is said to be the only person who knows the secret place of this _madhu_ besides Tvaṣṭar. They persuade him with the promise that he need not have any fear of Tvaṣṭar because they have invented an excellent remedy against his fury, viz.

the head of a horse. They substitute the horsehead for his own head and with this head he tells them the secret. When Tvaṣṭar becomes aware of this he is very angry, beheads Dadhyañc and conceals this horsehead. Dadhyañc, however, receives his own head again from the Aśvins, but the twin gods know the secret of the mead. This ancient story is incorporated in the mythology of Indra, because the tradition relates that the mighty god discovers in the Saryānavat pool in the mountains the severed horsehead with which Dadhyañc betrayed the secret. With the bones of this head Indra defeats the ninety-nine Vṛtras. In the post-Vedic tradition it is said that Tvaṣṭar fashioned from the bones of Dadhicā (i.e. Dadhyañc) the thunderbolt with which Indra killed Vṛtra; Macdonell, 1897 p.141-142.

The following observation can be made with reference to this myth. The mead has a central place in it. The secret of the mead is given away to the Aśvins who have a special connection with it as becomes clear from many of their epithets, such as e.g. 'drinkers of honey' (madhupā); see Macdonell, 1897 p.49-50. In ṚV.1.119.19 it is mentioned that a bee betrayed the secret of the madhu. In the later tradition this connection between the bees and the Aśvins has been preserved; cf. Meyer, 1937 III, p.236. In the course of time soma has superseded the mead; the term madhu is then also used for the soma drink. However, it is beyond doubt that mead as a sacred beverage in the history of the Indo-Iranian people has a more archaic tradition than the soma; Tvaṣṭar must have played an important role in the cult of mead because he is regarded as the guardian of the secret of mead. Moreover, it becomes clear that he even has had malevolent aspects of olden times. The kind of relationship between Tvaṣṭar and Dadhyañc is not elucidated, but the patronymic of the latter ātharvaṇa, i.e. son of Atharvan, seems to indicate that he is a fire priest; cf. Macdonell, 1897 p.141 f. Why the Aśvins wanted to know the secret does not become clear.

11. TVAṢṬAR AND THE ṚBHUS

It cannot be the place here to deal extensively with the obscure mythology of the Ṛbhus. I shall restrict myself, therefore to the fragments concerning their conflict with Tvaṣṭar. When we reconstruct the myth with the help of the fragmentary traditions of ṚV.1.20.6; 110.3; 161.2-5; 4.33.5-6; 4.35.4; 36.4 we get the following picture. The Ṛbhus, the artisans of the gods (Gonda, 1960 p.62), are at the order of the gods invited by Agni to fashion four new soma cups to replace the soma cup of Tvaṣṭar. When they receive the promise that they will get a share in the soma sacrifice they agree and make four beautiful cups. When Tvaṣṭar sees these soma cups he becomes jealous, conceals himself among the wives of the gods (gnās) and broods on revenge because the Ṛbhus have reviled his soma cup and have undermined his position by this act. When he wants to kill them they adopt new names at the soma sacrifice. By this trick they evade his revenge.

Just as in the other conflicts the sacred intoxicant has an essential place. Tvaṣṭar raises objections to the replacement of his one soma cup by four other ones which are made by order of the gods. Although the gods seem to be the real opponents of Tvaṣṭar in their endeavour for soma, his aggression turns against the Ṛbhus, the mortal executors of the order. When they fashion the cups by means of which the gods will become independent of the soma cup of Tvaṣṭar they will also receive a share of the soma. Although the gods do not like their human smell they get their portion in the evening libation of the soma. This implies their deification which is corroborated by the tradition that they have received immortality from Savitar; ṚV.1.110.3; 3.60.3. All these data point to the fact that the Ṛbhus were mortal beings who had an active share in the innovation of the soma ritual in which four soma cups were introduced instead of the one of Tvaṣṭar. This implies that in the ritual the gods got access to the soma independent of Tvaṣṭar. It does not seem improbable to me that the Ṛbhus were priests (cf. also Potdar, 1952 p.21 ff.) belonging to groups who promoted this new cult centred round the warrior god Indra. Their warm friendship for Indra is stressed in many texts; cf.e.g. ṚV.3.60.1 ff. When the poets of the Ṛbhu hymns describe the deeds of these heroes they often use terms which are also characteristic of the activities of Tvaṣṭar; Macdonell, 1897 p.132 f. The resistance of the Ṛbhus against the old creator god is expressed in these hymns by their rivalry with him as 'artisans'.

Another interesting feature in the myth is the fact that Tvaṣṭar conceals himself among the wives of the gods. Above we have described the god as a veritable friend of the wives; he worked closely together with them in the procreation of man and animal. Because he is mentioned together with them as one group receiving together a share of the soma (e.g. ṚV.1.15.3; 2.36.3) it is plausible to suppose that he was eliminated from his former official place. He does not have an independent place in the new soma sacrifice, but survives among the wives. The fact that Tvaṣṭar conceals himself among the wives where he settles himself, may be explained from the view-point that religious notions of earlier ages which have been eclipsed by new faiths may survive in the marginal cults; cf. e.g. Lewis, 1971 p.96. Some texts seem to refer to these marginal cults in which women play an important role. In the ritual context of TS.6.5.8.3. f. the god is mentioned in connection with the wives because of procreation. The gods, however, sought to slay Tvaṣṭar, but he escaped and went to the wives. They did not want to deliver him to the gods, because men do not give up even one who is worthy of death, who has come for help. The old creator god being once the mighty owner of the sacred intoxicant soma is removed from his position and pursued by the other gods until he finds rest in the rooms of the women. There he preserves his limited functions in the sphere of procreation.

12. TVAṢṬAR, THE FASHIONER OF THE THUNDERBOLT (VAJRA) OF INDRA

As mentioned above, Tvaṣṭar was reduced in the course of time to a god of fertility and the artisan of the gods. In that last capacity he is often described as the god who has shaped the weapon of Indra, the thunderbolt; ṚV.1.32.2; 52.9; 61.7; 85.9; etc. According to ṚV.4.17.13, however, it is Dyaus, the father of Indra (cf.st.4) who hurls the vajra. The old creator god who is worsted in his fight against Indra returns under the regime of his son as subordinate to him. Dyaus has delivered his weapon to his son and with this he has delegated his authority. Tvaṣṭar fashions the weapon of his former aggressor and has become the artisan among the gods. This specific quality which belonged to the creator-god of olden times does not form in itself an explanation of this fact. By fashioning the weapon of his former aggressor the vanquished father identifies himself with the conqueror Indra and shares in his glorious deeds. By taking this position the father maintains a subordinate place under the new regime of his son. By delivering his vajra, symbol of fertility and male sexuality, the father abandons his primacy in favour of his son Indra, who releases the waters, symbol of female fertility. The son takes care of the continuity of life. The submission of the father to the son is not pushed so far that all the characteristics of the former creator god are completely retouched or eliminated; cf. ṚV.1.80.4; 10.49.10.

13. UNITARIAN AND DUALISTIC CONCEPTIONS OF THE WORLD

As mentioned above (par.2), Bergaigne was of the opinion that Savitar-Tvaṣṭar was a manifestation of the 'father god'. He was the main representative of a unitarian conception of the world in which good and evil were reduced in the last resort to his sovereign will. In some texts he is called Dyaus and mighty Asura. Originally he had an important place in the cult. In the family sacrifice underlying the Āprī hymns he was eulogized as the creator who shaped heaven and earth and all beings. He bestowed progeny upon man and beast and as such he was responsible for the continuity of life. An important supporting task in this process was attributed to the waters, his wives. They were the source of life at which the whole creation was fed and in that capacity they were called mothers; cf. e.g. ṚV.1.23.16 ff.; 10.9.1 ff. These waters had their origin in heaven where they were contained in a heavenly reservoir; cf.e.g. ṚV.10.98.5,6,12. From there they flowed as rivers to this earth giving as 'mothers' their milk to the creatures; cf. also Lüders,1959,II p.588 f. Among these divine waters which are also called healing mothers, Sarasvatī takes an important place. It seems plausible to me that mother Bṛhaddivā, i.e. 'she who lives in the high heaven', and who is named in one breath with father Tvaṣṭar in ṚV.10.64.10, should be regarded as this heavenly water-spending source; cf. also ṚV.2.31.4 and 5.42.12. The old creator god was the husband and the owner of this water-giving source and of the waters flowing as rivers to this earth. They were personified as female deities. In the unitarian conception he was also conceived of as the father of the two sacrificial deities Agni and Soma who had a mediating function in the cult in which he had a central place. The Aṅgirases, the ancient race of priests officiating in the fire cult, regarded him as their mythical father; Macdonell, 1897 p.142 f.; Schmidt, 1968 p.42 ff. In Ṛ̣V.10.70.9 Tvaṣṭar is described as the companion of the Angirases. All these data point to an elaborated cult centred round this 'father god' with an official priesthood. Generally this god must have been regarded as a benevolent being considering the prayers in the Āprī hymns, but malevolent traits were not absent in his character. The ancient myth of Dadhyañc alludes to these aspects. The fact that Tvaṣṭar is qualified as <u>viśvarūpa</u>, i.e. 'he who contains all forms', forms another indication of this unitarian idea. Because many parallels of the gods functioning in the Tvaṣṭar mythology are found in the Avesta it is likely that this unitarian conception of the world finds its origin in the Indo-Iranian period.

With the debut of Indra on the stage of Indian religious history the situation changes. The son of the old creator god carries off the <u>soma</u>, drinks the intoxicant and is strengthened by it so that he is able to slay all his foes. Although RV.4.18.12 relates that Indra murdered his father, the central theme of his mythology is his victory over Vṛtra, the demon of obstruction, who encloses the life-giving waters and threatens the continuity of life. The power of chaos is personified as a dragon and Indra, like Saint George and other mythical heroes, slays this monster; cf. Kuiper, 1975 p.110; Gonda, 1978 p.55. By his victory over the powerful demon - according to the <u>brāhmaṇas</u> Vṛtra was created by Tvaṣṭar - Indra respores the cosmic order and secures the continuity of life. He seizes the power of his father by taking away his *soma* and he clears the chaos of the *ancien régime* of Tvaṣṭar. Besides this deed of cosmic importance ṚV.4.18 makes mention of Indra's victory over Vyaṃsa, a *dāsa* whose head he smashed. These *dāsas,* the aboriginal population, are regarded as the enemies of the Aryan tribes, because they form an obstruction to the acquiring of more living space. In the Vedic tradition all kind of demonic qualities are attributed to these aboriginals. The god of war destroys them and he restores order in the disintegrated world. Evil is dispelled outside the cosmos, but not definitively. Therefore one should be vigilant and strengthen the god in his fight against the demons and foes of the 'Aryans'.

In this myth Indra is the representative of a dualistic conception of the world in which good and evil are opposed to each other and not reduced to one origin. Indra breaks with his father and revolts against him because the old creator god who contains all forms (*viśvarūpa*) is in the last resort responsible for the decay of the *ancien régime*. In the escalation which follows the unreliable ambivalent 'father god' is murdered, but in the course of time this version is retouched. His totalitarian aspect is split off and hypostatized in his son Viśvarūpa, who is described as a monster with three heads and six eyes; cf. Schmidt, 1968 p.134. In order to limit the crisis, originally described as a family conflict, Vṛtra is introduced as embodiment of chaos and destruction. Indra is no longer accused of patricide and the drama is redressed. The partisans of the father Asura who did not submit to the regime of Indra are demonized and in the *brāhmaṇas* they form a coherent group of demons, the Asuras, who must be expelled by the gods from the cosmos. In these texts, however, their existence is accepted and becomes legitimated by connecting them with the concept of a new unitarian creator god Prajāpati. The gods of the old regime who choose the side of Indra and submit themselves keep their position or get a new role. In the late ritual version of the conflict in ṚV.10.124 Agni and Soma choose the side of Indra on condition that they receive a share of the sacrifice. Tvaṣṭar maintains some harmless functions and finds rest in the apartments of the ladies. In this way the reintegration within the dualistic conception of the world get its final shape; for the various phases in this process see also Turner, 1974 p.38ff.It is, however, evident that with the development in the society the various themes in this drama were rearranged in accordance with the ideology of the group which tried to reinforce its position. In the brāhmaṇas the priests relate that Indra, the god of the warriors, becomes dependent on the two sacrificial deities, Agni and Soma. Moreover, it is stressed that he is in fact an inferior being because he murders the brahmin Viśvarūpa, the son of Tvaṣṭar, cf. par.1.

It is a very difficult problem to give an adequate interpretation of the mythological drama which with the help of the scattered fragments in the ṚV. I have tried to reconstruct in outline in terms of social processes. Bergaigne observed that the unitarian and the dualistic conception of the world were both found in the ṚV. In discussing these fragments I tried to show that Tvaṣṭar should be conceived of as an old creator god who must have been very popular considering the cult centred round him. Originally Savitar must have been one with him. Moreover, he was sometimes named the ancient Asura or the sage Asura or the father Asura. Because this old creator god was localized in heaven he was also called Dyaus. This god is described with these various names depending upon the aspect which one wanted to stress. That he has his origin in the Indo-European period is clear from the parallels in the traditions of other Indo-European languages; cf. for

Dyaus Benveniste, 1969, I p.210. I do not share the opinion of Brown (1965 p.23) that Tvaṣṭar is not Indo-European in origin, but seems to have been acquired by the Aryans after leaving their homeland; see also Mayrhofer, 1976, III p.728.

Compared to Tvaṣṭar Indra is a newcomer. There are no data which plead for the same high antiquity. In the myth this relation is expressed by qualifying him as the son of Tvaṣṭar. In the advance of Indra and the decline of Tvaṣṭar the soma plays an important role. When the young hero has drunk the intoxicant he is strengthened, kills Vṛtra and releases the life-giving waters which were enclosed. This advance of Indra should be seen in connection with the alterations in the nomadic pastoral society of the mainly cattle-breeding 'Aryans' The fact that the warrior god comes more and more to the front and concludes a covenant with the 'Aryans' in their fight against their foes points to their increasing conflicts with neighbouring peoples. Although skirmishes between neighbour tribes were not uncommon in olden times, the intensity of these conflicts can be explained only if one takes into consideration that the 'Aryans' were threatened in their existence. The most important cause of this was the increasing dryness of the changing climate. By this dryness the people were forced to move with their stock to areas with enough water supplies. Hauschild (1964 p.63 f.), basing himself upon the research of Russian archaeologists, mentions two periods of prolonged dryness, one between 2000 and 1800 B.C., and one which was even more serious about 1250 B.C.; cf. also Ehlers, 1971 p.7 ff.; Ghirshman, 1977 p.22 f. On account of these periods of dryness the Indo-Aryans moved with their horses and chariots in undulatory motions from their homeland in the steppe between Dñepr and Volga to new areas with enough water for their herds. Thus they caused a chain reaction among the other peoples

(Ghirshman, 1977) and with this chaos. The lack of water which threatened these pastoral nomads in their existence is the main theme in the myth of Indra and the dragon. Indra kills the demon of obstruction who does not want to share the life-giving waters which are essential for the 'Aryans'.

In the brāhmaṇas Vṛtra is called a devourer of food (ŚB. 1.6.3.11,17) and it is mentioned that all plants and roots became alive again after his death (TS.2.5.3.2.,3). Moreover, Vṛtra is identified with the hunger that one feels in the belly; cf. TS.2.4.12.6,7. In Mbh.5.10.15 Vṛtra is described as the all destroying heat which makes the whole creation suffer. All these texts allude to Vṛtra as a demon of chaos who holds back the waters and causes death and destruction. The brāhmaṇas and the Mbh. are unmistakable clear about the origin of the demon: Tvaṣṭar has shaped Vṛtra! The old creator god is implicitly accused in these texts of the chaos caused by the detention of the waters, his wives. ŚB.11.1.6.24 elucidates the meaning of the waters in the following way:

> '..for the waters are the law: hence whenever the waters come (down) to this (terrestrial) world everything here comes to be in accordance with the law; but whenever there is drought, then the stronger seizes upon the weaker, for the waters are the law.' (transl. Eggeling, ŚB.V. p.18).

According to Lüders (1959,II p.588 ff.) the seat (or womb) of the cosmic law (ṛtásya yóni) is localized in the primeval heavenly waters. Because Tvaṣṭar contains all forms and can be conceived of as the owner of the waters he is responsible for death and destruction, as I have mentioned above. That is why he acquires the characteristics of a malevolent totalitarian tyrant against whom the son, esp. the young hero Indra, revolts.

It seems plausible that the generation conflict between the gods and the change in relative powers reflects the change in the traditional family relations. The necessity to migrate to new areas brought the Indo-Aryan tribes in conflict with neighbouring peoples. Their young qualified warriors (marya) functioned in these fights as storming-troops. Wikander (1938 p.74) regarded the Maruts, the wild heavenly companions of Indra, as a reflection of these warriors. According to him, they were organized in an 'arische Männerbund':

> 'Die Maruts reflektieren eben den kriegerischen Aspekt, den die Männerbünde bei dem arischen Stämme der Wanderungszeit und Eroberungszeit vorzügsweise entwickelt haben.'

Indra, the great chariot-fighter, is acknowledged by these young men as their god. He destroys the enemies and clears away the obstructions. He gives his people new space to live in. The murder of Tvaṣṭar by Indra should be conceived of from this point of view as the destruction of the demonic creator god who has turned against his creation. Indra's fight against the chaos monster is mentioned in many passages of the RV. After his liberation of the waters he has generated light, the sun and the sky. He has supported the earth and propped up the sky; Macdonell, 1897 p.61. Indra's weapon, the vajra, indicates that he also must have had connections with fertility; Gonda, 1978 p.61 f. The Maruts are not only young heavenly warriors, but also storm-gods who bring the heavy rains.

Since the beginning of the migration of the Indo-Aryan tribes from their original homeland a transformation must have taken place to a dualistic conception of the world. This transformation has been incorporated in the cult. Tvaṣṭar, the old creator god, is cast off from his fatherly throne and Indra assumes the government. The old generation becomes dependent upon the young one. In the new cult with Indra as central deity soma plays an important role. The warrior god is strengthened by it. According to Wasson (1968 p.10 f.) soma has hallucinogenic qualities and is prepared from the fly-agaric (Amanita muscaria Fr. ex L.). Wikander supposes that it was drunk by the young fighters before their campaigns. By drinking it they felt themselves invincible, because they disposed of 'Riesenkraft'. It is plausible that the priests gradually elaborated the soma cult. The fashioning of the four soma cups by the Ṛbhus seems to be an indication of this.

14. CONCLUDING REMARKS

With the settlement of the Indo-Aryan tribes in the north of India the balance was gradually restored and a new phase was introduced in their way of living. With this the relation between the warrior class and the priestly class changed. After the victory over the enemies and the occupation of their territory a new organization of society became important. The priests stressed their primacy in this process with respect to the warrior class in their brāhmaṇas. New conceptions are elaborated embracing the older ones. Prajāpati is in these texts an important god and can be conceived of as a new representative of the unitarian conception of life. He is identified with Savitar (Macdonell,1897 p.33), but also with Tvaṣṭar; e.g. Mbh.5.9.3,40; see also Van Buitenen and Dimmitt, 1978 p.294. In their endeavour to corroborate their claims the priests picked up ancient themes and reinterpreted them to their advantage. Indra becomes the murderer of the brahmin Viśvarūpa and virtually it is he who induced Tvaṣṭar to create Vṛtra by stealing the soma and drinking it. According to these traditions he becomes depressed on account of his guilt, so that he cannot act for the benefit of the world and conceals himself. In this way he is humiliated by the priests to their own advantage.

In this paper an attempt is made to outline the ideas connected with the drama concerning Tvaṣṭar. It may, however, be worthwhile to end with the words of Morgan (1877 p.5):

> 'The growth of religious ideas is environed with such intrinsic difficulties that it may never receive a perfectly satisfactory explanation.'

NOTES

1. The brāhmaṇas are theological treatises in which the hieratical class expounds its views. They date from the ninth century B.C.onwards and correspond to the separate Vedas. They give injunctions (vidhi) and explanations (athavāda) with reference to the seperate hymns and formulas which are contained in these Vedas, especially with respect to their employment in the sacrificial ritual.
2. Surā is a spirituous liquor; cf.Gonda, 1980 p. 64 f.
3. Indraśatru ; when the first member of this compound is accentuated it is called a bahuvrīhi and it denotes: 'having Indra as enemy (conquerer)'. If Tvaṣṭar, however, had stressed the second member of the compound the pronunciation of the curse would have been correct and its meaning would have been: 'Enemy (conquerer) of Indra, grow'.
4. The soma flowed in all directions from his nose, ears, etc. The Asvins cured Indra by a special sacrificial ritual called sautramaṇi; cf. Gonda,1980 p. 87 ff.
5. Ṛ̣V. 3.55.19; 9.81.4; 10.10.5
6. Ṛ̣V. 1.110; 111; 161; 4.33-37; 7.60. See also 3.60
7. Cf. also Griswold, 1971 p.276: 'If a mythological synonym, then Tvaṣṭar may have been originally an epithet of Dyaus, just as in two passages Savitar is an epithet of Tvaṣṭar'. Note 1.
8. In the context of the Āprī hymns the verbs piṃśati, 'he carves out (esp. meat), he prepares, he unites'. (Ṛ̣V.10.110.9) and samanakti, 'he anoints, he joints, he melts together' (Ṛ̣V.1.189.9) are chosen as a characterization of the activities of Tvaṣṭar; cf. also Van den Bosch, 1983 ch.4.9.
9. In the paradox the father is conceived of as the sky, while the rain bringing cloud is his udder; see also Geldner, 1951 p.331-332 with notes.

BIBLIOGRAPHY

Ammer, K., 1949: Tvaṣṭar, Ein altindischer Schöpfergott. Die Sprache I, Wien p.68 ff.

Bergaigne, A., 1878: La Rēligion Védique d'après les Hymnes du Rigveda I, Paris.

Bergaigne, A., 1883: La Rēligion Védique d'apres les Hymnes du Rigveda II and III, Paris.

Bergaigne, A., 1889: Histoire de la Liturgie Vēdique. Journal Asiatique 13, Paris.

Van den Bosch, L.P., 1981: Some reflections on the Āprī Hymns of the Ṛgveda and their interpretation. Lecture given at the fifth World Sanskrit Conference held in Benares. To be published in the Proceedings of the Conference.

Van den Bosch, L.P., 1984: The Āprī Hymns of the Ṛgveda and their Interpretation. In: Indo-Iranian Journal.

Boyce, M., 1975: A History of Zoroastrianism I, Leiden. Handbuch der Orientalistik.

Boyce, M., 1977: A Persian Stronghold of Zoroastrianism, Oxford.

Von Bradke, P., 1885: Dyaus Asura, Halle.

Brown, W.N., 1942: The Creation Myth of the Rig Veda. Journal of the American Oriental Society (JAOS), vol.62.

Brown, W.N., 1965: Theories of Creation in the Rig Veda. JAOS, vol. 85.

Brown, W.N., 1974: Prelude to the Indra-Vṛtra Battle (ṚV.10.124). Journal of I.E. Studies, vol.2.

Van Buitenen, J.A.B. and Dimmitt, C., 1978: Classical Hindu Mythology. A Reader in the Sanskrit Purāṇas, Philadelphia

Caland, W., 1924: Das Śrautasūtra des Āpastamba, vol.2, Amsterdam. Royal Academy.

Dandekar, R.N., 1979: New Light on the Vedic God, Savitar. In: Vedic Mythological Tracts, Delhi.

Ehlers, F., 1971: Klimageschichte und Siedlungsgang in Vor- und Frühgeschichtlicher Zeit in der Turkmenensteppe Nordpersiens. Arch.Mitt. aus Iran, NF.4, S. 7ff.

Eggeling, J., 1972: The Śatapatha Brāhmaṇa, vol. I-V, Delhi. Repr. of the first edition, I (1882), II (1885), III (1894), IV (1897), V (1900). Sacred Books of the East.

Geldner, K.F., 1951: Der Rig-Veda, aus dem Sanskrit übersetzt und mit einem laufenden Kommentar versehen, 3 vols., Cambridge (Mass.). Harvard Oriental Series vol.33-35.

Gershevitch, I., 1959: The Avestan Hymn to Mithra, Text with an English Translation and Notes, Cambridge.

Ghirshman, R., 1977: Iran et la Migration des Indo-Aryens et des Iraniens, Leiden.

Gonda, J., 1960: Die Religionen Indiens, I, Veda und älterer

Hinduismus, Stuttgart.
Gonda, J., 1974: Dual deities in the religion of the Veda, Amsterdam. Royal Academy.
Gonda, J., 1975: Vedic literature, Wiesbaden. Hist. of Indian Lit., fasc. I, 1.
Gonda, J., 1978: Die Religionen Indiens, I. Veda und älterer Hinduismus. Revised edition.
Gonda, J., 1980: The mantras of the Agnyupasthāna and the Šautrāmaṇi, Amsterdam. Royal Academy.
Grassmann, H., 1964: Wörterbuch zum Rigveda, Wiesbaden (4 unveränderte Auflage).
Griswold, H.D., 1971: The religion of the Rigveda, Delhi (repr. ed. 1917).
Haug, M., 1890: Essays on the sacred language, writings and religion of the Parsees, London (3 ed.).
Hauschild, R., 1964: Völker und Sprachen Kleinasiens, Berling. Sitzungsberichte Sächs. Ak. der Wiss. zu Leipzig, Band 109.
Hillebrandt, A., 1929: Vedische Mythologie II, Breslau.
Hillebrandt, A., 1965: Vedische Mythologie I,II. Repr. Nachdruck. ed. 1929, Hidesheim.
Keith, A.B., 1914: The Veda of the Black Yajus school, entitled Taittrirya Sanhita, Cambridge (Mass.) H.O.S. 18:and:19.
Keith, A.B., 1925: The religion and philosophy of the Veda and the Upanishads, 2 vols., Cambridge (Mass). H.O.S. 31 and 32.
Kuiper, F.B.J., 1975: The basic concept of Vedic religion. Hist. of Rel. vol.15, Chicago.
Lewis, I.M., 1971: Ecstatic religion, an anthropological study of spirit possession and Shamanism,Harmondsworth.
Lüders, H., 1951: Varuṇa, I, Varuṇa und die Wasser, Göttingen.
Lüders, H., 1959: Varuṇa, II, Varuna und das Ṛta, Göttingen.
Macdonell, A.A., 1897: Vedic mythology, Strassburg. Grundriss Indo-Ar. Phil. und Altertumsk.
Macdonell, A.A., 1917: A Vedic reader for students, London Repr. Madras, 1971.
Mayrhofer, M., 1956-1976: Etymologisches Wörterbuch des Altindischen, I (1956), II (1963), III (1976), Heidelberg.
Mayrhofer, M., 1964: Über Kontaminationen der Indo-Arischen Sippen des a.i. taks-, tvaks-, tvarś-. In:Indo-Iranica, mélanges présentés à G. Morgenstierne, Wiesbaden.
Mayer, J.J., 1937: Trilogie altindischer Mächte und Feste der Vegetation, Leipzig/Zürich (3 vols.).
Morgan, L.M., 1877: Ancient society, Chicago.
Nobel, J., 1957: Namen und Sachregister zur Übersetzung des Rigveda von K.F. Geldner, Cambridge (Mass.). H.O.S.

36.
O'Flaherty, W.D., 1975: Hindu myths, Harmondsworth.
O'Flaherty, W.D., 1980: Women, androgynes and other mythical beasts, Chicago.
O'Flaherty, W.D., 1981: The Rigveda, an anthology , Harmondsworth.
Oldenberg, H., 1897: Savitar. In: ZDMG 51 p.473-484 (Kleine Schriften I, Wiesbaden, 1967 p.714 ff.).
Oldenberg, H., 1905: Noch einmal der Vedische Savitar. In: ZDMG 59 p.253 ff.) (Kleine Schriften II, Wiesbaden, 1967 p.790 ff.).
Oldenberg, H., 1970: Die Religion des Veda, Darmstadt. Repr. ed. Stuttgart, 1917.
Potdar, K.R. 1945-1946: The Āprī hymns of the Rigveda, a study and a theory. Journal of the University of Bombay, sept. 1945 (I) and sept 1946 (II),
Potdar, K.R., 1952: The Ṛbhus in the Ṛgvedic sacrifice. Journal of the University of Bombay.
Renou, L., 1951: Les litteratures de l'Inde, Paris.
Rönnow, K., 1927: Trita Aptya, eine Vedische Gottheit, Uppsala. Thesis Litt.
Ryder, W.A., 1901: Die Ṛbhus im Ṛgveda, Gütersloh. Diss. Phil. Leipzig.
Schmidt, E.P., 1968: Bṛhaspati und Indra. Untersuchungen zur Vedische Mythologie und Kulturgeschichte, Wiesbaden.
Turner, V., 1974: Dramas, field and metaphors. Symbolic action in human society, London.
Varenne, J. , 1967: Mythes et legendes extraits des Brāhmaṇas, Paris.
Wasson, G.R., 1968: Soma, the divine mushroom of immortality, New York.
Wikander, S., 1938: Der arische Männerbund, Lund.

List with some abbrevations:

AV.	Atharvaveda
Mbh.	Mahābhārata
ṚV.	Ṛgveda
ŚB.	Śatapatha Brāhmaṇa
TS.	Taittiriya Saṃhitā
Y.	Yasna.

Feminine versus Masculine. The Sophia Myth and the Origins of Feminism

I. P. Culianu

Undoubtedly, as Th.P. van Baaren says, 'religion is a function of culture' (Drijvers-Leertouwer, 1973 p.160) - although a delimitation of 'culture' as a phenomenon that is both outside religion and inclusive of it, may not correspond to the current situation in which religion is culture, as an expression of both ecological (Harris, 1977; Lincoln, 1981) and anthropological (or even anthropogonic) factors (Morin, 1973).

This basic principle of the 'Groningen group' has led to a radical reconsideration of the phenomenology of religion. Indeed, if religion is merely to be studied in connection with that culture of which it is a 'function', then the problem of categories and patterns does not make sense any more. I can fully agree with H.J.W. Drijvers and L. Leertouwer, who find that 'a totally different method of comparison must be developped than that of phenomenology' (Drijvers-Leertouwer, 1973 p.163). This explicit statement is necessary, since in my paper I am obliged to deal with materials that hardly could call either upon a 'common origin', or upon any lineage whatsoever. However, I have many reasons for claiming that my approach is strictly historical, in so far as it is based on unequivocal facts, although a merely genetic perspective is not able to provide a valid explanation thereof. These facts ought to be faced as such, and it is not our methodology that must try to get rid of them if they do not fit into it, but they that are supposed to enlarge and modify, if necessary, our methodology. For, as H.J.W. Drijvers puts it, 'the historical method does not exist; there are only methods, which are used in the discipline of history in accordance with the problem from which the researcher takes his start and the subject he is working on' (Drijvers, 1973 p.58).

I. The Myth of Sophia

The subject on which I started working a long time ago was the Sophia myth and its place in different gnostic systems. I found out that, with the exception of the Valentinian gnosis (Stead, 1969), there is no corpus of the Sophia myth, a shortcoming of research which this article, as imperfect and incomplete it may be, tries to supply. I also found out that most of the scholars who have dealt with this myth were greatly interested in determining its origin (Bousset, 1907; Quispel, 1974; Schenke, 1962; Stead, 1969; MacRae, 1970; Rudolph, 1980), and only occasionally did they show a certain concern for its interpretation, usually in psychoanalytic terms (Meslin, 1970 and 1973; Pagels, 1979). However, no one seemed to take notice of the fact that the basic situation reflected in the Sophia myth - namely that responsibility for the deterioration of the human condition in the actual world is attributed to an original sin and to a subsequent 'passion' of a female entity - is not confined to gnosticism. On the contrary, such a myth, showing very surprising analogies with the myth of Sophia, is very wide spread, and, if I chose only a few examples to make my point, it was certainly not because I was running short of materials.

The occurrence of this myth in very different cultures must not be lightly dismissed as irrelevant to the case in point. On the contrary, it seems to belong to precisely that sort of problems of which those historians and anthropologists who believe that 'religion is a function of culture' should be mostly fond of, since a solution thereto can only be expected from a cultural comparison, transcending a merely genetic perspective. Needless to say, such an approach was possible here only in broad outline, and it could involve only a very restricted number of social and anthropological factors. That is why no final statement should be expected, besides the fact that the Sophia myth and its parallels seem to indicate that a certain pattern of 'feminism' occurs in archaic cultures and has the tendency to take analogous shapes in different environments.

1 THE CORPUS OF THE SOPHIA MYTH

This corpus, although not exhaustive, is however the most complete that has been established to date. According to the role devoted to Sophia in gnostic myth, three sorts of testimonies can be distinguished: A. Testimonies in which Sophia is a fallen entity (by far the most numerous and representative); B. Testimonies in which Sophia is exclusively the highest aeon of the unfathomable Father; C. Testimonies in which Sophia is replaced by a male entity, called Logos.

A SOPHIA AS A FALLEN ENTITY

a Testimonies from the Heresiologists

The name Sophia does not occur in the gnosis of Simon Magus. However, it is there that the immediate source of the Sophia myth should be sought for.

According to Irenaeus (I 23,2), the Ennoia (Mother-of-All) of the Father (Supreme-Power), emanated by the latter, 'descended into the lower regions and generated angels and powers by whom .. this world too was made. After she had generated them, however, she was held prisoner by them, due to envy, since they did not want to be regarded as the offspring of anyone else. He himself (Simon) was completely unknown to them, yet his Ennoia was held in bondage by the powers and angels emitted by her; and they subjected her to every form of humiliation to prevent her from hastening back to her Father. So far did this go that she was even confined in a human body, and for centuries, as if from one vessel to another, transmigrated into other female bodies'. After being Helena of Troy, 'finally she arrived even in a brothel' (tr. Haardt-Hendry, in Haardt, 1971 p.33). Simon came to redeem her and raise her up. (Note that Simon's lady was entitled to bear, as a spiritual entity, the titles of Mother and Virgin, while she was actually a whore; note also that the whole story was not that extraordinary in hellenistic context, since tradition concerning Pythagoras' transmigrations usually attributed to him reincarnation as 'the beautiful prostitute Alco').

The same doctrine, according to Irenaeus (I 23,5), was held by Menander, Simon's successor.

In the gnostic systems reported by the heresiologists, the Sophia myth occurs, besides the Valentinian gnosis, in the gnosis of the Barbelo-gnostics of Irenaeus (I 29,4), the Ophites of Irenaeus (I 30,3-4) and the Book of Baruch of Justin the Gnostic, according to Hippolytus (V 26,19-21), which is, however, only a further variant of the original myth.

Irenaeus's notice concerning the Barbelo-gnostics was based on the Apocryphon Johannis (Till, 1955 p.33; Giversen, 1963 p.282), extant in four coptic versions, of which one belongs to the Papyrus Berolinensis 8502 (BG) (Till, 1955 p.78-195), and the other three to the finding in Nag Hammadi (Krause-Labib, 1962): codex II,1 (Giversen, 1963; F.Wisse, in Robinson, 1977 p.98-116), III,1 and IV,1 (see also Krause-Labib, 1962).

Irenaeus' notice runs as follows (I 29,4 Harvey; also apud Giversen, 1963 p. 284) :'Deinde ex primo angelo (qui adstat Monogeni) emissum dicunt Spiritum sanctum, quem et Sophiam, et Prunicum vocant. Hunc igitur videntem reliqua omnia conjugationem habentia, se autem sine conjugatione, quaesisse cui adunaretur : et cum non inveniret, asseverabat et extendebatur, et prospiciebat ad inferiores partes, putans hic invenire conjugem. : et non inveniens, exsiliit taediata quoque, quoniam sine bona voluntate patris impetum fecerat. Post deinde simplicitate et benignitate acta generavit opus, in quo erat ignorantia et audacia. Hoc autem opus ejus esse Proarchontem (Protarchontem) dicunt, fabricatorem conditionis hujus : virtutem autem magnam abstulisse eum a matre narrant, et abstitisse ab ea in inferiora, et fecisse firmamentum coeli, in quo et habitare dicunt eum. Et cum sit ignorantia, fecisse eas quae sunt sub eo potestates, et angelos, et firmamenta, et terrena omnia. Deinde dicunt adunitum eum Authadiae, generasse Kakian, Zelon, et Phthonum, et Erinnyn, et Epithymiam. Generatis autem his, mater Sophia contristata refugit, et in altiora secessit et fit deorsum numerantibus octonatio. Illa igitur secedente, se solum opinnatum esse, et propter hoc dixisse : Ego sum Deus zelator, et praeter me nemo est. Et hi quidem talia mentiuntur.'

This text, being particularly important, deserved being quoted here at full length. In it, Sophia, also called Prunicos, a name that could be translated as 'The Prurient', being an indication of her sexual desire, is deprived of a syzygos. Therefore, she looks for a syzygos in the lower parts of the universe, and, being ashamed of her deed, she brings forth by herself the Protarchon of the lower Hebdomas. The Protarchon, whose syzygos is his own Presumption (Authadia), generates a number of vices. Sophia runs away from this disorderly creation and withdraws in the Ogdoas, i.e., above the Hebdomas.

In Irenaeus' account of the doctrine of the so-called Ophites, Sophia is a 'left-power' deriving from a leak of light from the left side of the Mother of the Living, who could not store in herself the whole mass of fertilizing light that flowed out of the Father of All and his Son (I 30,1-2). Sophia is also called Left, Prunicos, and Male-Female. She comes down on the motionless waters, sets them in motion, and takes a watery (i.e., material) body from them. Weighed down by matter, she tries to escape from the waters, but is unable to do so. She spreads out like a covering, and forms the visible sky out of her body (Haardt, 1971 p.77). After this, she dwells for a while under the heaven, but eventually puts off her watery body (also called Woman) and ascends above the sky. She is said to have a son, Ialdabaoth (whose name, according to Giversen, 1963 p.200, is correctly rendered by the coptic form Altabathô, found in NH II 67,29; 71,36; 72,12 and deriving from the Hebrew ʾel-taʾbôth, 'God of the desires' or 'longings'), who generates six other archons (Iren.I 30,3-5). This Hebdomas corresponds to the seven planets (ib.I 30,9). Sophia constantly helps mankind against the heavenly Rulers, seizing every occasion to deceive the latter (ib.30, 6.7.9.10). However, being unable to put an end to the tyranny of her Son, she calls upon her heavenly Mother, who makes that Christ (Sophia's brother, being the 'right-power' who asscended to the Pleroma) descends and, becoming Sophia's syzygos, redeems mankind through Jesus Christ (30,12-13).

According to the Book of Baruch of Justin the Gnostic reviewed by Hippolytus (V 26,1-37), a female entity, called Eden, similar in her functions to Sophia, is abandoned by her husband Elohim, the Father of Creation, who ascends with his angels to the unfathomable Father and sits at the right hand of the second male principle, called Good. This primordial divorce between Elohim and Eden has cosmic repercussions, since Eden, who is thenceforth the only supervisor of creation, tortures the _pneuma_ of Elohim in man by means of the angels Babel (Aphrodite) and Naas. Aphrodite incites 'among men adulteries and divorces', while Naas torments 'the Pneuma of Elohim with every form of punishment, in order thereby to punish Elohim himself through the Pneuma, (since) he had broken the marriage covenant entered into by him and abandoned his wife' (_ib._,20-21,tr. Haardt-Hendry).

The most extensive pieces of evidence provided by heresiologists in connection with the Sophia myth belong to the Valentinian gnosis. As they have been thoroughly studied by G.C. Stead (Stead, 1969), they do not deserve here a close investigation. They are represented by the accounts of Irenaeus (I 1,1-8.4), preserved in Greek version by Epiphanius (_Panarion_, 31), Hippolytus (V 29-36), and by the fragments of the Eastern Valentinian Theodotus preserved by Clement of Alexandria. As far as the fragments of Heracleon are concerned, preserved by Origen in his commentary to the Gospel of John, they belong to another group of testimonies (see further, under section C).

Irenaeus and Hippolytus use two sources of the Valentinian myth, commonly known as A and B: Irenaeus prefers A, taking however incidental notice of B (29,2.3); Hippolytus prefers B, using A in a few places (22,2;29,3;30,4;31,3). 'In both versions Sophia transgressed by acting presumptuously without her consort; but in version A she desires to penetrate the mystery which surrounds the supreme power, an attempt which nearly proves fatal; in version B she attempts to imitate the creative power of the Father by generating without her consort, so that a defective being results. In version A the next episode is played by Sophia's guilty thought, now discarded and in some way personified; in version B it is Sophia's formless, because fatherless, offspring, the ἔκτρωμα . It may perhaps be noted that at this point version B resembles the Barbeliote myth, in which Ialdabaoth is the fatherless offspring of Sophia, whereas A suggests the Ophite myth in which a second female power results from the first, so to speak, through the fragmentation of her personality when she is unable to bear the excess of light' (Stead, 1969 p.78). Further on, according to Stead, A presupposes a 'Pythagorizing' origin, while B was more influenced by Philo of Alexandria (Stead, 1969 p.79-80). However, 'both A and B represent late developments of Valentinian teaching which are considerably more complex than the system of Valentinus himself' (ibid.,81). G.C. Stead has attempted to reconstruct the evolution of the Sophia myth in Valentinian thinking (ib. 96-103), which meets, however, with very serious difficulties. According to him, Valentinus himself, as well as his pupil Ptolemaeus, were only marginally influenced by dualism, which they actually tried to avert. In the original doctrine of Valentinus, Sophia was an unfallen entity, a consort-Spirit of God (ib. 87,103). Therefrom developed the theory of a lower Sophia 'who fell from blessedness but was healed by divine intervention' (ib.103). 'Finally the concept of the perfect Sophia was abandoned, and the stories of upper and lower Sophia were assimilated one to another, so that they lost all useful distinctiveness, except that their difference served further to heighten the contrast between heaven and earth' (ib.103).

This evolutionary view tries to simplify the Valentinian puzzle in which, as G.C. Stead himself noticed very well, there are five distinct conceptions of Sophia: '1. Sophia as God's perfect consort. 2.Sophia as essentially the source of matter, evil and death. 3. Sophia who falls and leaves the heavenly world, but is pardoned and restored. 4. Sophia who sins and is pardoned, though without leaving the Pleroma. 5. Lower Sophia, who remains outside the Pleroma, but is pardoned and awaits restoration' (ib. 93).

As we will see further, all these five conceptions occur in the original gnostic texts from which, no doubt, the Valentinians took their inspiration. In this case, the preference for one or another version of the Sophia myth becomes a matter of choice between different positions, a view that ostensibly clashes with any attempt at an evolutionary reconstruction of Valentinian thinking. The Valentinians speculated upon a given gnostic system, represented, among other treatises, by the Apocryphon Johannis. Discarding, averting, or, on the contrary, stressing the dualistic presuppositions of different basic gnostic systems was a matter of personal interpretation which should not be transformed into a chronological sequence. Within the Valentinian school, the position of different thinkers, ranging from an abeyance of dualism to a plenary admission thereof, seems to be determined by the personal concern of every individual author (also according to the school to which he belongs) as to whether the relation to the Grosskirche has to be saved or not. This concern seems to play a more important role in the Italian school, in agreement with the teaching of Valentinus himself. However, the (late) Valentinian systems described by Irenaeus and Hippolytus, as well as the testimonies belonging to the Anatolic school, do not hesitate to put at jeopardy the relation with the Catholics. According to whether or not the dialogue with the Grosskirche had to be kept up, the Valentinian gnosis has known a process that hardly could be qualified as an evolution, being rather a contextual modification resulting from a higher or lower degree of admission, within different Valentinian systems, of the basic preexistent tenets of gnosticism.

b Original gnostic testimonies

Among the original gnostic testimonies in coptic language two deserve a particular attention: The Apocryphon Johannis, on which Irenaeus' notice about the Barbelo-gnostics was based, and the first two books of Pistis Sophia of the Askew codex. The latter are almost entirely devoted to the story of fall and restitution of Sophia.

It has been told above that the Apocryphon Johannis is extant in four versions, two long (NH II,1 and IV,1) and two short (BG 2 and NH III,1), all of them largely concording with one another. With some inconsequential differences of vocabulary, the myth of Sophia is presented in all four version in identical terms: 'But (δέ) Epinoia's (ἐπίνοια) Sophia (σοφία), since she is an aeon (αἰών), conceived a thought from herself with the invisible (ἀόρατος) spirit's (πνεῦμα) Enthymesis (ἐνθύμεσις) and Prognosis (πρόγνωσις) ; she would reveal an image from herself without the will/ of the spirit (πνεῦμα) although he did not approve (εὐδοκεῖν) it and /without/ her fellow and without his thought. But (δέ) thought it without (χωρίς) the will of the spirit (πνεῦμα) and the knowledge of her fellow she brought it forth. But (δέ) because of the invincible power in her her thought was not ineffective (ἀργός) and an imperfect thing was revealed from her, and it was different from her appearance because she had created it without her fellow, and it bore no likeness to the mother's hope and it had another figure (μορφή) (NH II,1 p.57, 25-58,7 Giversen). This dragon with a lion's face, called Ialdabaôth (or, as in several places of NH II,1, Altabathô: cf. Giversen, 1963 p.200), is the first archon, the demiurge of the lower world. Together with his own Non-Sense (ἀπόνοια) ;cf.BG 2,118 Till;

NH III,1,15,9-16 Krause-Labib), the Protarchon generates 12 ἐξουσίαι and seven kosmokratores, Rulers of the Universe, who are the planetary Hebdomas and have as syzygiai seven attributes of God from the Old Testament (cf.BG 2,124-8 Till etc.). The total number of the ἀγγελία is 360 (cf.BG2,39,14-15 Till,etc.). At this point, Sophia, who had tried to conceal her miscarried child from the aeons, realizes the consequence of her fault and, in dismay, begins to go to and fro (cf.NH II,1,p.61, 14 Giversen, etc.) and repents (μετανοεῖν).

The repentance of Sophia is the major subject of the first two books of the coptic treatise Pistis Sophia of the Askew codex. The terminus post quem of this treatise is the first half of the IIIrd century C.E., since Pistis Sophia contains five Odes of Salomo, and H.J.W. Drijvers demonstrated that these Odes, whose background is an anti-marcionite polemic, were written in Syriac at the beginning of the IIIrd. century (Drijvers, 1978).

The cosmic drama and the restoration of Sophia form the core of the teachings of Pistis Sophia. The text, which could be certainly called farraginous , is based on a crude and primitive cosmology. Since the authors of the bad heimarmene of man are the kosmokratores, salvation is viewed as a process of breaking down the regularity of the motions of the heavenly rulers. This conception of salvation presupposes a vivid polemic against astrology.

The story of the fall and restoration of Sophia is presented here in rather unusual terms. From the beginning on, Pistis Sophia is installed outside the Pleroma of the 24 of Light, and, at the same time, above the 12 aeons ruled by the archons of the great τύραννος Adamas, which obviously represent the twelve signs of the zodiac. Thus, Sophia abides in the 13th. aeon, beneath the border of the Pleroma and above the seats of the τύραννοι (PS ch.29,p.25 Schmidt-Till). Not only the archons hate her, but also the τριδύναμος Authades, who resides in the 13th aeon. To spoil Sophia and deprive her of her light, Authades emanates a force with a lion's face, and, from the ὕλη of this force, he emanates several other προβολαί that are ὑλικοί. He sends the latter in different τόποι of the χάος. Casting a glance below, Pistis Sophia sees the light of the leontocephalic force, and takes it for a representative of the Pleroma. Without asking her *syzygos'* permission, she goes down to that deceiving light, thinking that, if she could incorporate it, she would make of it an aeon of light and use the latter as a vehicle to ascend to the Pleroma. On the contrary, it is the leontocephale who swallows Sophia's *dynamis* of light, whose excreted *hyle* becomes, in the chaos, an archon with a lion's face, called Ialdabaoth. The body of the latter is made of fire and darkness (PS ch.31, p.28 Schmidt-Till). Deprived of her light, Pistis Sophia becomes very weak, and, repenting several times, she calls upon the Pleroma to help her in her distress. To save Pistis Sophia from all her followers, the aeon Christ is eventually dispatched by the Pleroma.

The myth of the fall of Sophia occurs further in several coptic gnostic treatises discovered at Nag Hammadi, although seldom in its complete form.

In the myth of the *Hypostasis of the Archons* (II 94,4-8,tr. Bullard, in Robinson,1977 p.157), where several female characters occur - Incorruptibility, Spiritual Woman of Mother of Living, Carnal Woman or Eve, Norea and Zoe - it is told that Pistis Sophia 'wanted to create something, alone without her consort'. She is also mother of Zoe (95,6ff) and supervisor of life and justice in the lower world (96,1-4).

In the treatise of Codex II,5 which was given the title

On the Origin of the World, Pistis Sophia is also held responsible for having created the demiurge Yaldabaoth, who is 'lion-like in appearance' (100,8,tr.Bethge-Wintermute in Robinson,1977 p.163).

In *The Second Treatise of the Great Seth* (VII,2) the aeon Sophia is called *whore* (50,28), a term that cannot be explained without a reference to her being 'prurient' (which is still the most probable translation of the Greek *prounikos*) and, as such, being the cause of devolution within the Pleroma. This might also explain the occurrence in the gnostic (?) library at Nag Hammadi of a text like *Bronte*, *Perfect Mind* (VI,2), which is probably an aretalogy of Isis and has nothing gnostic in it. However, a gnostic reader might have easily recognized Sophia in Bronte, who claims to be both 'the whore and the holy one' (13,19 tr. MacRae in Robinson,1977 p.271). There is no clear explanation of the fall of Sophia in the *Second Treatise of the Great Seth*, except that she acted without consulting the Pleroma and thus the product of her work was perishable (VII,50,26ff). However, when seeing the deeds of the Savior, some of the archons were persuaded by Sophia to leave the lower world ruled by the Cosmocrator (cf. the *Book Baruch* of Justin the Gnostic, cited above). The motif of the repenting archons is not uncommon in gnosticism. For instance, in the *Hypostasis of the Archons* (II 95,13ff), it is Sabaoth who defects Matter, joining Sophia and her daughter Zoe. However, in the *Second Treatise of the Great Seth* it is told that these archons were equally ignorant, since they believed that Sophia herself was the Supreme Power in the Pleroma (VII 52,34). As a matter of fact, the Supreme Power is male, not female, it is a Father, not a Mother. It is not unusual that gnostic texts insist upon the superiority of the male upon the femal principle: 'femaleness existed, but femaleness was not first' (The First Apocalypse of James, V 24,29 tr. Schoedel in Robinson, 1977 p.243).

The Letter of Peter to Philip (VIII,2) reports the fall of Sophia in sharp terms: 'When the disobedience and the foolishness of the mother appeared without the commandment of the majesty of the Father, she wanted to raise up aeons. And when she spoke, the Authades (Arrogance) /followed/. And when she left behind a part, the Authades laid hold of it, and it became a deficiency' (135,12ff,tr.Wisse in Robinson,1977 p.396). Men are those 'who have suffered at the transgression of the mother' (139,23).

In The Thought of Norea (IX,2), deficiency is attributed to Norea, who, as a female entity also occurring elsewhere in gnostic treatises, might be identified in this case with Sophia.

In A Valentinian Exposition (IX,2), which could not belong to the school of Heracleon, as E.H. Pagels claims (in Robinson, 1977 p.435), since the replacement of Sophia by Logos was fundamental in Heracleon, the Sophia myth cannot be clearly reconstructed, because of the very lacunary text on page 32.

B SOPHIA AS AN UPPER AEON

At least in one of the coptic testimonies, the Sophia Jesu Christi, extant in four versions (NH III,3 and 4; V,1;BG 8502,3), of which two (III,3 and V,1) bear the title of Eugnostos the Blessed and are slightly different from the other two, Sophia is exclusively viewed as an upper aeon, a syzygos of Man, who is the first emanation of the Propator, the unfathomable Father. Gnostics are said to be those who do not simply invoke a Father as an archē of the All, but an Urvater (Propator), who is anarchos, without any beginning (Till,1955 p.222-3). This is an extremely interesting transcendental motivation of gnostic 'anarchism'.

Though the text of the Sophia Jesu Christi contains several allusions to the fault of a woman (e.g.BG 8502,118,15-16 in Till,1955 p.276-77), this is probably Eve, not Sophia. The latter is simply an Urmutter, Mother of All, πρωτογενέτειρα (Till,1955 p.238), also called ἀγάπη. The hypostasis of Sophia, is, however, duplicated, since she is figured out as both syzygos of Man and mother of Son of Man (Eugnostos III 77,tr. Parrott in Robinson, 1977 p.214a) and syzygos of son of Man (ib.,218a; cf.Sophia,ib.214b and 218b). Eugnostos goes even further, ascribing the name of Sophia to the female parts of all of the six androgynous beings begotten by the syzygos of son of Man: All-wise Sophia, All-Mother Sophia, All-Begettress Sophia, First-Begettress Sophia, Love Sophia, Pistis Sophia (ib.,218a). There are, thus, eight Sophias united in perfect syzygiai with male principles. According to both Eugnostos and Sophia (ib.,223), Sophia the consort of Man is also called Silence, which recalls the Valentinian aeon Sigé.

The Sophia Jesu Christi contains an allusion to the coming to existence of the demiurge of the lower world, who proclaims himself Almighty (ib.,219b-220b). The name of Sophia also occurs in connection therewith, but she is ostensibly cleared of any responsibility for the fall of the demiurge.

The Mother of All may also be introduced, in gnostic treatises belonging to that kind of speculations very developped among the Sethians of Hippolytus, as an androgynous being in which femaleness is, however, predominant: 'I am androgynous (I am both Mother and) Fahter since (I copulate) with myself. (I copulate) with myself (and with those who love)me, (and) it is through me alone that the All (stands firm). I am the Womb (that gives shape) to the All by giving birth to the light that (shines in) splendor. I am the Aeon to (come.I am) the fulfillment of the all, that is, Me (iroth) ea, the glory of the Mother' (Trimorphic Protennoia XIII 45,tr. Turner, in Robinson,1977 p.467). Trimorphic Protennoia seems also to belong to those treatises in which Protennoia-Barbelo is exclusively viewed as an upper female entity.

However, a Sethian version of the fall of Sophia is preserved in the Paraphrasis of Sêem (VIII,1), namely in the story of how Derdekeas the Savior suscitated the forms of the universe from the cosmic womb: 'And I said to her "May seed and power come forth from you upon the earth". And she obeyed the will of the Spirit that she might be brought to naught. And when her forms returned, they rubbed their tongues with each other; they copulated; they begot winds and demons and the power which is the form of fire and the Darkness and the Spirit. But the form which remained alone cast the beast from herself. She did non have intercourse, but she was the one who rubbed herself alone. And she brought forth a wind which possessed a power from the fire and the Darkness and the Spirit' (VII 21,tr. Wisse in Robinson,1977 p.317-18).

Gnosticism - and not only Valentinian - abounds in examples in which female entities are both viewed as important hypostases of the Pleroma (e.g., Mother of Living) and as lower principles that caused the devolution of the Pleroma and called the inferior world into being. The distinction is very clear in The First Apocalypse of James (V,3): 'But I shall call upon the imperishable knowledge, which is Sophia who is the Father (and) who is the mother of Achamoth. Achamoth had no father nor male consort, but she is female from a female. She produced you without a male, since she was alone (and) in ignorance as to what (lives through) her mother because she thought that she alone existed' (35,tr. Schoedel in Robinson, 1977 p.246). The same opposition between a higher Sophia (Echamoth) and a lower one (Echmoth) occurs in the Gospel of Philip (II,3): 'Echamoth is one thing and Echmoth another. Echamoth is Wisdom simply, but Echmoth is the Wisdom of death which is the one which knows death, which is called 'the little Wisdom' '(60,tr. Isenberg in Robinson, 1977 p.136).

The same reduplication of the female hypostasis is obvious in the Barbelognostic systems, where Barbelo is the image of the unfathomable Father (e.g., Apocr. Joh., BG 8502,27,11-13 in Trill,1955 p.94), whereas Sophia is the lowest aeon belonging to the fourth and last Great Light, ruled by the angel Elêlêth. Being prurient, she thinks without her syzygos' permission and produces Ialdabaoth (Till, 1955 p.114-116).

Sometimes, reduplication of female beings has a systematic character in gnostic treatises, such as The Hypostasis of the Archons (II,4). It is perhaps because two accounts of creation, of which the second is clearly Barbeliote, are mixed up in this text, that the number of female entities is so high. In the first part of the treatise, the main oppositions involve the Spiritual Woman *versus* the carnal Woman, and Eve *versus* Norea. In the second part, three female entities are concerned: the Virgin Spirit (παρθενικὸν πνεῦμα) is usually the name of Barbelo: cf.Till, 1955 p.94), Sophia-Pistis, who caused the lower world to be, and Zoe, Sophia's daughter. Both Norea and Zoe play a positive role in the history of salvation, though being daughters of fallible female beings. The two series of characters are perfectly symmetrical and represent the duplicate of one another on different planes: on the spiritual plane, Sophia is the antithesis of the Virgin of Spirit, whereas Zoe is in some way the restoration of her mother Sophia to a prelapsary state; on the plane of creation, the carnal Woman (Eve) is the shadow and the antithesis of the spiritual

Woman, whereas Norea is the one who contributes to free mankind from the Rulers of Unrighteousness.

C SOPHIA REPLACED BY LOGOS

In his *Commentary on John* (II 14,in John I 3), Origen ascribes to Heracleon, a teacher of the Western Valentinian school, the idea that the lower world has been created *through* Logos (τὸν δι᾽οὗ) and not by Logos (οὐ τὸν ἀφ᾽οὗ ἤ ὑφ᾽οὗ). As a matter of fact, it is the Demiurge who created the lower world, but Logos caused him to do that. In a passage reported *verbatim* by Origen, Heracleon states that Logos has formed the spiritual men κατὰ τὴν γένεσιν (Orig. II 21), by planting in them the pneumatic seeds deriving from the Pleroma. This is enough to understand, from this highly attendible source, that Heracleon replaced, in the Valentinian myth of creation, the entity Sophia by the entity Logos. Heracleon's case was unique in the history of gnosticism. Its uniqueness has been recently confirmed by the fact that such a doctrine of Logos occurs in only one of the Nag Hammadi treatises, the *Tractatus tripartitus* (I,5), which has rightly been ascribed either to Heracleon himself or - which is more probable - to his school.

The author of the *Tractatus tripartitus* is extremely careful in clearing Logos-Sophia of any guilt, although such a result cannot obviously be reached without internal contradiction. He claims that Logos acted out of *free will* (1 75,35), a statement that seems hardly conceivable before Origen, the more so as Logos' free will has a parallel in the αὐτεξούσιον of the origenian νοῖ, their free will being that which actually determined their fall (Crouzel, in Bianchi-Crouzel, 1981 p.47:8). It has been said that Origen's doctrine is conditioned 'par le désir de donner une réponse philosophique aux présupposés cosmogoniques des gnostiques pour sauver à tout prix le libre arbitre' (Documento finale, in Bianchi-Crouzel, 1981 p.305). As far as the Tractatus tripartitus is concerned, one could say that it is conditionné par le désir de donner une réponse gnostique aux présupposés philosophiques des chrétiens. This seems to imply both that Origen's doctrine of free will already existed, and that the Tractatus tripartitus is moving out of the deep concern of meeting this doctrine in a point where no contradiciton between gnosticism and the Grosskirche would subsist. As a matter of fact, the Tractatus tripartitus is no less christian than Origen himself was gnostic.

'The intent of Logos was something good', states the Tractatus tripartitus (76,3-4,tr. Atridge-Pagels in Robinson, 1977 p.68). However, this aeon was the last of the Pleroma 'and he was young in age', i.e. unexperienced. 'Therefore it is not fitting to criticize the movement which is the Logos, but it is fitting that we should say about the movement of Logos, that it is a cause of a system, which has been destined to come about' (77,6ff). If the Logos failed in his attempt to 'grasp the incomprehensibility' of the Father, it was because he was programmed to fail, so that the inferior world could come into being. This is actually a platonic view of the fall, and could be ascribed only to a gnostic who was anxious both to please the Grosskirche and at the same time to keep up gnostic myth in almost its full extent. For Logos takes over Sophia's adventures and, being rejected by the Limit, he produces deficiency 'for he was not able to bear the sight of the light, but he looked into the depth and he doubted. Therefore it was an extremely painful division and a turning away because of his self-doubt and division, forgetfulness and ignorance of himself and of that which is '. (77,18ff).

J. Zandee has argued that the occurrence of Logos instead of Sophia in the Tractatus tripartitus could be explained as a choice between two possible translations of the Hebrew word ḤKMH, Wisdom (Zandee, 1967). As a matter of fact, in Philo the word ḤKMH is translated both as σοφία and as λόγος. G.C. Stead has shown that a branch of Valentinianism had undergone the influence of Philo (Stead, 1969 p.79-80). However, Heracleon's choice of Logos instead of Sophia has nothing to do, either with the Jewish ḤKMH or with Philo. Origen reports that Heracleon was commenting upon the Gospel of John, and this is already enough to explain why he kept up Logos in his system and put aside the common gnostic aeon Sophia. As far as the Tractatus tripartitus is concerned, this gnostic treatise goes so far to meet the doctrine of the Grosskirche, that it would be superfluous to enquire further about the origin of the aeon Logos - which is simply the Logos of the Gospel of John, to which the features of the gnostic aeon Sophia are ascribed. The Tractatus tripartitus is a very sophisticated piece of gnosis, which could be defined as not gnostic any more, and not christian yet. However, neither christians nor neo-platonics could, in their turn, resolve the contradiction in which the Tractatus tripartitus does not hesitate to incur: if Logos acted out of free will, then he is the sole responsible of the existence of the lower world, but the latter remains nevertheless an arbitraty and deficient product of Logos' fall; however, if the fall of Logos was already foreseen and programmed by the Father, then the world is not an arbitrary creation any more, but the free will of Logos becomes absurd. How a world which is bad and good at the same time was created through the free will of an entity beyond any responsibility of his superiors, who, however, knew that that was to happen and wanted it to happen, this is an uncomfortable juridical situation, in which, however, any unbiased judge would say that the superiors are morally responsible for the creation of the world. After all, the gnostics themselves were logically more coherent in supposing that this world was not to be, but Sophia caused it to be. Thus, one could really doubt whether the unfathomable Father was almighty and omniscient, but would not declare him guilty of the existence of this world.

2 THE ORIGIN OF THE SOPHIA MYTH

I consider that Bousset's interpretation of the character of Sophia in gnostic myth is paradigmatic for the religionsgeschichtliche Schule as a whole. Bousset thinks namely that Sophia-Barbelo (which he interprets as a corruption of παρθένος) is a duplicate of the Near Oriental Great Mother, known under the names of Ishtar, Attargatis, Kybele, Anaitis (Anahita), Astarte, etc. (Bousset, 1907 p.26). Obviously, this generic statement does not account for the existence of a lower Sophia, which Bousset relates to an iranized babylonian astrological lore (Bousset, 1907 p.43; for a criticism of this theory, see Culianu 1982).

After World War II, the theory of the Jewish background of the Sophia myth became very influential, and remained unchallenged up to date. Gilles Quispel was among the first scholars who argued that gnostic Sophia, already present in the gnosis of Simon Magus under the name of Ennoia, was nothing but the Jewish ḤKMH (Wisdom) which, in Samaria, was conceived as a cosmogonic power (Quispel, 1974 p.163). In his article Der gnostische Anthropos und die jüdische Tradition (1953; quoted here according to the revised version of 1974), Quispel attempted a bold reconstruction of the evolution of the Sophia myth. The 'primitive' form of the jewish gnostic myth was the following:

'Gott schafft aus dem Chaos die 7 Archonten durch Vermittlung seiner Chokma, der humectatio luminis oder Lichttau '(Iren. I 30). Die Chokma wirft ihr Eidolon, ihr Schattenbild, auf die Urwasser des Tohuwabohu. Daraufhin bilden die Archonten die Welt und den Körper des Menschen, der auf der Erde wie ein Wurm kriecht. Die Chokma schenkt ihm den Geist' (Quispel, 1974 p.178). Later on, Sophia is replaced, in her cosmogonic function, by an anthropos. Gnostic theodicy, whose expression is the myth of the lower Sophia and of her fall caused by Eros, is explained by Quispel as an outcome of orphic-platonic dualistic speculations (ib.,191).

Hans Martin Schenke resumed and continued Quispel's theory. According to Schenke, the idea of reflection of a spiritual entity into the lower waters, which is fundamental in Quispel's 'primitive' version of gnostic myth, derives from Genesis 1,26 (Schenke, 1962 :72ff). Schenke agrees with Quispel that the cosmogonic role devoted to an anthropos represents a later development within gnostic myth (ib.,32). Schenke draws a further distinction between gnostic systems in which two Urmenschen occur (Gott, Stammvater), and systems in which three Urmenschen occur (Gott, himmlischer Urmensch, Stammvater) (ib.64-5).

In his survey of Jewish and gnostic evidence, George W. MacRae comes to the conclusion that there are many similarities between ḤKMH in Jewish sources and Sophia in the Sethian-Ophite cosmogonies. The most important analogies between the two are: their personal character, their intimate contact with god, their dwelling in the clouds, their identification with the Holy Spirit, their role in communicating wisdom and revelation to men, their descent into the world of men, their reascending to their heavenly abodes, their role in Adam's creation and sustenance, their identification with life or with the tree of life (MacRae, 1970 p.88-94). However, MacRae considers that Jewish sources could not account for the idea of the fall of Sophia. According to him, the fall of Sophia represents a gnostic reinterpretation of the biblical fall of Eve (ib., 99; Rudolph, 1980 p.227-8).

To sum up: Jewish speculations on ḤKMH-Wisdom and allegorical interpretations of the Book of Genesis provide a satisfactory explanation of the upper Sophia in gnosticism and of her creative power. However, the gnostic tale of the fall of Sophia is not likely to be explained from Jewish sources, though a certain contamination with the biblical fall caused by Eve should not be overlooked (Rudolph, 1980 p.228).

3 INTERPRETATIONS OF THE SOPHIA MYTH

The feministic implications of the gnostic Sophia myth have been analyzed by E.H. Pagels in her puzzling book (Pagels, 1979:54ff). Mrs. Pagels claims that the existence of the upper female divinity, God-the-Mother, in gnosticism, is symmetrical to the important role devolved to women in gnostic community. This statement is perhaps a bit too hasty, since worship of a Great Goddess is not incompatible with the most patriarchal forms of social organization. Furthermore gnostic treatises themselves seem very concerned to avoid misunderstandings, in their insistence upon the fact that the first principle is always a Father of All. Mrs. Pagels also overlooks the fact that it is precisely Sophia's fall, and not Sophia as a Great Mother, to play an outstanding role in gnostic myth. It is true that lower Sophia helps mankind against her own son, who, being the divinity of the Old Testament, is obviously a Father. In this case, it is a Mother-figure to bring remedy against a situation of discomfort set off by a Father-figure. This does not mean, however, that Sophia herself is perfect, and gnostic texts may occasionally warn against the temptation of holding Sophia for a supreme divinity.

Sophia is basically an ambiguous character, a 'repented whore', to put it in genuine gnostic terms, whose positive features and sincere repentance fail, however, to mask the gravity of her guilt.

Mrs. Pagels took notice of the interesting aspects of the phantasmic scenery of gnostic myth, and recommended a psychoanalytical approach thereof (ib.,133). Such an approach has been already attempted by Michel Meslin (Meslin, 1970 p.141-2 and 1973 p.206-7).

Eros is certainly important in the myth of Sophia, who is called 'The Prurient' and, in the sethian version, is represented by a form emerging out of the cosmic womb, a form that being without consort, 'did not have intercourse, but... was the one who rubbed herself alone' (VII,21). The being alone of Sophia is here emphasized over other features that account for her fall in other treatises, i.e. her being the youngest and last aeon at the periphery of the Pleroma and her desire to know the Father-of-All, her thinking without the permission of her syzygos, her spontaneous revolving towards the abyss or her being led astray by the archons to look down into the abyss. Among these explanations of the fall of Sophia, Meslin chose the first one as being the most relevant. Thus, the freudian interpretation of the Sophia myth became self-evident and convincing: 'Il apparaît clairement que ce mythe original repose sur une structure psychologique à phantasmes, et qu'il est susceptible d'une transcription psychanalytique freudienne. Sophia a le complexe d'Electre. Elle est l'expression absolument directe de l'inconscient féminin. En voulant se fondre dans la personne du Père, elle manifeste un sentiment très profond de l'inceste. Elle a beau savoir qu'il ne faut pas, que cet amour désordonné ne peut conduire qu'à sa perte, elle sent que si cela était permis, un tel amour lui donnerait la plénitude de l'être' (Meslin, 1973 p.206-7).

II. The Sophia Myth as a Cultural Problem

It seems that all questions concerning the Sophia myth have been asked and solved. New interpretations may arise, but no one of them would ever part from the basic presupposition that the myth of Sophia is an original gnostic myth, whose background is, in all probability, Jewish.

However, there is still one question which has never been asked, a question that may be crucial to the case in point: is really the Sophia myth an original gnostic myth? Even those who emphasize the Jewish origin thereof, confess that they were unable to discover such a myth in Judaism. On the other hand, neither Near Oriental, nor Greek mythology, could be relied upon to determine its background. Under these circumstances, it seems safer to state that the Sophia myth is originally gnostic.

A simple summary of the Sophia myth, picked up from the gnostic environment, will show that things are much more complicated. The main stream of that gnosis which is derived from the doctrine of Simon of Samaria postulates that the lower world, the human world, came to existence through the fault of a female entity. This fault is the hybris of a woman and is or could easily be qualified in sexual terms. As a matter of fact, this woman either is deprived of a consort or acts without permission from her husband, she wants to get nearer to her father than the family rules in the Pleroma would permit, and from her behavior (which, in different versions of the myth, is specified as being _autoerotic_ rather than incestuous), an anomalous, miscarried, male child is born, who is to be held responsible for the creation of the lower world. Toward mankind, the mother of the demiurge has an ambivalent attitude: on the one hand, had she not committed that primordial sin, mankind either would not exist at all, or, if existing, would not know its present misery; on the other hand, she is precisely the one who conferred upon mankind a spiritual prestige which is higher than that of the demiurge, and she constantly helps men to be relieved from the tyrannical power which the demiurge exerts upon them. _In absoluto_, Sophia's fault ends up in a mess, which needs the intervention of a Savior to be cleared up; but in its relationship to mankind, her guilt is a _felix culpa_.

I believe that Sophia's guilt could properly defined as a guilt of _feminism_: in the beginning, she revolts against the _régime_ of the world installed by her father and also against the rule according to which she must ask in all circumstances her husband's permission before doing anything. (That, obviously, if she has a consort; otherwise she might neglect to have sexual intercourse with a partner, which is still worse, since she takes an autoerotic behavior). When this first revolt proves fatal, she again revolts against her own son, and helps mankind to escape his tyranny.

Were gnostics feminist? In a way, those of them who ever asked themselves about the origin of patriarchalism, may have fostered feelings that could be defined as 'feministic'. This issue belonged to their rejection of the Old Testament, whose divinity was male and in which it was said that, after the fall, women were cursed to be forever submitted to men (Genesis 3,16). Since this curse, according to the gnostics, is uttered by the bad demiurge of the world, it is obvious that the patriarchal *régime*, in which women are submitted to men, is wrong: this reasoning occurs in the *Apocryphon Johannis* (Till, 1955 p. 162).

However, our concern in this paper is not to determine whether and to what extent gnostics were 'feminists'. Once the conclusion has been reached that Sophia's fault could be defined in a way as a 'feministic' revolt against the patriarchal order of the universe - which is both the upright order of the Pleroma and the wrong order of the Demiurge of the lower world - the question that still has to be asked is whether that kind of fault is typically and originally gnostic.

In very different cultural environments, the myth of a female character whose revolt against patriarchal rules is qualified in sexual terms, having as a primary issue both men's fall from a happy but ignorant state and the origin of culture, occurs very often. Culture itself is usually viewed as an ambivalent process, which is both a major progress in comparison with man's natural condition, and an unlucky finding, in so far as it would not have been necessary if the fall had not altered man's primitive state of happiness.

In an older article (now in Culianu , 1981 p. 1-14), some examples of this myth have been analyzed: the myth of Wawilak sisters in Murngin culture (Arnhem Land, Australia), the myth of Muso Koroni in Bambara culture (West Africa), and the Greek myth of Demeter. Since then, material from Desana culture (Tukano Indians living in the forests of the Vaupès territory,Colombia Northwest Amazon; Reichel-Dolmatoff, 1971 p.30-32;p.35-36; p.73-75; p.99-103) has confirmed my basic assumption,namely that the myth of a sexual transgression of a female entity, leading both to the 'fall' of mankind and to the origin of culture, is well known in widely divergent cultural environments. I do not intend to resume here my view of the matter. I think that one example will be sufficient to show that the Sophia myth is nether typically nor originally gnostic. It is the Bambara myth of Muso Koroni (Culianu, 1981 p.4-7), of which I will present here only the most salient features.

The creation myth of the Bambara starts with an impersonal male entity, called Pemba or Bemba, who manifests himself as a balanza tree (Acacia albida) and then as a trunk (pembele). As a pembele, Pemba generates out of himself the 'little old woman with a white head', muso koroni kundye, who becomes his wife. Muso Koroni gives birth to all plants and animals, who worship Pemba as their creator (Ngala). She plants Pemba in the ground and he becomes a balanza tree again, which is the forefather of all trees, whose foliage gives shelter to mankind.

Mankind is not the product of Pemba, but of Faro, who, at the time when Pemba was an impersonal entity, was a vibration (fãro) that served to Pemba to create the sky, after which Faro fell to the earth in the form of rain and became master of the element water. Faro made men immortal. They received their nourishment from heaven, through Teliko, master of the air and guardian of the upper waters of Faro, who moved to the earth and became supervisor of the lower waters, on earth and beneath it. During the rainy season, Teliko sent to mankind 'a sort of stones from the seventh heaven, containing karite nuts, shi kolo' (Dieterlen, 1951 p.18). The tyrannical creator Pemba wants all women to have intercourse with him, and Muso Koroni becomes jealous. Therefore, she betrays him and ceases to cooperate in the process of creation. 'This was the origin of her fall, of her poorness and weariness, since the balanza tree cursed her for her betrayal and repelled her when she wanted to go back to him. She became so depressed, so hopeless, that she was seized by a sort of madness. She went through the skies, the space, the earth, from West to North and from South to East, planting pieces of wood in the ground, such as she had done for Pemba, in the hope that they also would become balanza trees' (ibid.). Her sexual life became irregular, and she produced the first menstrual blood. Moreover, she revealed to mankind 'all she had learned from Pemba and was to be kept secret. And to everything she touched, she transmitted the impurity she had contracted because of his betrayal. Because of her, earth became impure, a quality which became permanent' (ibid.).

Pemba and Faro pursue Muso Koroni. Faro catches her and tries to make her submit to her creator. 'But she refused and declared herself free. Thus, disorder interfered with the process of creation: evil, bad luck and death were introduced by her in the world' (Dieterlen, 1951 p.19). However, the role of Muso Koroni is not exclusively negative. She taught men language and agriculture. As far as language is concerned, it is an ambivalent matter, positive and negative at the same time. At the beginning of time, communication was possible without language. Language was necessary only after the fall caused by Muso Koroni (Culianu, 1981 p.6,n.29). Sound existed before language: it was a drone which was called 'inaudible word', given by Pemba in custody to Faro. But this uninterrupted buzzing was no language, since language is based on cuttings in sound, on irregularity. These 'cuttings' were caused by Muso Koroni's pride and disobedience, which provoked Pemba's anger. Pemba 'grabbed her neck and squeezed. Till then, she was integrated in the continuous sound. Now, she began screaming out of pain and produced inarticulated but distinct sounds.

These are the beginnings of words and languages'(Zahan, 1963 p.16).

To sum up:in Bambara myth, Muso Koroni is a female character who revolts against the wrong 'male' order of the world. Her revolt could be generically defined as a quest for freedom, but could also be more specifically interpreted in sexual terms (her 'betrayal' of Pemba is actually adultery or autoeroticism). Muso Koroni's fall determines the fall of mankind from primitive immortality and happiness to a postlapsary condition in which evil, bad luck and death irrevocably belong to human fate. However, Muso Koroni helps mankind in pain by teaching them language and agriculture, i.e., 'culture' in broad outline.

The analogies between the Sophia myth and the Bambara myth of Muso Koroni are too obvious to be mentioned. However, since a genetical filiation is, in this case, out of question, a broad cultural explanation must be found to account for the surprising similarities between these myths.

CONCLUSION

The myth of Sophia is neither typically nor originally gnostic. It is the wide spread myth of a female entity interfering with the male order of the world. Out of her fault, mankind undergoes downgrading and has to suffer. At the same time, the same entity relieves man's postlapsary painful condition, being thus a benefactor of mankind.

Such a myth is the expression of complex cultural and social factors, to which the traditional phenomenological and comparative approaches cannot provide a satisfactory explanation.

The principal presupposition of this myth is that the order of the world is patriarchal and in some way unfair toward the female main character. Her revolt is usually not deprived of a certain justification. On the other hand, her connection with the fall of mankind, with the passage from an immortal and innocent state to a condition marked by suffering, sexuality and death, is very typical to another well known character of the mythologies of the world, i.e. the Trickster. Sophia, Muso Koroni, and the other characters briefly mentioned above are to some extent female Tricksters. Their fault is expressed in sexual and 'feminist' terms, which is one of the most constant features of this myth, present even in the case of the Greek goddess Demetra, who revolts against the order of Zeus.

Tricksters are always ambivalent: they are producers of a disorder ending up in death, suffering, sexuality. But they supply at the same time fallen men with all the cultural techniques necessary in order to survive. Fall is, for men, a deleterious event, but also an improvement.

The Sophia myth is expressive of the same ambivalent attitude toward culture: had Sophia not committed any fault, mankind would not exist, but gnosis would not exist either. Of course, only gnostic dualism could go so far as to state that total absence of mankind would be the greatest benefice for mankind itself.

Speaking of 'feminism' in connection with the myth of a female Trickster may lead the reader to the conclusion, that the author of this article shares Mrs. Pagels'view on gnosticism. Therefore, a specification is needed: the female Trickster herself is 'feminist', and her fault could be equally defined as 'feministic', i.e. as an affirmation either of her rights as a woman or of her specific sexuality. That means precisely,that the myth codifies here a set of socially unacceptable attitudes, whose finality is nothing less than to provide an explanation of the origin of evil. The function of the myth is thus clearly antifeminist.

However, the situation in so far as gnosticism is concerned

is further complicated by the existence of the demiurge, Sophia's son. Several authors have shown that the gnostic demiurge shares the main features of a male Trickster, and that the myth of the pride and ignorance of a Trickster is wide spread (Culianu, 1979). That means that gnosticism operates actually with two instead of one Trickster: a female one(Sophia) and a male one (the demiurge). Their relationship is ambivalent, since the demiurge is Sophia's son; but it is only slightly ambivalent, in so far as Sophia has completely rejected her miscarried progeny. Since the male Trickster is here both the immediate author of the existence of an evil world and an adversary of the female Trickster, this ends up in a reconsideration and restoration of the female character from the viewpoint of mankind. However, if Sophia was worshipped by the gnostic, it was certainly not because she was a feminist, but on the contrary, because she was able to repudiate the evil product of her being-feminist and thus to convert to antifeminism, which was the accepted attitude.

One final word should also be spent about the explanation of the myth of the female Trickster. A sociological explanation accounting for a pluri-genesis of similar myths within social environments which were also similar in broad outline is very likely. The idea that feministic initiatives would end up in a mess must be common to any patriarchal society. It provided occasionally a good explanation of the origin of evil in the world. On this plane, the female Trickster had one concurrent only: the male Trickster, who was actually, to a certain extent, a representative of male qualities.

May these statements not be misunderstood: both male and female Trickster can be explained as religious 'projections' of social factors (see the contribution of Th.P. van Baaren in this volume) which actually has something to do with the mythical narratives in which they occur, but not with the meaning thereof. The myth of a Trickster is meant to explain the origin of evil, which is a very important, deep, and tangled matter, though modern man has pragmatically cut this Gordian knot, by saying that theodicy is absurd. Characters in this myth are likely to be explained in sociological perspective; but such an approach is of little epistemological use, if it is not able to recognize the significance and the intention of the myth, which are, n'en déplaise, metaphysical.

BIBLIOGRAPHY

Bianchi, U. and Crouzel, H. (Eds.), 1981: Arché e Telos. L'antropologia di Origene e di Gregorio di Nissa. Analisi storico-religiosa (Studia patristica mediolanensia 12), Milano.

Bousset, W., 1907: Hauptprobleme der Gnosis (FRLANT 10), Göttingen.

Culianu, I.P., 1979: Review to U. Bianchi, Prometeo, Orfeo, Adamo (Rome, 1976) In: Aevum LIII p.172a-176b.

Culianu, I.P., 1981 : Iter in silvis. Saggi scelti sulla gnosi e altri studi, vol. I (Gnosis II). Messina.

Culianu, I.P., 1982: L'"Ascension de l'âme" dans les mystères et hors des mystères. In: Bianchi, U. and Vermaseren, M.J. (Eds), La soteriologia dei culti orientali nell'Impero Romano (EPRO 92), Leiden.

Dieterlen, G., 1951: Essai sur la religion Bambara, Paris.

Drijvers, H.J.W., 1973: Theory formation in science of religion and study of the history of religions. In: Van Baaren, Th.P. and Drijvers, H.J.W. (Eds.), Religion, culture and methodology, The Hague-Paris p. 57-77.

Drijvers, H.J.W. and Leertouwer, L., 1973: Epilogue. In: Van Baaren and Drijvers, 1973 p.159-168.

Drijvers, H.J.W., 1978: Die Oden Salomons und die Polemik mit den Markioniten im syrischen Christentum. In: Orientalia Christiana Analecta 205 (Symposium Syriacum 1976), Rome, p.39-55.

Giversen, S., 1963 : Apocryphon Johannis. The coptic text of the AJ in the NH Codex II, with translation, introduction and commentary by S. Giversen, Copenhagen.

Haardt, R., 1971: Gnosis. Character and testimony. Transl. into English by J.F. Hendry, Leiden.

Harris, M., 1977: Cows, pigs, wars, and witches. The riddles of culture, Glasgow.

Krause, M-L.P., 1962: Die drei Versionen des Apokryphon des Johannes im koptischen Museum zu Alt Kairo, Wiesbaden.
Lincoln, B.,1981:Priest,warriors and cattle. Berkely/L.A./London.
MacRae, G.W., 1970: The Jewish background of the Gnostic Sophia myth. In: Novum Testamentum XII (1970) p.86-101.
Meslin, M., 1970: Le Christianisme dans l'empire Romain, Paris.
Meslin, M., 1973: Pour une science des religions, Paris.
Morin, E., 1973: Le pradigme perdu: la nature humaine, Paris.
Pagels, E., 1979: The Gnostic gospels, New York.
Quispel, G., 1974: Gnostic studies I, Istanbul.
Reichel-Dolmatoff, G., 1971: Amazonian cosmos, Chicago
Robinson, J.M., 1977: The Nag Hammadi library in English. Under the editorship of J.M. Robinson, Leiden.
Rudolph, K., 1980: Sophia und Gnosis. Bemerkungen zum Problem "Gnosis und Frühjudentum". In: Träger, K.W., (Ed.) Altes Testament Frühjudentum - Gnosis, Berlin p.221-237.
Schmidt, C-Till,W.,1954: Koptisch-gnostische Schriften. Erster Band: Die Pistis Sophia. Die beiden Bücher des Jeû. Unbekanntes altgnostisches Werk, hrgg. von C. Schmidt. 2.Auflage, bearbeitet von W. Till, Berlin .
Schenke, H.M., 1962: Der Gott "Mensch" in der Gnosis. Ein religionsgeschichtlicher Beitrag zur Diskussion über die paulinische Anschauung von der Kirche als Leib Christi, Göttingen.
Stead, G.W., 1969: The Valentinian myth of Sophia. In: Journal of theological studies, N.S. XX (1969) p.75-104.
Till, W.C., 1955: Die gnostischen Schriften des koptischen Papyrus Berolinensis 8502, hrgg., übersetzt u. eingeleitet von W.C. Till, Berlin .
Zahan, D., 1963: La dialectique du verbe chez les Bambara. Paris-The Hague.
Zandee, J., 1967: Die Person der Sophia in der Vierten Schrift des Codex Jung. In: Bianchi, U. (Ed.) Le origini dello Gnosticismo, Leiden p.205-214.

Conflict and Alliance in Manichaeism

H. J. W. Drijvers

Manichaeism represents a system of religious symbols and practice that is based on a radical metaphysical conflict between two opposing principles and the salvation from that conflict through the alliance of the eternal divine mind and its parts which were scattered in man and the world during the successive phases of that basic struggle. Conflict and alliance, therefore, are not interpretative categories to explain some aspects of Manichaeism, but they belong to the key notions of the Manichaean doctrine and mythology (1). Manichaeism as a religious movement in the Roman Empire originated in a conflict in an Elchasaite community in Southern Mesopotamia, in which Mani pretended to give the right interpretation of Elchasai's words, rules, and revelations, so that he actually made an alliance with Elchasai against the latter's followers (2). The Manichaean attitude towards all former religions was exactly the same: Mani proclaimed himself the Apostle of Jesus Christ and the Paraclete,the fulfilment of Jesus' promise, and in this manner opposed established Christian belief and practice of his days (3). The history of the Manichaean church is a concatenation of conflicts and persecutions which characterised the mission of this universal religion. No wonder, that conflict and struggle were an essential part of Manichaean Selbstverständnis (4).

Manichaeism, therefore, is quite evidently an excellent case for the study of possible relations between conflict and alliance in the world of the divine and in the body social, of relations between religious concepts and their eventual counterparts in social reality. Several methods are available and current to tackle that problem, although not all are rewarding because they do not give access to a given social context, in our case to Manichaeism as a religious movement in the Roman Empire that started about 240 A.D. in Mesopotamia and rapidly spread by virtue of an intense missionary practice.

Since the Manichaean mythology and doctrine is based on the fundamental opposition of primeval light and darkness which is developed in a complicated system of binary oppositions that form the structure of the world and man, Manichaeism seems an excellent case for a structuralistic analysis. That methodological approach ,however, will not lead to a better understanding of the social context in which Manichaeism arose and of the possible reasons why the Manichaeans mapped out man and world the way they did, but will only reveal once more the 'universal grammar of the human intellect' which structuralism is all about. Structuralism is not interested in particular men in their particular historical circumstances, but only in Man written large, a fundamentally a-historical being (5).

A functionalist approach in general constitutes a better link between religious concepts and social reality, but functionalism as such generally does not pay much attention to the contents of religious concepts, but only to their function in a social context, so that functionalism is only marginally interested in historical research (6). In our case that would mean, that a functionalist analysis of Manichaean concepts of conflict and alliance would conclude that they mirror conflicts and alliances in the body social, but would not indicate what they are about. It is the case, therefore, that an actor-oriented description and interpretation is to be preferred to all other interpretations. Our description and interpretation is based on the formulae Manichaeans used to define what happens to them, since these formulae provide the best interpretation of their experience of their history and of the way they felt human life in the world (7). In the case of Manichaeism such a working-method is in particular obvious, since Manichaean writings swarm with various notions that refer to conflicts and alliances on different levels of world history and human existence. Actually conflict, struggle, and their counterpart, an all-embracing alliance of light and grace which guarantee a final victory with peace and eternal rest after a life-long struggle are a basic experience of Mani and his community. It is, however, not our aim to rewrite the whole of Manichaean mythology and history with conflict and alliance as leading ideas, nor to carry out a thorough semantic analysis of all notions of conflict and their counterparts on various levels of Manichaean cosmology and anthropology, however much that would be worth doing.

Our only purpose is a description as precise as possible in terms of the interpretations to which Mani and his followers subjected their experience of conflict and alliance as basic notions of world history and human existence. Since such a description, which is at the same time an interpretation, must be actor-oriented, it will be based exclusively on authentic Manichaean documents, in the first place the Coptic manichaica and the Cologne Mani Codex and any other remnants of Mani's original writings (8). This interpretative description will naturally lead our investigation around to the problem of the specific social context in which that experience arose and to its functioning. What kind of people were attracted by Mani's preaching and for what reasons? Were these religious notions of conflict and alliance rooted in social conflicts and attempts to overcome these? Conflict and alliance in Manichaean ideology and in Manichaean history might, therefore, make visible the tangent planes and limits of various explanatory models and ways of understanding.

For Mani and his followers the whole of world-history from its very beginning till its last moment is one continuous war that started with the initial conflict of darkness and light, when the former attacked the latter. The Kephalaia summarizes

Mani's teaching for his disciples in the following way:

> He (i.e. the Paraclete) revealed to me (i.e. Mani) the mystery of Light and Darkness, the mystery of Combat and of War and of the Great War....... that the Darkness caused (9).

This primordial attack brought about counter-measures from the side of the Father of Greatness, the god of Light, who sent the Primordial Man harnassed with his armour of light elements to the Darkness in order to repel its attack. The Primordial Man, however, was conquered by the Darkness and obliged to leave behind his armour of light elements, the Living Soul. Struggle and Defeat of the Primordial Man is called by Mani the 'mystery of Combat' and that is the first phase of the war between light and darkness that is the cause and essence of world history. In a sense the defeat of the Primordial Man means the victory of Darkness, but on the other hand the light elements that were mingled with the darkness held it back from rising up to the world of light, and thus stopped its assault. The Light is a deadly poison in the Darkness and in the end it will completely lame its activities. This first phase necessitates the delivery of the light that was left in the darkness and the bringing about of such a final situation that the darkness will never again be in the position to make an assault on the world of light. The dualism of light and darkness in Manichaeism, therefore, is an optimistic dualism. World history is based upon a cosmic alliance of Light and all its particles that will never be left alone in the dark world, but are being helped to return to their original state of harmony and rest. Darkness is an evil power with strictly limited possibilities and effects, whose final defeat has been certain from the very beginning of its longing for the world of light on. In Manichaeism Light and Darkness, therefore, are not equivalent entities, but their powers are quite uneven (10).

The initial defeat of the Primordial Man stirred the whole machinery of the delivery of light which caused the creation of the world and man as instruments in this process. The first step was the liberation of the Primordial Man from the evil powers of Darkness. The world of light called into being a new trias, the Beloved of Lights, the Great Architect and the Living Spirit. It was the task of the Living Spirit to liberate the Primordial Man, and she, therefore, called him, whereupon he answered. Call and Answer form a pair of hypostases that symbolizes the essence of deliverance. The answer to the call from the world of light is deliverance from the world of darkness, just as the Primordial Man was rescued by being called by the Living Spirit and by answering that call. He returned to the world of light, but left his armour consisting of light particles behind. Their liberation is the final aim of all following actions undertaken by the world of light, whereas the darkness does all it can to keep them imprisoned. Mani calls this process of liberation 'the mystery of war' which forms the essence of history.

The next step is the liberation of all light particles that were left behind. The Mother of Life and the Living Spirit descend into the realm of darkness and conquer the archons of darkness. Out of their dead bodies they create the cosmos, all heavens and worlds. The Living Spirit shapes Sun and Moon out of refined light, and fixes Planets and Signs of the Zodiac on the wheel of the spheres. They are the (astral) Archons who contain a large quantity of light. It is noteworthy that there is a gradual increase or decrease of light according to cosmic levels. Sun, Moon and Planets contain the largest quantity, but in lower spheres and on the earth there is lesser light. We would like to emphasize that creation as such is in Manichaeism not an activity of an evil demiurge, but is a positive act brought about by divine beings who played a paramount role in the whole process of light deliverance. In contradistinction to all other gnostic systems in Manichaeism creation is a means to liberate the divine light particles and not to imprison them. That is another confirmation of the aforesaid optimism, which is based on the conviction that in the end the divine is a coherent whole that uses its agents to annihilate evil powers. The creation of man, Adam and Eve, is part of the next phase in this cosmological conflict. After the construction of the cosmos as an instrument, a machine, for the purification of light, the Father of Greatness calls the Tertius Legatus into being, with whom the third phase of world history begins, when he sets the whole apparatus in motion (11). He, therefore, seduces the Archons by appearing to them as a fair woman or a beautiful young man and in their sexual excitement they gave up the light that was imprisoned in them. The light of the male archons fell on the earth and gave birth to all kind of plants. The female archons delivered abortions that walked around on earth and ate from plants and trees. In order to prevent the liberation of their light particles Saklas and Nebroël, the leaders of these abortions, devoured their children, had sexual intercourse and procreated in this way Adam and Eve, who were intended to torture the light particles and to keep them imprisoned in their bodies (12). Man, therefore, is created as a product of the evil archons who tried to save their light from liberation, and functions in this way as a target for all divine helpers, whose only aim is the rescue of light. He forms a special battle area in the cosmos on which the conflict is fought. The whole world, however, is the scene of a cosmic war between light and darkness, since light particles were also scattered in plants and trees, in North African Manichaeism identified with Jesus in his appearance as Jesus Patibilis (13). Nature, therefore, is not dead matter, but like man, the focal point of a life-and-death struggle between cosmic powers. Hence, man's alliance with nature, in which light is imprisoned like in himself, an alliance that in particular comes to light in Manichaean tales (14). Man's hatred for matter as such and for the created cosmos has often been emphasized in studies on Manichaeism, but it should at least be corrected a little. Manichaean religious attitude knows a deeply felt emotional solidarity with all living creatures and all nature: this is one of the main characteristics of the famous story on Mani's conversion in the Cologne Mani Codex (15). That solidarity is still corroborated by the Manichaean view that man and world have not been left alone in their struggle, but have been permanently helped by divine persons, who constructed the universe in such a way that it functions as an enormous machine for the liberation of light, and by divine messengers, who brought their message of the great war and man's place and role therein. Their appearance, however, was always accompanied by a war or conflict, since the powers of darkness took their counter-measures. The second Homily in the Coptic Book of Manichaean Homilies is devoted to the theme of the Great War and gives a lively description of these conflicts throughout world history (16). All apostles in their turn preached that war and suffered for it:

> All apostles cried, they preached
> this war in every book, from Adam on....
> till to-day .... (17).

It is, therefore, not surprising that Mani's coming also aroused several conflicts that were not accidental, but constituted an essential element in his appearance. His vocation meant a conflict with the Elchasaites on the function of washing and baptism and on purity (18). Mani's coming and preaching at Babylon was resisted by the powers of darkness and by all evil men according to his own description preserved in the Kephalaia:

> From that place I went to the region of Babylon, the city of the Assyrians, walked in it and entered its cities. I spoke in that Truth of Life that is with me, and preached in it the Word of the Truth and of Life. With the voice of preaching I separated in it Light from Darkness, Good from Evil... the powers that reign over the world. They sow their envy into the hearts of kings and leaders. They and the sects on every place resisted me. As you see yourselves, they fought with me great wars.... If I had not the protection of the Father... who does not help the impious, but always helps me, they would not have let me walk one day in their country Babylon (19).

Mani's struggles and conflicts are consequently no private matters, but part of the war between light and darkness, in which light a priori was, is and will be victorious. A Middle Persian text (M 224 I) thus calls the Apostle of Light 'the ruiner of the enemies': 'Behold, the ruiner of enemies comes, who destroys and disperses them. You, Father, Lord Mani, are worthy of praise and blessing, and the gods and the Elements of Light....' (20).

Even when persecuted and suffering in the world, Mani himself, as well as all his followers, are actually invincible, because they wear the armour of wisdom:

> I (i.e.Mani) clothed them with the armour of wisdom, so that you will not find a single person among men... and he will conquer them. As nobody in the whole world could conquer me, so nobody will be able to conquer my sons (21).

The all-embracing alliance of light protects all Manichees like Mani himself against their enemies, because they actually belong to the world of light that is invincible by nature. Mani and the Manichaean church are instruments in the process of liberation and have in this way close and special ties with the world of light. Just as Mani had his Twin Spirit, his heavenly double, who guided and protected him, so every Manichee has his divine helper in his war. Mani is addressed as follows:

> We do reverence to Jesus, the Lord, the Son of Greatness, who sent you, dearest one, to us. We do reverence to the praised Maiden, the Light Twin, who in every battle was your helper and companion (22).

In this way the Manichaean church and each individual Manichee could put all that happened to them, all persecution and sufferings into a cosmic context of struggle, in which their fate gained sense and meaning and the victory was theirs, even if it was not visible. Fragment 10 of Mani's <u>Epistula Fundamenti</u> dealing with Christ's Crucifixion put it this way:

> The enemy, who hoped that he had crucified this Saviour, the Father of the Just, has been crucified himself. Because at that time what happened was one thing, and what one saw, something else (23).

Suffering in Manichaean view has something ambiguous and paradoxical. On the one hand it is the result of persecution and hatred of wicked enemies and the reason for many litanies and complaints. On the other hand suffering is salvation, and the deaths of countless Manichaean victims of persecution and political murder are as many defeats of the eternal enemy, darkness and his evil powers. Such a deep-rooted conviction provided the Manichaean community with the strenght to survive. Their enemies had been defeated already; their power was merely illusion and lacked real vigor (24).

Hence there is a strong eschatological element in Manichaean doctrine. Mani's Šābuhragān, his only work written in Middle Persian, contains an apocalyptic portion which has partly been preserved. The end of the world will be foreboded by the Great War, a time of bitter conflicts, when most of the light will have been rescued out of the world. It is pictured in glaring detail in the Homily on the Great War. Then will follow the Second Coming of Jesus, the judgment, the separation of the righteous from the sinners, after which the Great Fire will destroy the world and the last particles of Light will ascend to the New Paradise. Matter will be incarcerated and Gods and the redeemed, Light re-united, will behold the Father of Greatness, who had hidden his face ever since the struggle between Light and Darkness began (25). The war is an intermezzo limited and enclosed by the power of Light, which upholds its alliance with all its particles.

This confidence in the final victory is, however, not the source of an really optimistic view of life, in which man can take his leisure, because nothing actually is left for him to do. He is not only an onlooker who interprets what happens to him and others without taking an active share in it, but he himself is a conflictridden creature. The parties at war fight their battle on a microcosmic scale in him, just as they fight in the whole created cosmos on a macrocosmic scale. Manichaean anthropology gives a characteristic symbolic expression to that analogy by relating the parts of the human body to various parts and elements of the cosmos and by using the allegory of an army camp as wel for the cosmos as for the human body (26). Kephalaia ch. 70 offers a circumstantial description of the corresponding parts with full anatomical and astrological details (27). Just as the archons fight against each other in the cosmos, so the human body which was created by those archons is characterized by the same revolt and struggle. Just as the whole cosmos is divided into five encampments over which the five sons of the Living Spirit reign, so the body of the electus is likewise divided into five encampments. Just as the five sons of the Living Spirit suppress the revolting archons each in his own region, so the Light Nous, an emanation or appearance of Jesus Ziwa, guards the encampments of the body and restrains the sensual lusts that reside in them. The electus who masters one of these lusts is like one of the sons of the Living Spirit. He, who controls his sexual desire, his 'womb', is compared with Adamas of Light, the most prominent fighter against matter and the evil in it (28).

A variant of the same army camp allegory occurs in Kephalaia ch. 56. The archontic creators put the five senses into the human body, which are specified as the enthymesis of the ear, the eye, the smell, the taste, and the sense of touch. These organs function as gates through which evil can pass. Since the appearance of the Light Nous, however, these gates are open for the good. Although the Saviour opens the gates, man, the inhabitant of the camp, can let the good in, or keep it outside. Actually the human body is a camp in which evil is encamped and which from the outside is besieged by the Light Nous. Whether the good de facto will enter into man, depends on the human nous which can be activated by the Light Nous (29). On a microcosmic scale the salvation of each individual human being in whom the new man is born through the enlightment of his nous is an exact analogue of the salvation of the Primordial Man by the Living Spirit. Just as the Living Spirit called the Primordial Man, whereupon he answered, so the Light Nous calls the nous to arms against the body and its evil lusts. It should be emphasized that Manichaean anthropology in this respect fundamentally differs from current gnostic views. In all gnostic systems the body belongs to the sphere of the evil demiurg and is dominated by astral archons who enslave it. In Manichaeism the body is a battle scene where the new man is born when the nous conquers all bodily lusts. In a certain way the body is a conditio sine qua non for salvation, since it is the very place where the nous can demonstrate its triumph over darkness and matter. This whole complex of symbolism has, therefore, its organic place in Manichaean doctrinal teaching and exhortation (30).

Human life is a permanent battle, a continuation of the Primordial fight. A Parthian text gives the following description:

> To you I will speak, my captive soul, remember your (real) home. .... Remember the devouring ... that bit you asunder and devoured you in hunger .... Remember the hard battle of old and the many wars you had with the Powers (?) of Darkness (31).

Mani himself fought that battle, which ended with his death, when he won eternal rest and final triumph. Another Parthian text offers a striking description of his death :

> Just like a sovereign who takes off armour and garment and puts on another royal garment, thus the Apostle of Light took off the warlike dress of the body and sat down in a ship of Light and received the divine garment, the diadem of Light, and the beautiful garland (32).

The Manichaean community has a deep sense of alliance and solidarity with all its forerunners, apostles of light and truth, and with all its living members, who so to speak, belong to a cosmic army fighting against evil powers. That sense of community finds its expression in particular in the liturgy, especially of the Bema feast, during which the Manichees honour their Paraclete (33). One of the many Bema hymns contains a characteristic eulogy:

> (we will praise).... and the fortunate ancestors who

> are the light chariots, the brave hunters and the keen (?) helmsmen, the praised apostles, the great arrangers and the very strong powers, the spirits created by the (divine) word, the fortunate sovereign, the light forms, the very best gods, the great saviours, the good helpers, the joy-giving deliverers, the keen (?) warriors and the strong battle-stirrers who have smitten death and conquered the enemies, and who have been led up in victory and arranged in peace: may they ever be praised through the praise of the light Aeons, and may they be praised through the strong praising of the Holy Religion so that their great peace, their pious protection and nourishing full of life can be arranged all over the Holy Religion, particularly over this place and (this) blessed assembly .... (34).

This sense of alliance was the strength of the Manichaean community during its many persecutions in East and West. Actually the Manichees were the only heretics who were executed in the Early Church and who were persecuted by Christians and pagans alike (35). That fate linked them with the whole chain of apostles of light who proclaimed the great war and were themselves persecuted and killed (crucified). Their personal fate was viewed against the background of the cosmic conflict between light and darkness and their persecutors were consequently the representatives of the evil darkness, whereas they considered themselves as messengers of the world of light and, therefore, as invincible, however much they suffered under oppression and persecution. The question is extensively dealt with in Kephalaia ch. 38, in which Mani gives an explanation of his appearance, power and divine mission which makes him and his church insuperable in the world and even more powerful than kings and sovereigns (36). This conviction of alliance with, and lasting support from, the world of light gives enormous self-confidence to Mani and his followers and must have been a strong unifying element in the community, the more so as it labels all opponents as representatives of evil darkness and, therefore, a priori as powerless against the world of light. It provides the Manichaean church with clear borders and a zone of conflict that lies without. A Parthian hymn says:

> Who will take me over the flood of the tossing sea - the zone of conflict in which there is no rest? (37).

It is a typical example of a social structure in which group is strong and grid weak, as Mary Douglas puts it, which is in complete accordance with the bodily symbolism used to express the most fundamental assumptions about the cosmos and man's place in it (38). In such strong group, where grid is weak, ascetic attitudes reject what is external and controls bodily enjoyment and the gateways of sensual experience (39).
It is, therefore, not surprising that all Manichees, even those who are known by name, do not show a personally coloured individual physionomy or personality, but on the contrary a certain uniformity and a standardized language and behaviour. The Manichaean electus is more a type than an individual human being.

Manichaeism was, notwithstanding many persecutions and opposition the only missionary religion of a gnostic character. Gnostic groups in general were not engaged in conscious mission, but spread their ideas along intellectual paths, more parallel with the spread of books and ideas. Manichaeism, however, propagated its gospel through mission, to which Mani himself gave the command and the example. He travelled widely to make his gospel known and sent out a whole range of missionaries to East and West. The explanation of this missionary zeal is debated and has given rise to various views. J.P. Asmussen thinks that political reasons cannot be ruled out, since 'The Motives of conversions to a religion, whose tendency to renounce life and state is obvious, are difficult to explain !' (40). According to H.-Ch. Puech Manichaean mission originates in the instabilitas loci that characterizes a saint who is not attached to earthly life and comfort, and does not have a permanent abode, but is a wandering monk (41). Both scholars stress the Manichaean's detachment from earthly life, but that as such provides an insufficient explanation of Manichaean mission. It seems to me that their relatively optimistic dualism, which considers the cosmos as a coherent whole due to the activity of a good demiurge who, in creating the world, contributed to the liberation of divine light particles, offers a better answer to the question of Manichaean mission. Their strong loyalty to all dispersed light in the world, combined with their feeling of a cosmic alliance of light that was all - embracing, brought about a loyalty to mankind which was in need of salvation. They did not simply renounce life and did not hate the body without more ado, but on earth and in the body the eternal struggle between light and darkness was fought by them. Just as they used all their efforts to control bodily senses and enjoyment, so in their mission they tried to control the whole world, to lay hands on all particles of light, to master all events and to incorporate mankind into their group, in other words to extend their group to the borders of the world, as part of their struggle against evil and darkness.

In this way they limited the zone of conflict and expelled evil power from the world.

Manichaean mission as part of manichaean religious behaviour brings us to the question of activities that are characteristic of a gnostic ascetic religion as Manichaeism was. It is customary practice to view Manichaeism as a religion that is characterized by a deep hatred for and abhorrence of earthly life and by the certainty of a gnosis of divine origin that brings salvation. It is described as a religion of the _nous_, as a mere intellectual approach to the paradox of human existence (42). It seems, however, that Manichaeism appealed to other human feelings and activities as well. Manichees were not only pale and ground down ascetics, filled with a deep hatred and mistrust towards earthly life and carnal sensuality, but they were also driven by an ineradiable inner urge to combat evil on its own territory just as the Primordial Man once did. In a sense they formed a forerunner of the Salvation Army ! A Manichee praising Mani said: May I belong to the point of your army ! (43). Salvation, therefore, is not only an intellectual process proceeding automatically from the enlightment of the _nous_, but salvation is being realized through active taking part in the combat against darkness in the world (44). In this context the notion of sin and the practice of confession of sins should be understood , although it at first glance seems illogical. How can the real self of a man, his divine soul, be responsible for evil that is inherent in matter and, therefore, in his body ? His human existence is tragic, since he is not guilty of evil in the world. Sin, however, is the result of the actual situation of the soul which is mixed with the body, and, therefore, can be seduced by the _concupiscentia_ that is the essence of evil matter. Sin consequently has a temporal reality and is caused when the soul does not resist carnal seduction, although the soul itself is not capable of sin and so cannot be blamed for sin and evil. The function of the _nous_ is the activation of the soul, so that she will resist every seduction. The enlighted and activated _nous_ is in Pauline terms the new man who permanently fights against the old man, the fleshly seduction which is the nucleus of the material body (45). The confession of sins functions as an instruction and admonition. It reminds the soul of its real self, it dispels oblivion, it arms the soul with its quinquepartite spiritual armour to 'fight with Āz (i.e. Greed) and Ahrmēn (i.e. the devil)'(46).

Manichaeism, therefore, was the only gnostic movement with an extensive liturgy, official feasts and sacramental rites within a strictly hierarchic ecclesiastical organisation, precisely because religious practice based upon, and activated through, myth and doctrine was an essential element in the process of salvation (47). This institutional structure was in the first place meant to instil a fixed and ritualistic behaviour into the members of the Manichaean community. The endless hymns and praisings which combine doctrinal elements with lamentations about the actual state of the soul, and the elevated poetic depictions of its ultimate happiness, rest, and joy, enforce a stylized ritualistic behaviour which embodies the central value system of Manichaeism. They combine traditional paideia in a master - pupil relationship with a strong loyalty towards Mani, the divine teacher (Paraclete!) par excellence, who is always present among his followers (48).

The importance of ethics and religious acting in Manichaeism should be stressed, the more so since moral conduct is a much neglected element in gnostic studies in general. For according to traditional views salvation was brought about by intellectual contemplation, so that gnostic ethics as such strictly speaking could not exist (49). The oldest strain of gnosticism, however, is characterized by asceticism, which is not only inspired by mere abhorrence from material reality, but also by a fervent attempt to master evil in the world and to lay hold on visible reality (50). Asceticism certainly as it was practised by Manichees, was a kind of heroism inspired by their deep-rooted conviction that evil had been conquered by the light world and, therefore, can and will be conquered by anybody in his private life as part of an all-embracing strategy.

The basic pattern of Manichaean religious experience is that of a conflict of metaphysical dimensions, of which the outcome is certain. Manichaean heroic ascetic behaviour and fervent mission was given support by its reliance on victorious light that never will fail to help its disciples. That is not a tragic experience, but far more it bears evidence of a cosmic optimism, of forming part of the triumphant alliance of light.

Conflict and alliance in the divine world bring about a characteristic behaviour of the Manichees in their world, full of conflicts and persecutions. Notwithstanding their severe sufferings, their mission was carried on and their ecclesiastical organisation kept intact (51). In this respect their fate and history is to be compared with the nascent Christian church, and an indication that the general term gnosticism covers a very wide range of religious doctrines and groups which are only partly comparable with each other and surely not all akin.

In what specific social circumstances do these ideas on conflict and alliance originate ? Although fervent personal and social struggles formed part of the whole history of the Manichaean movement, there are no indications at all that a specificic social conflict was the starting point for the development of the dramatic central myth of Manichaeism in order to provide a this - wordly conflict with cosmic and metaphysical dimensions. Mani's conflict with his Elchasaite group centered around the problem of sense and meaning of human actions in relation to the real nature of this world. The cleansing rites of the baptists did not do away, in Mani's view, with the evil irrational, even chaotic character of all wordly phenomena (52). Mani's attitute gives evidence of a thorough disbelief in traditional patterns of religious explanation and at the same time of a persistent attempt to giving sense to all what happens in this world. This characteristic mentality was born in intellectual and literate circles for which it was utterly impossible to accept a chaotic and irrational reality. Against all outward appearance of a chaotic evil world ruled by demonic powers, Manichaeans adhered to a rational and noetic character of this cosmos which, although invisibly, is sustained by the everlasting loyalty of an alliance of divine light. Manichaean doctrine of conflict and alliance was born in a crisis, but it also is a valiant victory over the same crisis. That is the social aspect of the salvator salvandus myth ! (53). Manichaean gnosticism was not a withdrawal from this world in order to devote oneself to reflection and meditation on an extra-mundane salvation of Asian origin, as Max Weber held to be the case, but a restless activity to help light to its visible victory (54).

Current myths and religious doctrines of traditional character did not meet the needs of minds longing for an all-embracing harmony in a world where political powers exercised an often cruel authority with complete disregards of individual liberty and dignity. The result was a sharp and often unbearable tension between belief in divine rule and empirical reality, giving rise to all kinds of Traditionskritik of which Manichaeism is a variant (55). It re-interpreted baptismal views, Christian belief, Iranian traditions and Buddhism, since all covered only part of the world or misinterpreted it completely. It broke up traditional communities and formed new groups bound together by their common mentality and spirit that in principle aimed at the whole world and all people (56). It was of particular importance that the individual was not left alone within the rather uniform group, but acquired his personal divine helper, his heavenly alter ego assisting him in his life-long struggle. It provided him with a cosmic sense of safety and security.

This universal solidarity brought Manichaeism into conflict with almost every political power of its time, of which it was a natural opponent. Karter felt that very keenly and did all he could to eliminate the Manichees as an organised group in the Sassanid empire just as Diocletian did in the West (57). Manichees were outsiders by nature and, therefore, a permanent threat to all established power. It is not surprising that persecution of Manichees increased when Christianity became the official religion of the Roman Empire and part of its established value system.

Historical developments in the third century and earlier gave rise to an outburst of disbelief in the rationality of the world that was proclaimed by all traditional beliefs. That is a crisis of the traditional value system which is at the same time a social crisis deeply felt in particular by an intellectual elite. Their response was a thorough rethinking of all known religious systems incorporating various elements of philosophical, astrological and scientific learning into a new all-embracing and all-explaining system. Manichaeans did not withdraw from the world but tried to overcome this world by systematic reflection and severe ascetic practice. They demonstrated that a perfect harmony between religious values and religious practice is possible by exerting mind and will which are part of a divine mind willing man's salvation from his bodily and intellectual conflicts.

NOTES

1. On Manichaeism - Puech,H.-CH.: Le manichéisme, son fondateur, sa doctrine, Paris, 1949; Widengren, G.: Mani und der Manichäismus, Stuttgart, 1961; Klīma, O.: Manis Zeit und Leben, Prag, 1962; Widengren, G. (ed.), Der Manichäismus, WdF CLXVIII, Darmstadt, 1977; Puech, H.-Ch.: Sur le manichéisme et autres essais, Paris, 1979; Die Gnosis, Band III, Der Manichäismus, eingeleitet, übersetzt und erläutert v. Böhlig, A., Zürich, 1980; Tardieu, M.: Le manichéisme (que sais-je?), Paris, 1981.

2. The relevant information stems from the Cologne Mani-Codex (CMC), edited by A. Henrichs and L. Koenen - Henrichs, A. and Koenen, L.: Ein griechischer Mani-Codex (P.Colon.inv. nr. 4780), ZPE 5, 1970 p. 97-216; ZPE 19, 1975 p. 1-100; ZPE 32, 1978 p. 87-200; ZPE 44, 1981 p. 201-318; ZPE 48, 1982 p. 1-59; Cameron, R. and Dewey, A.J. (ed./transl.): The Cologne Mani-Codex 'Concerning the origin of his body', Scholars press, Missoula, 1979; cf. Henrichs, A.: Mani and the Babylonian baptists: A historical confrontation, HSCP 77, 1973 p. 23-59; Rudolph, K.: Die Bedeutung des Kölner Mani-Codex für die Manichäismusforschung. In: Mélanges d'histoire des religions offerts à Henri-Charles Puech, Paris, 1974 p. 471-486; Koenen, L.: Augustine and Manichaeism in light of the Cologne Mani-Codex. In: Illinois Classical studies 3, 1978 p. 154-195; Henrichs, A.: The Cologne Mani Codex reconsidered, HSCP 83, 1979 p.339-367; Henrichs, A.: Literary criticism of the Cologne Mani-Codex. In: The rediscovery of Gnosticism, ed. Layton, B., vol.II , Leiden, 1981 p. 724-733; Koenen, L.: From baptism to the Gnosis of Manichaeism. In: The rediscovery of Gnosticism, vol.II p. 734-756.

3. Cf. Böhlig, A: Die Gnosis, Band III, Der Manichäismus, 23 ff.; Koenen, L.: Illinois classical studies 3, 1978 p. 161-176; Stroumsa, G.G.: Aspects de l'eschatologie manichéenne, RHR CXCVIII 2, 1981 p. 163-181.

4. See e.g. Kephalaia, Band I, Stuttgart, 1940, Kap.XVIII; Man.Homilien, Polotsky, H.J. (ed) , Stuttgart, 1934 7 ff.: Der Sermon vom grossen Krieg.

5. Cf. Geertz, C.: The interpretation of cultures, New York, 1973 p. 345-359 for a fundamental criticism of Lévi-Strauss' structuralistic approach.

6. Bellah, R.N.: Religious evolution. In: American sociological review 29, 1964 p. 358-374 clearly demonstrates the difficulty of combining a functionalist approach with historical research.

7. Cf. Geertz, C.: The interpretation of cultures, 14 ff.

8. The Coptic manichaica, i.e. Polotsky, H.J. (ed.): Manichäische Homilien, Stuttgart, 1934; Böhlig, A. (ed.): Kephalaia, Band I, Stuttgart, 1940 , zweite Hälfte Lieferung 11/12, Stuttgart, 1966; Allberry, C.R.C. (ed.): A Manichaean psalm-book, part II, Stuttgart, 1938 were originally written in Syriac and through a Greek version translated into Coptic; cf. Baumstark, A.: Oriens Christianus 36 (review of A Manichaean psalm-book), 1941 p. 117-126; the Cologne Mani-Codex too is the product of translation from Syriac; cf. Henrichs, A.: The Cologne Mani-Codex reconsidered, HSCP 83, 1979 352 ff.; Mani's original writings are only fragmentary preserved cf. Klīma, O.: Manis Zeit und Leben, 401 ff.; Böhlig, A.: Die Gnosis, Band III p. 221-239 (transl.); Tardieu: Le manichéisme p. 45-67; they were all originally written in an East Aramaic dialect, very close to Syriac except the Šābuhragān, cf. Rosenthal, F.: Die aramaistische Forschung, Leiden, 1939 p. 207-211; Mackenzie, D.N.: Mani's Šābuhragān, BSOAS 42, 1979 p. 500-534; BSOAS 43, 1980 p.288-310 published the preserved fragments of this mainly apocalyptic work.

9. Kephalaia 15 p. 3-5; cf. Böhlig: Die Gnosis, Band III p.85.

10. For a survey of Manichaean cosmology - Cumont, F.: Recherches sur le manichéisme I. La cosmogonie manichéenne d'après Théodore bar Khôni, Bruxelles, 1908; cf. Böhlig: Die Gnosis, Band III p. 103-108 (German transl.) Theodor bar Khoni gave excerpts from original manichaean writings, most likely the Pragmateia, cf. Tardieu: Le manichéisme 94 ff.; Puech : Le manichéisme 74 ff.; Polotsky, H.J.: Manichäismus, PW, Suppl.VI p. 240-271 = Der Manichäismus, WdF CLXVIII Widengren, G. (ed.), Darmstadt, 1977 112 ff.; Böhlig: Die Gnosis, Band III 29 ff.

11. The Tertius Legatus most likely is identical with Mani, cf. Stroumsa, G.G.: RHR CXCVIII 2, 1981 p. 172 and n. 40; cf. Tardieu: Le manichéisme 106; cf. however Böhlig: Die Gnosis, Band III,57.

12. Polotsky: Der Manichäismus p. 120-121; Böhlig: Die Gnosis, Band III.

13. On Jesus Patibilis - Puech, H.-Ch.: Sur le manichéisme et autres essais, Paris, 1979 p. 56-57 and p. 165-166; Augustin: Contra Faustum, XX 2 p. 536 , p. 21-23; 552,22 - p.553, 15; Böhlig: Die Gnosis, Band III p. 57-58.

14. Henrichs, A.:"Thou shalt not kill a tree" : Greek, manichaean and Indian tales. In: Bulletin of the American society

of Papyrologists 16.1-2, 1979 p. 85-108; cf. the remarkable story on a converted Manichee which now feels free to kill ants, text in Roediger, A.: Chrestomathia syriaca, third edition, Halle, 1892 p.85.

15. CMC 6,2 - 10,12: when a baptist took vegetables from the garden they were 'wailing like human beings, and, as it were, like children. Alas ! Alas! The blood was streaming down from the place cut by the pruning hook which he held in his hands. And they were crying out in a human voice on account of their blows '. Cf. Henrichs and Koenen: ZPE 19, 1975 p. 11-13; Augustin: Contra Faustum 6,4, p. 289,18: dolorem sentire fructum, cum de arbore carpitur; Augustin: De haer 46.

16. Man.Hom. p. 7-42; cf. Puech: Sur le manichéisme 86 ff.

17. Man.Hom. 14,29-31.

18. CMC 79,14-99,8 ; cf. in general Koenen, L.: From baptism to the gnosis of manichaeism 734 ff.; Henrichs, A.: Mani and the Babylonian baptists: A historical confrontation, HSCP 77, 1973 p. 23-59.

19. Kephalaia 186 p. 25-187,10.

20. Andreas, F.C. and Henning, W.: Mitteliranische Manichaica aus Chinesisch - Turkestan II, SPAW, 1933 p. 322; Asmussen, J.P.: Manichaean literature. Representative texts chiefly from Middle Persian and Parthian writings, New York, 1975 p.52.

21. Kephalaia, Ch.XXXVIII 89,18-102, 12 in particular 101,13-17.

22. Henning, W.: Ein manichäisches Bet- und Beichtbuch, APAW 1936 10, Berlin, 1937 p. 20,322-328 = p.27; cf. Asmussen: Manichaean literature, p. 66.

23. Euodius: De fide 28 (Zycha, J. ed.), CSEL 25 p. 964,7-10: ...inimicus quippe, qui eundem salvatorem iustorum patrem crucifixisse se speravit, ipse est crucifixus, quo tempore aliud actum est atque aliud ostensum.

24. On persecution of manichees - Brown, P.: The diffusion of Manichaeism in the Roman Empire, JRS, 1969 p. 92-103 = Religion and society in the age of Saint Augustine, London, 1972 p. 94-118.

25. Šābuhragān (Mackenzie , D.N. ed.) p. 399-402 : and he who shall do the will of the gods (and) be a travelling-companion and helper (of the religious and he) too who (is) well-disposed to them .. shall be .. with the gods in Paradise ..; cf. Man.Hom.41 p. 12-20.

26.Cf. Nagel, P.: Anatomie des Menschen in gnostischer und manichäischer Sicht. In: Studien zum Menschenbild in Gnosis und Manichäismus (Nagel, P. ed.), Martin-Luther-Universität Halle-Wittenberg Wiss. Beitr., 1979/39 (K5), 1979 p. 67-94.

27.Kephalaia, 169 p.24-175, 24; cf. Nagel: Anatomie des Menschen 89 ff.

28.Kephalaia,172 p.4-20; cf. Bar Khoni, T.: Liber Scholiorum XI, CSCO 69, 316,23-317,2 on Adamas of Light; Tardieu: Le manichéisme, 100; Böhlig: Die Gnosis, Band III p. 107.

29.Cf. Nagel: Anatomie des Menschen p.86; Puech, H.-Ch.: Péché et confession dans le manichéisme. In: Sur le manichéisme et autres essais p. 169-178.

30.Cf. Böhlig, A.: Probleme des manichäischen Lehrvortrages. In: Mysterion und Wahrheit, Leiden, 1968 237 ff.

31.Andreas, F.C. and Henning, W.: Mitteliranische Manichaica aus Chinesisch-Turkestan, III, SPAW, 1934 p.876 (M 33); Amussen: Manichaean literature p. 49.

32.Andreas and Henning: Mitteliranische Manichaica, III 860 f. (T II D 79); Amussen: Manichaean literature p. 55.

33.On the Bema feast - Allberry, C.R.C.: Das manichäische Bema-Fest ZNW 37, 1938 p. 2-10 = Der Manichäismus, WdF CLXVIII p. 317-327; Ries, J.: La fête de Bêma dans l'église de mani, REA 22, 1976 p. 218-233; Puech, H.-Ch.: Sur le manichéisme et autres essais p. 301-304 and 389-394.

34.Henning: Ein manichäisches Bet- und Beichtbuch p. 21-22 (from M 801 p. 7-8); Asmussen: Manichaean literature p. 64.

35.Cf. Brown: The diffusion of Manichaeism in the Roman Empire 92 ff.

36.Kephalaia 89 p. 19-102,12; Böhlig: Die Gnosis, Band III 81 f.

37.Boyce, M.: The Manichaean hymn cycles in Parthian, Oxford, 1954 p. 81 (Huwīdagmān IVa); Asmussen: Manichaean literature p.83.

38.Douglas, M.: Natural symbols. Explorations in cosmology, London, 1970 140 ff.

39.Douglas, M.: Natural symbols p. 143.

40.Asmussen: Manichaean literature p. 24.

41.Puech, H.-Ch.: Der Begriff der Erlösung im Manichäismus. In: Der Manichäismus, WdF CLXVIII 192 f.

42.Puech: Der Begriff der Erlösung p. 157 and 163-164.

43.Man.Hom. 5, 6-7.

44.Cf. Schottroff, L.: Animae naturaliter salvandae, zum Problem der himmlischen Herkunft des Gnostikers. In: Eltester, W. (ed.), Christentum und Gnosis, Beiheft ZNW 37, Berlin, 1969 83 ff.; Böhlig: Die Gnosis, Band III 36 f.; Cramer, M.: Zur dualistischen Struktur der manichäischen Gnosis OrChr 39, 1955 p. 93-101, esp. 93 f.

45.Puech, H.-Ch.: Péché et confession dans le manichéisme. In: Sur le manichéisme et autres essais p. 169-178; Asmussen, J.P.: XuĀSTVĀNĪFT. In: Studies in Manichaeism, Copenhagen, 1965 p. 167-199.

46.Andreas and Henning: Mitteliranische Manichaica aus Chinesisch-Turkestan II, SPAW, 1933 p. 307 (M 49 IIR, 6-7); Asmussen: Manichaean literature p. 10.

47.Cf. Puech: Liturgie et pratiques rituelles dans le manichéisme In: Sur le manichéisme et autres essais 235 ff.

48.Peter Brown in an unpublished paper The saint as exemplar in late antiquity brilliantly described this relationship and the paradigmatic function of the late antique saint with whom Mani shows great resemblance (letter of September 25, 1981).

49.Cf. Kippenberg, H.G.: Intellektualismus und antike Gnosis. In: Max Webers Studie über das antike Judentum. Interpretation und Kritik, (Schluchter, W. ed.), Frankfurt (M), 1981 209 f., referring to Weber's view of gnosticism.

50.Cf. Rudolph, K.: Die Gnosis. Wesen und Geschichte einer spätantiken Religion, Leipzig, 1977 p. 258-264; Stroumsa, G.G.: Ascèse et gnose. Aux origines de la spiritualité monastique. In: Revue Thomiste LXXXI,4, 1981 p. 557-561.

51.Brown, P.: The diffusion of Manichaeism in the Roman Empire 98 ff.

52.CMC 83 p. 20-84,9: 'Therefore,(make an inspection of) yourselves as to (what) your purity (really is. For it is) impossible to purify your bodies entirely - for each day the body is disturbed and comes to rest through the excretions of feces from it - so that the action comes about without a commandment from the Savior.'

53.Cf. Colpe, C.: Die gnostische Anthropologie zwischen Intellektualismus und Volkstümlichkeit. In: Studien zum Menschenbild in Gnosis und Manichäismus p. 31-44; idem, art. Gnosis II (Gnostizismus) RAC XI,611 and 637 f.

54.Cf. Kippenberg, H.G.: Intellektualismus und antike Gnosis p. 201-215.

55.Koenen, L.: From baptism to the Gnosis of Manichaeism. In: The rediscovery of Gnosticism II p. 734-756 actually interpreted nascent Manichaeism as a form of Traditionskritik of elchasaite concepts of purity and cleansing.

56.Colpe: Die gnostische Anthropologie p. 39; Kippenberg: Intellektualismus und antike Gnosis p. 215.

57.Brown: The diffusion of Manichaeism in the Roman Empire p. 94-98.

How Dualistic Beliefs are Performed by Shi'is: The Stages of Kerbala

H. G. Kippenberg

SOCIAL CONFLICTS AND DUALISTIC BELIEFS

The different Iranian religions provide classical examples for the subject of this volume 'Struggles of Gods'. The ancient prophet Zarathustra taught a continuing struggle between truth (Aša) and lie (Drug), the good and the evil spirit (Spenta Mainyu and Angra Mainyu). Later Zoroastrianism identified the good spirit with Ahura Mazdā, the God of heaven himself. His fight with Ahriman lasts the whole time of the world. In the Islamic period Iranians likewise stuck to this subject. The Shi'i relations about Husayn and his fight at Kerbala against Yazid found sympathy especially with Iranian peoples. Although the success of Shi'i religion in Iran in the 16th century A.D. was due to political reasons, its elective affinity with older Iranian dualism probably promoted its spread.

Many scholars took this Iranian inclination to dualism as self-evident and not in need of an explanation. But there were also prominent scholars who looked for social conflicts explaining dualistic beliefs. I will mention three hypotheses that seem to me quite reasonable. C. Colpe related the ethical dualism of Zarathustra to a conflict between predatory nomads and settled stock-farmers. J. Duchesne-Guillemin suggested as background a ritual organization, dividing the inhabitants of the settlements into two competing parties. H.S. Nyberg placed the dualistic ideas of Zarathustra in the context of a struggle between two cult-communities (1). If you enter into the details of the reasoning, you soon detect a certain gap in the line of the argument. There can be no serious doubt

that the aforementioned conflicts really existed. But do they account for the origin and spread of dualistic ideas ? If several conflicts existed, which was the decisive one and why this one and not the other ? Suppose the same type of conflict existed also elsewhere - and it did! - without generating similiar ideas, how to explain this ? The main problem seems to me the tacit assumption that there is a causal relation between social conflicts and dualistic ideas. I became convinced by an article of A. MacIntyre that there is no causal relationship between actions and beliefs. Imagine you are engaged in a conflict with predatory nomads or with a competing party or with a rival cult-community: it remains your own decision to describe this conflict in terms of dualistic beliefs or not. There is no law for describing it in this way or another. In itself, the existence of a conflict cannot explain why people choose this belief and not another one to give expression to it. Instead of looking for causes of the origin and spread of dualistic ideas we must study the use people made of them. Is there evidence that Iranians described social conflicts in terms of dualistic beliefs ? Is there evidence that such descriptions were institutionalized and part of a public idiom?
Only if these questions are answered can a relationship between social conflicts and dualistic beliefs be established (2).

Whether by chance or by necessity: the recent political events in Iran provide us with material illuminating the relationship between social conflicts and dualistic beliefs. The manifestations there in the years 1978 and of course later made abundant use of the beliefs of the Imami Shi'a. The traditional mourning rites and especially the Muharram-processions came to be powerful political manifestations against the Shah regime. But also beyond these occasions demonstrators made extensive use of Shi'i concepts. I mention three examples:

- people who died fighting against the troops of the Shah were regarded as martyrs like those of Kerbala;
- during the revolution banners proclaimed: 'Every day is 'Ashura and everywhere is Kerbala';
- photos taken of manifestations show participants conceiving their own actions as performances of the traditional passion play (ta'ziya).

What strikes us is the fact that the actions on the streets were interpreted as a ritual performance. The Shi'i beliefs that were used in describing the conflict with the Shah regime derived primarily from ritual and not from theology. I mention this because there were scholars claiming that Shi'i theology denied on principle the legitimacy of all political rule. This assertion, which indeed seemed to explain the use of Shi'i concepts by the opposition, turned out to be wrong. Quite the other way around Shi'i theology backed mostly political quietism. Not theology but the popular performances of the battle of Kerbala provided first and foremost the model of the demonstrators. Moreover the revolutionary theologians Khomeyni and Ali Shari'ati also relied more on Shi'i rituals than on a genuine theological theory about the state. Therefore we have to study Shi'i rituals if we look for an institutionalized relationship between social conflicts and Shi'i concepts. Are there indications that the ritual reality recollecting the battle of Kerbala became infused with social actuality (3)?

If we take such a possibility seriously we have to examine our term 'ritual' and its implications. Annually on the 10th of the month Muharram (the 'Ashura day) the Shi'i remember the tragical events of Kerbala. These rites belong to a widespread type of feasts suspending the rules of everyday life. They are called rituals of rebellion or reversal. M. Gluckman,a hard-boiled functionalist, attributed to these rituals the function of a steam valve preserving the established order by permitting protest. Since the publication of Gluckman's article a lot of work has been done in this field. E. Norbeck, V. Turner and B. Babcock, who contributed to these studies, discerned in the symbolic inversion genuine wants and experiences that otherwise are not publically permitted. B. Babcock even subscribed to the idea of Marx, that we must regard these ritual rebellions 'as a significant step in the development of a revolutionary class consciousness'. Of course we cannot apply these views mechanically to the 'Ashura rituals. But they can open our eyes for meanings that are obscured by a functional approach (4).

TRADITIONAL STAGES OF KERBALA: CONFLICTS BETWEEN CITY-QUARTERS

The 'Ashura-processions originated in pre-Safawidic times and we possess quite detailed accounts of Tabari and Rumi referring to the mourning rites in memory of Husayn. But only European travellers visiting Safawidic Persia wrote comprehensive reports about 'Ashura-processions they happened to observe at different times and places. These early accounts were supplemented by subsequent travellers and by anthropologists. All these sources enable us to describe these processions as a social fact (5).

The processions obtained their recruits from different quarters of the Iranian cities and were organized by rich and distinguished men of these quarters. The committee (hay'at) that arranged the Muharram-feasts, arose from the circle of believers around a mosque, from followers of a cleric or from

Ill.1: Group of an 'Ashura procession

Ill. 2: Presentation of the defeat of Kerbala

partisans of a rich co-believer. Primordial loyalties, obeyance to a mujtahid, patron : client relations, kinship and guilds were the stuff the organizing committees were made of. The individual group of the procession - called daste - was constituted by members of the guilds. E. Aubin took a photo of such a daste in the beginning of our century (ill.1). Particularly noticeable is the standard, around which the group flocks together. It is a fanar from Tehran. A drawing of it was published by Van Vloten in 1892. And Van Vloten added the comment:

> 'The quarters formed groups of twenty up to more than a hundred persons, which group themselves around their appropriate flag ('alam). It is unusual that two of such groups meet without a clash arising from it' (6).

The groups were not constituted by individual decisions but by primordial loyalties. The ritual organization reiterated a social order arranging individuals not in horizontal classes but in hierarchical coalitions. This fact is of special importance for the understanding of the 'clashes', Van Vloten speaks about. The participants in these processions firmly believed that they underwent the same experience Husayn and his followers had undergone. Young men scourged themselves with chains and swords. Some of them wore shrouds demonstrating their willingness to die for Husayn. Eventually they submitted this willingness to proof in street-fighting. Already an early traveller, P. Della Valle gives us a vivid description of the occurrences at Isfahan in 1617:

> 'All men of the neighbourhood watch these things, holding in their hands long and thick sticks that serve to fight with the members of the other processions coming toward them, if they happen to meet - and this not only in order to gain priority over them, but also to make a performance, I believe, of the scuffle in which Husayn died. They are persuaded that one who dies in the quarrel, since he dies for Husayn, would go directly to Paradise. They say, moreover, that during all the days that 'Ashura lasts, the gates

> of Paradise are open at all times, and all Mohammedans who die during those days go straight there, with their shoes and clothes still on' (7).

All essential traits mentioned by Della Valle are corroborated by later observers: the fight happened between different processions, it arose out of disputes over superiority, was considered as reiteration of the battle of Kerbala, its victims were regarded as martyrs matching the heroes of Kerbala, and people believed the gates of heaven to be open at 'Ashura.

We owe further instructive information concerning the nature of the struggles to J. Chardin and J.T. Krusinski. J. Chardin who visited Isfahan in 1684/85 gives a reason for the disorder:

> 'Le Grand-Prévôt étoit au milieu de la place avec trente gardes à cheval & autant de valets à pied, pour empêcher le desordre; car comme la ville d'Ispahan est d'ancienneté partagée en Factions, comme l'on a dit, il arrive souvent qu'en de pareils jours, des Quartiers se battent de bonne façon l'un contre l'autre & alors c'est un furieux desordre pour la Fête.'

About forty years later the Jesuit J.T. Krusinski gave further details about the urban factions. Already the former Shah Abbas (1587-1629) had fostered in each town of his empire the spirit of faction and stimulated the forming of two factions.

> 'These two factions, one of which was called Pelenk and the other Felenk and which were distinguished from one another by the particular colour that each chose for the neckbands of their shirts, were equally distributed in every town, where they formed, as it were, two different nations, that had no relation with one another; the one party not being able to contract marriage or even to eat with the other. Each of these factions had their estates separate.......... It was especially at the celebration of the famous feast of Husayn, Ali's son-in-law, that the enmity of the two parties broke out in a more remarkable manner, by means of the permission that was then given them to fight. Though they did it without arms, because they were not suffered to make use of anything else but stones and sticks, it was with so much fury and blood-shed, that the king

> was often obliged to employ his guards to separate them with drawn swords: and hard was it to accomplish it even with a method so effectual, insomuch that at Ispahan in 1714 they were under a necessity before they could separate the combatants to put above three hundred to the sword on the spot.' (8) .

So far Krusinski in his unique account about the ritual fights at 'Ashura and their political and social background. It relates - as Chardin did - the struggle in the streets to previous factions tolerated or stimulated by the government. The existence of such urban factions is a recurrent phenomenon in the history of the Middle East cities and is emphasized in all studies about the cities of the Middle East. The 'Ashura ritual confirms it. The commemoration of Husayn provided an example how people must act in the situation of a conflict : they are obliged to fight and must accept suffering and death. So the account of the events of Kerbala were used to describe own experiences. The performances connected with this commemoration reflect a social conflict typical for the premodern Iranian society (9).

SELF-SACRIFICE IN THE PASSION-PLAY (TA'ZIYA)

The accounts we owe to the European travellers reflect of course an observer's point of view. We must therefore try to base our interpretation on notions of the Iranian Shi'is themselves. The material we are looking for can be found in the so-called ta'ziya. It is well known that in the second half of the eighteenth century a passion-play came into existence arising from the recitations and preachings during the Muharram processions and that since then the annual commemoration was accompanied by ta'ziya performances.

The ta'ziya speaks quite often about sacrifice and salvation. But these terms must not be interpreted as salvation in the sense of Christian theology. The action of the salvator Husayn is effective only if followed by the believers. Incessantly the different persons say to each other: 'May I be your ransom'. This is not an empty phrase. Solemnly Ali Akbar and Qasem (followers of Husayn) promise: 'For Husayn I give my life as ransom'.The notions fedā (ransom) and qorbān (sacrifice) refer to a reciprocity between Husayn and his followers. But only the free young men are worthy of martyrdom, are chosen to be sacrificed for their fathers (so the Ismael myth).

The sacrifice is not an individual and subjective act, but answers to an objective necessity. Payment of ransom is a typical institution of the Middle East protecting the agnatic groups from disintegration. The heroes of Kerbala support their kinsman Husayn and do what everybody ought to do. Even if they have no chance of winning they are obliged to do so. Their martyrdom is an act of loyalty: of loyalty towards Husayn but also to heaven, that is responsible for tyranny and oppression. The martyr therefore expects to enter paradise immediately. We heard about such expectations already in the accounts about struggles in the street during 'Ashura. Now this motive returns in the passion-play and reveals the social norms the passion-play is referring to. It refers to a permanent social necessity for solidarity, whether it succeeds or fails. What tells is the heavenly reward. The apocalyptic expectation also influences the representation of the adversaries of Husayn. These men who slaughtered the Imam and his family so cruelly address Husayn with the solemn words: 'May I be your ransom, father of the heaven of glory'. They are addressing one another in the very meanest terms. The ta'ziya anticipates in this way the apocalyptic end of the bad and the victory of the good. There is no better illustration of this apocalyptic certainty than a Persian lithography deriving from a ta'ziya manuscript.

In front of Imam Husayn you see the corpses of the members of his family. He himself and his horse are hit by numerous arrows. But their effectiveness is so to speak destroyed: by placing them externally on the skin - by the halo round the head of the Imam - by the rose growing beneath the horse of the martyr. The representation of the defeat of Kerbala reflects the apocalyptic victory of the Imam over his enemies (ill.2).

The ta'ziya plays are apt at illustrating the actor's point of view regarding the conflicts bursting out during the 'Ashura processions. I wish to emphasize two items. Firstly martyrdom is at once a heroic deed and a fatality. Secondly the victory of the martyrs is an apocalyptic one. The struggle is going on until the end of the world. As a good believer you must accept this as destiny. This actor's point of view reflects a peculiarity of Iranian society Paul Vieille has pointed out. This society did not submit social rivalries between different vertical groups to the institution of contract as happened in European history, but gave them free play. This free play reappears in the ta'ziya as fatality and in the 'Ashura processions as street-fighting (10).

MODERN STAGES OF KERBALA:STRUGGLES AGAINST COLONIALISM

By the end of the nineteenth century we observe a certain change in the meaning connected with the commemoration of Husayn. At that time the Shah was eager to sell the Iranian tobacco concession to an Englishman. The large-scale protests against this purpose were for the first time led by Shi'i clergymen, 'Ūlamā. A fetwā was announced from Mujaddid Shirazi, then marja'-e taqlīd (supreme authority of the Shi'i) directing all believers to abstain from smoking. The text read simply: 'In the name of God, the Merciful, the Forgiving. Today the use of tanbāku and tobacco in any form is reckoned as war against the Imām of the Age (may God hasten his glad Advent)'. During the protests in Tehran in January 1892 the bazaar was closed and about four thousand people massed round the citadel led by a sayyid (alleged descendant of the prophet) and dressed in shrouds as if ready for jihad. The ta'ziya often calls the shroud a ceremonial dress that the martyr put on as his bridal dress. At that time intellectuals acqainted with European liberalism began to justify it as genuine Islamic. In a letter to Shi'i 'Ūlamā one of the most influential anticolonial agitators Jamāl ud-Dīn wrote in March 1892:

> 'When this Shah, this viper and man of sin, obtained control of the kingdom, he began gradually to infringe the rights of the 'Ulamā, lower their status, and diminish their influence, on account of his desire to exercise despotic authority in his vain commands and prohibitions, and to extend the scope of his tyranny and oppression'.

The 'Ashura paradigm (the struggle against tyranny) was filled with new political experiences. Humiliations inflicted upon 'Ulamā and merchants were described by means of the old account of Husayn defeated at Kerbala. But this new content of the account also profoundly changed its performance. Political manifestations against the tyranny became now the genuine performance of the account of Husayn. We find this conception back in the Persian revolution 1905-1909 and on the occasion of the manifestations in 1963. I do not need to enter into details because the recent events in Iran testify abundantly to this new interpretation. It was developed and propagated by Dr. Ali Shari'ati, the Jamāl ud-Dīn of our days. He demanded the believers to turn black Shi'ism (the religion of mourning) into red Shi'ism: the religion of martyrdom.

"Ashura recalls the teaching of this continuing fact", he wrote in 1972, "that the present Islam is a criminal Islam in the dress of 'tradition' and that the real Islam is the

Ill. 3: Demonstrators displaying clothing with blood

Ill. 4: Demonstrator displaying bloodied hands

hidden Islam, hidden in the cloak of martyrdom." And in his book Shahadat he exposes the idea, that in the ever present battle of history, time and place all stages are Kerbala, all months are Muharram, all days are 'Ashura (11).

There is abundant evidence that the manifestations against the Shah-regime referred to this conception. Many demonstrators conceived a possible death in the fights against the troops of the Shah as the death of a martyr worthy of the highest rewards. This is corroborated by press-photos, first-rate sources concerning the use of 'Ashura-symbols. I choose two examples. To ill. 3 belongs the information : 'Demonstrators display what they say is a piece of clothing worn by one of the thirteen persons reported shot by troops 12/24'.
Another photo is explained by the following words: 'Demonstrator displays bloodied hands after Army troops opened fire on crowds protesting at a massive military display in Tehran 1/31 on the eve of the return of Ayatollah Khomeyni from 15 years of exile' (ill. 4).

There are a lot of parallels for both actions in the Shi'i passion-play. By showing the shirt stained with blood the persons shot by the troops are declared martyrs who fought as Husayn did against tyranny. And those displaying the clothing are playing the role Zaynab played at the stage of Kerbala: they testify to this martyrdom in public. Likewise the hands coloured red with blood (or perhaps henna ?) refer to the passion-play. Henna was used during the wedding celebrations. This usual custom had been transferred to the ta'ziya, because for the martyr 'the henna of the happiness of life is the blood'. The photos taken of these manifestations are in fact photos of a passion-play put into practice (12).

FINAL OBSERVATION

What does this all mean for an understanding of the relationship between dualistic beliefs and social conflicts ? I think there are two terms illuminating this relationship. The first one is the term 'stages' (sahne) of Kerbala used by Ali Shari'ati. The account of Kerbala is conceived as an account of a never-ending conflict. The real conflicts are the stages of the struggle of Kerbala. I do not think that Ali Shari'ati created this idea. On the contrary, already in precolonial times the account of Kerbala had its stages. But in colonial times the representation of the events of Kerbala became deeply altered. Besides the conflicts between urban groups based on primordial loyalties there arose another basic analogy of the Kerbala-struggle: the struggle against colonialism and imperialism. Now the struggle for independence became the appropriate means for the performance of the play. Ali Shari'ati did not create the idea of performance, but he pleaded for a new anticolonial meaning against the older one. This of course does not diminish his great achievement. The second term is 'performance'. In the beginning we maintained, that only if social conflicts are regularly described by dualistic ideas we can speak of an established relationship between the two. We are now able to specify this. What we are looking for is the performance tradition. In Shi'i Iran the dualistic ideas were part of a performance tradition (13). The question remains, whether there existed a continuity or discontinuity between this performance tradition and pre-Islamic ones. Is there evidence that already in pre-Islamic times the struggle between the good and the evil spirit, between Ahura Mazdā and Ahriman formed part of a popular public performance ? I have no answer to this question. But I am convinced that we have to scrutinize this possibility if we wish to ascertain a certain typical Iranian 'tradition', remaining identical from Zoroastrianism to Shi'i Islam.

I express my thanks to mrs. G. van Baaren-Pape for checking my English translation.

NOTES

1. Colpe, C.: Zarathustra und der frühe Zoroastrismus. In: Asmussen, J.P./Laessøe, J./Colpe,C. (eds.), Handbuch der Religionsgeschichte, vol.2, Göttingen, 1972 p. 338-341; Colpe, C.: Art. "Dualismus". In: Haussig, H.W. (ed.), Wörterbuch der Mythologie, vol.4, Stuttgart, 1982 p. 328; Duchesne-Guillemin, J.: La religion de l'Iran ancien, Paris, 1962 p. 189; Nyberg, H.S.: Die Religionen des alten Iran, Osnabrück 1966 p. 196 ff.

2. MacIntyre, A.: A mistake about causality in social science. In: Laslett, P. and Runciman, W. (eds.), Politics and society, Oxford, 1967 p. 48-70; this anti-naturalist approach and its opposite (the naturalist approach) has been discussed by Q. Skinner: "Social meaning" and the explanation of social action. In: Gardiner, P. (ed.), The philosophy of history, Oxford, 1974 p. 106-126.

3. With regards to the manifestations and their use of Shi'i concepts: Fischer, M.M.J.: Iran. From religious dispute to revolution, Harvard, 1980 chapter 5&6; Keddie, N.: Roots of revolution. An interpretive history of modern Iran, New Haven, 1981 p. 239-258; Tilgner, U. (ed.), Umbruch im Iran, Reinsbeck, 1979 p. 110-132; legitimacy - Algar, H.: The oppositional role of the ulama in twenthieth-century Iran. In: Keddie, N. (ed.), Scholars, saints and sufis, London, 1972 p. 231-255 and Arjomand, S.A.: Religion, political action and legitimate domination in Shi'ite Iran, fourteenth to eighteenth centuries A.D. In: Archives Européennes de sociologie 20 (1979) p.59-109 (Shi'i theology backing quietism).

4. Gluckman, M.: Rituals of rebellion in South-East Africa. In: Order and rebellion in tribal Africa, London, 1963 p. 110-136; Norbeck, E.: African rituals of conflict. In: Middleton, J. (ed.), Gods and rituals, Austin/London, 1967 p. 197-226; Turner, V.: The ritual process, Harmondsworth, 1974 chapter 5; Babcock, B. (ed.), The reversible world. Symbolic inversion in art and society, Ithaca/London, 1978 p.13-36 (Introduction; quotation on p. 22 f.).

5. Tabari - Müller, H: Studien zum persischen Passionsspiel, Freiburg, 1966 p. 40; Rumi - Mamnoun, P.: Ta'ziya. Shi'itisch-Persisches Passionsspiel, Wien, 1967 p. 13; survey of the sources - Kippenberg, H.G.: Jeder Tag 'Ashura, jedes Grab Kerbala. Zur Ritualisierung der Strassenkämpfe im Iran. In: Greussing, K (Hg.), Religion und Politik im Iran, Frankfurt, 1981 p. 217-256 on p. 222.

6. The principles of recruiting are described by I. al-Haidari: Zur Soziologie des schiitischen Chiliasmus, Freiburg, 1975 p. 41 f.; E.: Muharram-Bräuche im heutigen Persien. In: Der Islam 49 (1972) p. 249-272 on p. 259 f.; Aubin, E.: Le Chi'isme et la nationalité Persone. In: Revue du Monde Musulman 4 (1908) p. 457-490 (the photo on p. 472); Van Vloten, M.G.: Les drapeaux en usage à la fête de Huçein à Téhéran. In: Internationales Archiv für Ethnographie 5 (1892) p. 105-111 (quotation on p. 110).

7. Della Valle, P.: Letter, July 25, 1618 apud A. Bausani, Persia Religiosa de Zarathustra a Bahâ'ullâh, Mailand, 1959 p. 429 f. (transl. by I. Culianu).

8. Chardin, J.: Voyages du chevalier Chardien, vol. 2, Amsterdam, 1735 p. 248; Krusinski, J.T.: The history of the revolution of Persia, vol. 1, London, 1728 p. 91 f.

9. With regard to city quaters - Eickelman, D.F.: The Middle East, Englewood Cliffs, 1981 p. 110-116; Pearson, M.N.: Premodern Muslim political systems. In: Journal of the American Oriental society 102 (1982) p. 47-58.

10. On the different aspects of the ta'ziya - Chelkowski, P.J. (ed.), Ta'ziyeh. Ritual and drama in Iran, New York, 1979; examples for the idea of ransom - Virolleaud, Ch.: Le théâtre Persan ou le drame de Kerbéla, Paris, 1950; De Generet, R.H.: Le martyre d'Ali Akbar, Liège/Paris, 1946 p. 56 f.; p. 120-124; heaven responsible for tyranny - Virolleaud, Ch.: La passion de l'Imam Hosseyn, Beirut, 1927 Persian text p. 11; the martyr enters paradise immediately - De Generet, R.H.: l.c. p. 44 f. and 66 f.; plate - Monchi-Zadeh, D.: Ta'ziya. Das persische Passionsspiel, Stockholm, 1967 p. 89; Vieille, P.: Le feodalité et l'etat en Iran, Paris, 1975 p. 296-298.

11. Keddie, N.: Religion and rebellion in Iran. The tobacco protest of 1891-1892, London, 1966 p. 95 f. (quotation of the fetwā); Algar, H.: Religion and state in Iran 1785-1906, Berkeley, 1969 p. 214 (events January 1892); quotation Jamāl ud-Dīn - Browne, E.G.: The Persian revolution of 1905-1909, Cambridge, 1910 p. 24 f.; Thaiss, G.: Religious symbolism and social change. The drama of Husain. In: Keddie, N. (ed.), Scholars, saints and sufis (note 3) p. 349-366; Shari'ati, A.: Shahadat, Tehran, 1972 p. 104; Akhavi, S.: Religion and politics in contemporary Iran. Clergy-State relations in the Pahlavī period, Albany, 1980 p. 143-158.

12. With reqard to the roles of Husayn and Zaynab - Shari'ati, A.: Shahadat p. 104; henna - De Generet, R.H.: l.c. p. 80 f.

13. The term basic analogy is derived from V. Turner: Social dramas and ritual metaphors. In: Dramas, fields and metaphors Ithaca, New York, 1974 p. 26; performance tradition - Beeman, W.O.: A full arena. The development and meaning of popular performance traditions in Iran. In: Bonine, M. and Keddie, N.: Continuity and change in modern Iran, Albany, 1981 p. 285-305.

Catharism, Catholicism, and Magic. Rethinking Le Roy Ladurie's 'Montaillou'

Y. Kuiper

Social reality which is far removed from us, in time or distance, often possesses a certain charm. The tremendous interest which the general public has for Le Roy Ladurie's historical study 'Montaillou: village occitan de 1294 à 1324' can undoubtely be seen in this light (1). Both scientifically and as literature his book is considered by many to be of high quality (2).

The attraction of this book also lies in the fact that it fits into recent developments in European historiography: the rise of the 'history of collective mentalities' and the revival of 'narrative history' (3). The period in which historians from the French Annales-tradition especially concentrated on uncovering structures and recording developments in historical society in charts and graphs, seems to have come to a (temporary ?) end in the seventies.

An important aspect of Annales historiography is, that it is open to methods and research results from related disciplines. At the hight of 'structural history' economics, demography and sociology functioned as supporting sciences, now some Annales-historians derive their inspiration from disciplines such as anthropology and psychology. Le Roy Ladurie's 'Montaillou' is an obvious example of this. Anthropology in particular supplied him with a model for the study of a small, medieval village community. Thus he attempts in 'Montaillou' to depict the relationship between the social structure of the village, the economic relationships, and the mental, psychological world of its inhabitants.

In his reconstruction of the emotional and mental world of these villagers Le Roy Ladurie was able to use a unique source (4). Jacques Fournier, Bishop of Pamiers between 1317 and 1325, had as inquisitor in this period asigned himself to the task of completely exterminating the Cathar 'heresy' in his diocese. He was of the opinion that his accomplishments should be documented as precisely as possible by his associates. The village of Montaillou seemed to harbor many heretics and by way of the many extensive interrogations which the inhabitants were subjected to we are confronted not only with their Cathar ideas but also with other, sometimes associated, aspects of village life.

Thanks to Le Roy Ladurie's microscopic approach the historian of religion is extensively informed of the reality of Cathar religious experience - a subject about which less has been published than about the history of ideas of Catharism. In this article I will attempt to show how Le Roy Ladurie's study offers an important supplement to the already existent notions about Catharism, and in which way he partially corrects these notions. My attention will especially be directed to relations and conflicts between Catholicism, Catharism and popular religion. In the first part of this essay I will supply a summary of recent research into Occitanian Catharism, while in the second part those chapters of Le Roy Ladurie's book will be discussed which shed light on the reception of Catharism by illiterate peasants and shepherds from an isolated region in the French Pyrenees. Finally, in the last part of the article, a number of interpretations from previous parts will be evaluated and a few conclusions will be drawn.

CATHARISM IN OCCITANIA

Many researchers have dealt with the largest medieval Christian heresy, Catharism. There is some consensus among them about subjects such as its European area of distribution, its dualistic tenets and its rituals. In contrast, the question of the origins of Catharism continues to provide matter for heated debates. For this problem one may distinguish between two interpretations which, at first sight, exclude each other. The first emphasizes the diffusion of religious ideas. Dondaine and Werner, for example, think that the diffusion of the dualistic 'theology' of the Balkan Bogomils - in which Manichaean elements may be identified - led to the emergence of various heretic movements in Western Europe after the year 1000 (5). These movements resembled Catharism as it developed in Southern France and Northern Italy in the twelfth century. Both authors have pointed at clear similarities between the doctrine of the Bogomils and the dogmas of the heretical sects in Western Europe: baptism is rejected, meat is taboo, there is no respect for the cross and no special value is attached to marriage. They also make clear that these sects manifested themselves rather suddenly and that their followers were recruited from all layers of the population. Contrary to this point of view are the ideas of, among others, Morghen and Russell (6). They regard the early heretic movements first of all as a product of regional and local circumstances. Rather than a diffusion of Oriental religious ideas a wave of piety and a desire for reformation of the Catholic Church should have led to the emergence of these sects. Cathar dualism is in this view regarded as a consequence of the elementary opposition in Christian thought: the struggle between body and soul. In addition, some Cathar specialists have, in various ways, tried to reconcile these more or less extreme points of view (7). Others extended their historical approach to religious ideas with a more sociological approach of Catharism: for which social strata had Catharism most appeal, can we recognize in the repression of Catharism aspects of class conflict, or is, in a way, Catharism the ideology of regional groups opposing the growing state-formation process in France ? (8).

As appears from some original Cathar writings still at our disposal, the central characteristic of Cathar doctrine is its dualism (9). Within Cathar doctrine two tendencies may be discerned: a radical dualism and a moderate dualism. The first is reminiscent of Manichaeism, while the second seems to bear resemblance to the doctrine of the Bogomils.

Radical dualism assumes the existence of two independent principles which are in eternal opposition to each other: one representing good (or light) and the other evil (or dark). 'Satan' is seen as an autonomous power opposite to 'God', with 'God' ruling the spiritual and 'Satan' the terrestrial world. In the key-myths of radical dualism one is told that the devil, son of the god of darkness, seduced one third of the angels present in the heaven of the good god. Before these angels were expelled from heaven they had a tripartite constitution: body, soul and spirit. After their fall their souls were locked up in terrestrial bodies, created by the evil god, while their bodies and spirits remained in heaven. Out of pity the good god sent Christ - an angel with special gifts who always remained wholly spirit - to earth to save 'the lost sheep'. Only these fallen angels are 'the good people' on earth and only they can be saved. As long as their souls have not been released from their earthly prison they wandered from body to body (of human beings or animals).

Moderate dualism acknowledges one God who created both the spiritual and the material (although undifferentiated and formless) world. An angel - Lucifer - rebelled against God and was expelled from heaven together with his followers. Thereupon he shaped the evil world from originally good matter. In many forms of moderate dualism human beings and their souls are believed to descend from the bodies of Adam and Eve. Men of the Cathar community would certainly be saved although others were nor irrevocably lost because they were offered the possibility of a new incarnation through migration of souls. For them redemption could take place at a later point in time (10).

Another question, not easily answered, is which version the Cathars in Occitania (Languedoc) subscribed to. According to Nelli the Occitanians - just like the Cathars in northern Italy - remained, by and large, true to radical dualism (11). Wakefield however, recognizes a circular movement in Cathar history in Languedoc: before 1170 moderate dualism dominated; after 1170 Catharism radicalized along with a process according to which Cathars increasingly organized themselves ecclesiastically. (There were four orders of Cathars: bishop, 'filius major', 'filius minor', and deacon) (12).

When around 1250 Catharism - through the influence of the Crusades against the Occitanian Cathars, the mendicant orders and the Inquisition - no longer functions as the big anti-church, more scope for moderate dualism arises again within Cathar doctrine. In the meantime the impact of the movement has shifted from the cities to the countryside, so that at the end of the thirteenth century all kinds of popular belief and superstition turn up in Cathar doctrine (13). Nelli supposes that during this last period radical dualism was also toned by the influence of the Catholic Church. He nevertheless still believes that "mais en ce qui concerne l'essentiel, la doctrine n'avait pas tellement varié" (14).

But what facets did Catharism reveal in practice ? How was Catharism organized at the grassroot level and what were its rituals ?(15). Catharism knew a fundamental difference between a spiritual élite, a kind of priestclass - these priests were called 'perfecti','parfaits', 'bonhommes' or 'bon chrêtiens' - on the one hand, and a large group of followers ('credentes' or 'croyants') on the other.

The most important Cathar ritual was the 'consolamentum'. It was conducted by a parfait in the presence of fellow-bonhommes and a few other believers. The ritual consisted of two parts: in the first part the novice, at least 18 years of age, received the authority to say the Lord's Prayer; in the second part the actual baptism took place. In the baptismal ceremony the acting parfait held the book of Gospels above the believer's head while other parfaits placed their hands on his body. The ceremony ended with the Kiss of peace ('caretas') to each other (men to men and women to women) followed by a general confession of sins. In most cases the ritual was performed as a whole, but sometimes a period of fasting was inserted between the first part and the baptism.

When one had become a parfait, one was for the rest of his life obliged to refrain from sexual intercourse and eating meat (on danger of disturbing the metempsychosis), cheese, milk and eggs. The killing of people and certain animals and the taking of an oath were also forbidden. Only parfaits had the power to bless bread and in daily life they were respected in a special way ('melioramentum'): on greeting and parting the believers made three deep genuflexions in front of the parfait after which the latter said some formulas expressing the wish that the believers would be led to a good end (i.e. the 'consolamentum'). Thereupon the believers received the Kiss of peace and were blessed by the parfaits who as a rule travelled around as duos. In the beginning the bonhommes could be recognized by their black robes. After the Inquisition started to pursue them with the help of heretic-hunters, spies and informers, the parfaits used to hide a black cord under their neutral dress. If parfaits sinned against their vows they were often rebaptized. Most bonhommes led an exemplary life however, representing the 'Vita Apostolica' in a dignified way.

Ordinary believers did not receive the 'consolamentum' until they realized that death was near. The ritual was then reduced to more modest proportions and the emphasis was on the Lord's prayer. At the end of the 13th century, in the very last phase of Occitanian Catharism, this'consolamentum' of-the-ill was supplemented with the prohibition for the dying person to take any food or fluid. In this way his or her soul would be saved. This phenomenon ('endura') gave rise to many speculations. The phenomenon, often described as 'ritual suicide', is probably overemphasized in earlier literature about Catharism and the number of cases where 'endura' was applied is very likely overestimated. Different motives are mentioned: the one wants to underline the pessimistic view of life of the Cathars, the other takes the declining years of Catharism as a sign of decadence, still another wants to portray the last Cathars as 'desperate' (16).

Borst pointed out that for the original meaning of 'endura' one should turn to the period of fasting which sometimes preceded the normal 'consolamentum'. Haste necessitated a reversal of acts for the dying recipient, hence the fasting afterwards according to Borst. This author also wonders whether reports mentioning a prolonged death-struggle do indicate that they abstained from food but not from drinking, since medical research has shown that people under such conditions have about 75 days to live. (17).

The fact that an ordinary believer did not really become a Cathar until death was approaching gave some food for thought that these believers led a dissolute life, or at least lived by a double standard of morals. Wakefield properly notes that this is easier said than proven (18). A standard medieval Catholic criticism of Catharism was, for example, that since all was forbidden in Cathar doctrine, all was equally allowed; this encouraged sexual licence.

No doubt, Cathar thought is anti-sexual. For Catharism considers subjection to the flesh as the capital sin. Marriage, incest and any kind of perversion are even lumped together. In a way marriage attests of fornication and is regarded even more sinful than all other sexual relations. Pregnant women, even when approaching death, are not allowed to enter the sect. Many Cathars believe that the devil houses in a pregnant body. Borst notes in this context that contempt of marriage, women and also children was less visible in the later history of Catharism (19). He does not specify dates, but connects this milder attitude with the growth of the movement and the ecclesiastical institutionalisation of Catharism. Furthermore, it could be pointed out that female parfaits have also existed during some time, although they never occupied prominent positions in the movement's hierarchy. According to Lindeboom the parfaits in particular should be blamed for references to 'declining sense of morals' (20). They may have left wife and children behind to follow their call, while too much confidence - a fatalistic assurance as it were - in their own unassailable moral qualities may have tempted them into sensuality and indulgence. Finally, in this brief review of Cathar rituals the 'convenensa' could be mentioned, a ritual which is an extension of the 'melioramentum'. Since the middle of the thirteenth century a custom develops according to which the believer expresses the wish to receive the 'consolamentum' at the end of his life. Thereupon a parfait assures him that this will be granted even if he should loose his speech (21).

The history of Languedoc Catharism may also be placed within a political and social-economic perspective. From Borst's and Nelli's publications it appears that both authors perceive the same overall development, despite differences of interpretation of Catharism as such (22).

After Catharism found a response among large groups of the population around 1170, the following decades picture a development of the movement toward a clerical organization with its own intelligentsia who knows some Latin and owns books. In those times the Cathar movement also became an instrument in big politics: the counts of Toulouse and their following resist the influence of the French King and the Catholic Church. They mobilize in their campaign the Cathars who still had foothold among all layers of the population (high and low nobility: the powerful patrons of the Cathars; the rich middle class families who dominated the town councils; tradesmen, artisans and labourers in the towns and villages; and the peasants in the countryside). So a view of Catharism as a proletarian movement does not correspond with the facts. At this time there is not yet a gulf between town and country and mobility of population carried Catharism from one to the other and vice versa. In missionary practice family influence has always been the most important social factor and the impact of the Cathar missionaries on women has been probably decisive.

In 1209 an alliance of King (Philip August) and Church (pope Innocentius III) starts to fight the high Occitan nobility and Cathars. There is no room for Catharism in the emerging national state of France and the military battle may be considered as terminated when the last Cathar fortress, Montségur, is conquered by the alliance in 1244.

By participating in the Albigensian crusades the Church tries to exterminate a rivalizing religious organization; the result however is, that Catholic authority is made more subservient to the powers of the French national state. Already during the first years of the battle, the high nobility of the Languedoc disassociates itself from Cathar matters and rich citizens in the towns (bankers, lawyers and financiers) are becoming now the patrons of the movement. Yet Catharism continues to commit large groupings (low rural nobility, tradesmen, artisans and peasants). But after 1250, when the political and religious battle was definitely lost, Catharism as a real clerical organization collapses. Under pressure of the papal and episcopal Inquisitions and due to the success of mendicant orders (the Dominicans and the Franciscans) Catharism is forced to move out of the cities.

After the Fourth Lateran Council in 1215 (Rome) inquisitorial institutions and activities grew. Since heresy in the Middle Ages was seen both as a sin and as a crime, Churchmen and secular authorities had to cooperate in prosecuting and punishing the offenders. Sentences for heresy varied from heavy penalties like the stake and longtime imprisonment (confiscation of goods was almost invariably added to these penalties) to light convictions like compulsory pilgrimage and the wearing of clothes to which yellow crosses were stitched. Contrary to popular belief, notices Hamilton, the inquisitors handed very few persons over to the secular authorities to be burnt at the stake. According to this author's calculations, less than three people a year were burned at its average in Languedoc when the campaign against heresy there was fiercest (23).

From about 1250 onwards Cathars are mostly found in the countryside. Not the Cathar bishops but rather 'the elders' (itinerant folk-preachers) are now the leading authorities within the movement. Hence Borst writes about the social background of Occitan Catharism towards the end of the thirteenth century:

> "vor allem die Schreiber und Notare sind die katharische Führungsschicht. Die Masse der Anhänger wird vom Handwerk gestellt; das ganze Tuchgewerbe ist noch vertreten; Metzger, Gastwirte, und Gerber, Friseure, Arbeiter und Hirten, Dienstmägde, Wanderartisten und Dirnen sind die letzten Getreuen der katharischen 'Vollendeten'" (24).

But peasants are also among them - as appears from Le Roy Ladurie's 'Montaillou'. However, the way various authors view this final phase of Catharism is somewhat curious. It looks as if they feel obliged to describe rural Catharism with mixed feelings. Nelli speaks for instance about 'the degeneration of Catharism' and Borst asserts about the influence of popular belief on Cathar doctrine: "man hat sie mit skurrilen und blumigen Einzelzügen aus dem Volksdenken nur noch ausgeschmückt" (25). Probably they overlook the fact that there has always been in Cathar myths and stories tendencies to gross materialization of key themes and a strong vein to fantasy - especially in the interpretations of the sympathizers of Catharism.

What can be said about Catharism in quantative terms ? Great caution should however be exercised here. Estimate of the adherents of the movement (mostly based on Inquisition reports) vary immensely. However a certain consensus does exist about the number of parfaits. In this respect an important source is a treatise about Catharism - written in 1250 - of Rainier Sacchoni, a Dominican and an inquisitor, who once was an important leader in one of the Cathar churches in Lombardy (26). When confining ourselves to the publications of two cautious researchers, namely Borst and Wakefield, we encounter the following figures. Number of perfecti around 1200 (in southern France), Borst: c. 600 and Wakefield : 1000 to 1500; around 1250, both authors : c. 200 ; and after 1300: Borst c. 15 and Wakefield: less than 20 (27).

The number of believers can only be speculated upon, at least as far as the period 1200-1250 is concerned. Borst thinks that the movement had about the same amount of adherents in 1250 as around the change of the century, viz. about half a million. This figure is in strong contrast with Molinier's calculations of almost four million believers for the first decades of the thirteenth century (28). There is no difference of opinion among the various authors about the number of followers of Catharism in Languedoc after 1300: no more than about 1000. At that time Catharism experienced its last revival in the mountains of upper Ariège - a region where heresy had not penetrated until late. One of its centres here was the village Montaillou.

The leader of this revival is the notary Pierre Authiē a native of this region (29). In the years before 1300 he had taken refuge in Lombardy where he had been converted to 'true Christianity'. With the aid of his brother and his son he once more succeeds in inspiring the faithful of the villages. But in 1309 he too is arrested by the Inquisition, together with his relatives and some friends. In 1311 they make their appearance at the stake. Before the stakes are alighted Pierre Authiē's last words to the crowd seem to have been: "If it were lawful for me to preach, you would all accept my faith"(30).

One of his confidents, Guillaume Bélibaste, who, in spite of his criminal past, became a parfait - although he did not live the life of the perfect, he had for instance a mistress - manages to escape from the dungeons of the Inquisition in Carcasonne. He takes refuge in Catalonia and becomes the leader of a small colony of Cathar refugees. However, in 1321, through treason of one of his followers, Bélibaste falls into the hands of the Inquisition. Some years later southern French Catharism was dead. Or as Le Roy Ladurie writes on the last page of 'Montaillou': "Today Catharism is no more than a dead star, whose cold but fascinating light reaches us now after an eclipse of more than half a millennium" (31).

CATHARISM IN MONTAILLOU

'Montaillou: village occitan de 1294 à 1324' is not a study about Catharism, much less about its theology. Only the fact that so many 'heretics' lived in Montaillou and were pursued so obstinately by the bishop of Pamiers, Jacques Fournier (the later pope Benedict XII), enabled Le Roy Ladurie, as he writes himself, to trace the mentality of the peasants and shepherds from Montaillou and surrounding villages. Nevertheless Cathars play an important role in the book and they are just those heretics who are not treated quite seriously by some historians who wrote about the movement. Le Roy Ladurie's potrayal of them is rather at variance with the standard point of view. In his study the peasants of Montaillou appear not to be stupid and backward, but on the contrary, their oral tradition shows a delight in philosophical and metaphysical speculation.

Let me first summarize the information Le Roy Ladurie gives about non-religious aspects of life in Montaillou. After that sketch I shall return to religious matters.

Montaillou was (and is) a small village in the northern Pyrenees. About 250 people lived in this village in the beginning of the fourteenth century. Two somewhat larger cities in the vicinity were Foix and Pamiers, at respectively 50 and 70 kilometers from Montaillou; the village belonged to the principality of Comtē de Foix and to the diocese of Pamiers. In the first part of his book Le Roy Ladurie discusses the political and economical relationships in both the village and the region. Two ways of life are compared with one another: the cult of the 'domus' (or 'ostal' - a term which covers both the literal translation 'house' as well as 'household' or 'family') and the world of the shepherds; ways of life that are oriented around different means of survival, namely agriculture and herding sheep. Class distinctions did not exist in Montaillou. The village is an archipelago of 'ostals': each household owns its own ground and produces for private consumption. Great wealth is rare amongst these peasants. The composition of a household can be quite variable. Most possess a family structure; sometimes there is domestic personnel. The authority within an ostal rests with the male head of the family. Economically and emotionally the ostal is the central value in the lives of these villagers. In the case of death of a head of family bits of fingernails and hair are kepe to stress the continuity of the ostal. Not the whole village but only the ostal grieves for its death.

In this peasant community men usually married much younger women; there were many widows in the village. The relatively high dowries caused the heads of the ostals to indulge in marriage politics. In spite of this some people still did marry for love.

To depict the world of the shepherds Le Roy Ladurie especially relied upon the life history of the shepherd Pierre Maury from Montaillou. Shepherds are the bachelors of the Pyrenean villages; for varying periods of time they are in service of the owners of large herds. They travel with these herds from the summer meadows in the hills to the winter meadows in the valleys (some of which were situated in Spain). Their mobile existence places them in the position of mediatior for the different ways of life. Undoubtedly the transhumance played a role in spreading Catharism. Sometimes these shepherds even function as bodyguards or guides for traveling Cathar 'priests'. Although large differences in wealth were not common in Montaillou, there were important differences in influence and prestige between the ostals. These differences were based upon the nature of the relationships which were held with the outside world. In this way the Clergue family dominated village life through its contacts with authorities outside of Montaillou. Bernard Clergue actes as bayle for the Count of Foix. In this function he collected taxes for his master and acquired judicial authority. His brother Pierre represented church authority as the village priest (the Inquisition of Carcassonne and the Bishop of Pamiers). For years the brothers took advantage of the weak influence of the regional authorities in local matters. Although they did collect taxes they rarely actually passed these on. As the brothers also flirted with Catharism they managed to align themselves to the houses of many a heretic. Furthermore, the priest Pierre hardly led a virtuous life, had various mistresses (amongst whom the noble wife of the 'châtelain' of Montaillou, who lived in the little castle of the village: Bêatrice de Planissoles) and at times functioned as an agent of the Inquisition. In this last role he could easily dispose of troublesome enemies.

Not all ostals subjugate themselves to the Clergue regime. One of the remaining Catholic, anti-Clergue ostals (the Azéma family) even counts among its kin the Bishop of Pamiers, Jacques Fournier, the fanatic heretic persecutor. A bitter power struggle takes place between the Clergue's and the Azéma's (and their followers) - a fight between 'scorpions in a bottle' as Le Roy Ladurie calls it. It is not until about 1320 when Fournier himself starts to take part in the matters of Montaillou that the balance turns in favour of the anti-Clergue faction. Both brothers soon find themselves in the dungeons of the Inquisition and die in captivity. In this local power struggle each side makes use of intimidation and false witness in the Inquisition; occasionally not stopping even at murder.

In the second part of his study Le Roy Ladurie attempts to do what he dearly misses in other studies about life in the middle ages, namely to give the illiterate peasants a voice in the historical treatise (32). Over hundreds of pages we follow the people of Montaillou (and the surrounding villages) in their daily existence, are confronted with their ideas, their emotions, their aspirations and their fears. A multitude of topics are extensively addressed: love, sexuality, the position of women, violence, poverty, literacy, gestures, personal hygien, and many other subjects. Obviously there are also chapters on religion, magic and folklore - we will now restrict ourselves to these subjects.

Already at the beginning of his book Le Roy Ladurie states that he treats the difference between 'Cathar' and 'Catholic' in the way suggested by his source. Many passages indicate that this distinction had a flowing nature. Villagers changed their religious orientation during their lifetime. Although nearly all did so from the same motive: fear - fear for the Inquisition, but above all fear for (or finally faith in ?) the right salvation of their souls.

Before Fournier started to interfere actively in Montaillou in 1318, the Inquisition of Carcassone had already raided the village once before. In 1308 all villagers above the age of twelve had been rounded up and interrogated, whereupon the first victims fell. Montaillou was becoming 'the village with the yellow crosses'. The sword of Damocles has been hanging above the village ever since. When the faction conflict mentioned earlier is becoming more intense and the networks of priviliged villagers are intruded upon, the end of Catharism in Montaillou is approaching. Catharism was introduced into Montaillou through one of the ostals; the continuing struggle for power between the different ostals finally stamped out the heretic creed. Using the testimonies in the Fournier register Le Roy Ladurie reconstructs the following distribution of religious preferences in the village: 11 Cathar ostals, 5 Catholic ostals, a few mixed ostals, and a number of families of changing faith.

Le Roy Ladurie continually emphasizes that Catharism in Montaillou was a matter of the domus , and that, in a way, it reinforced the existing domus tradition. So Cathar meetings with or without visiting parfaits were held within the ostal. Moreover even paradise was imagined by a lot of villagers as an immense domus.

From a more general point of view Le Roy Ladurie contrasts the 'little tradition' of peasant Catharism and Catholicism with the 'great tradition' of urban and more official Catholic values. Cathars as well as Catholics in the countryside rebelled against clerical taxes and mendicant orders.

In order to understand the religious mentality of these villagers one could first take a look at the nature of Catholicism in the village and subsequently scrutinize Cathar convictions. Such an approach is in accordance with Le Roy Ladurie's thesis that Catharism is an extreme heroic variant of Christianity: here one becomes a Cathar when Catholicism falls short.

Almost everybody in the village participates now and then in churchlife, although many not enthusiastically. Mass is attended above all to maintain social contacts within the village. Reception of the basic sacraments (baptism, confession, first communion and marriage) is no indication of a strong bond with the Church. According to Le Roy Ladurie some of them should rather be seen as 'rites de passage' (youth, adolescence and adulthood). Nevertheless the reader of 'Montaillou' gets the impression that the Catholic calendar still regulates village life.

Almost every villager went to confession once a year. Confession was more highly regarded than the other sacraments because every one - Catholics and Cathars - thought that it might offer the means of salvation. But the heretics of Montaillou did not tell the whole truth in the confessional. "I make confession of my sins, except those I have committed in heresy, for I am afraid of losing all my possessions if I reveal that", said a woman of Montaillou in her deposition before the Inquisition. Sacraments which were almost totally absent in religious life in Montaillou were confirmation and extreme unction. When people were in danger of death, unless they were real Cathars, a priest would come to their bedside and questioning the dying believer on the articles of faith. What followed then were the acts of confession and communion.

Going on a pilgrimage and fasting were however religious practices widely observed. Common practices were also paying tithes and firstfruits, giving alms to pilgrims visiting the Virgin of Montaillou, making the sign of the cross before eating and sleeping, the reciting of the Pater Noster, genuflecting in church and taking the Easter communion. On the other hand remembrance of the dead - the saying of Masses for the repose of the souls of the dead - was a common practice in the towns of upper Ariège, but not in a village as Montaillou. A striking fact is also that some of the great developments in medieval (western European) Christianity hardly exerted any influence upon religious thought in Montaillou. For example many villagers, and not only the strict Cathars, had difficulties with millenarian theories; they rejected the idea of the end of the world, the Final Judgment and the general Resurrection. Even when the parfait Bélibaste, after a trip to Spain, enthusiastically told his followers there were rumours about "people will rise up against people and kingdom against kingdom: a descendant of the King of Aragon will graze his horse upon the altar in Rome", a woman from Montaillou only replied: "And when will that be, sir ?" (33). Generally speaking religious doubt was widespread here. People had considerable doubt about central tenets of the Church's teaching as the Virgin birth and the doctrine of transsubstantiation.

One of Le Roy Ladurie's more general conclusions is that a strong sense of sin is foreign to religious life in Montaillou. He suggests that the 'honour and shame' sentiments centred around the domus-complex have a much greater influence. In this respect Catharism and Catholicism are vey much alike. What is then the essential difference between believers of both persuasions ?

Catholics and Cathars differed in religious 'means' rather than in religious 'goals'. Their preoccupation with salvation in the other world was the same, but they disagreed about the answer to the question: <u>who</u> can save our souls? To the Cathars this was the parfait, to the Catholics the priest. So a Cathar from a village near Montaillou explained to his cousin: "The goodmen follow the path of God .... they alone can save souls. And all those who are received into their sect before death go straight to Heaven, whatever wickedness or sin they have committed". (34). As Le Roy Ladurie points out, the parfaits also have important social functions. In this segmentary, to anarchism tending micro society they connect ostals, suppress violence, show respect for another man's possessions and act as justices of peace. As a real Durkheimian Le Roy Ladurie also stresses the importance, viz. the social function, of ritual for Cathar mentality. Especially the consalamentum was the answer to an ancient problem: "comment gagner son ciel sans se fatiguer ?" (35). As the citation above already illustrated, there was no need for the adherents of the perfecti to worry about Christian moral as long as the hour of truth had not yet come. Besides, nothing terrible could happen to them as their 'saints' were always nearby. The Fournier register also shows that many Cathar believers compared their leading men with the Apostles. The ways of acting of the parfaits were directly linked to the Vita Apostolica with its ethics of poverty. This devotion to the Apostles was a general development in western European religion after the eleventh century. The depositions of the people from Montaillou demonstrate exactly how this theme was incorporated into popular devotion and specifically into Catharism.

The local churches in Montaillou and Prades d'Aillon (at a stone's throw distance of Montaillou) were dedicated to Saint Peter, probably for this reason, he was in this neigbourhood the most popular Apostle. But also the most respected? "Oh ! oh ! How can we do such a thing in the church of Saint Peter ?" said Bēatrice de Planissoles, in Prades, when she entered the local church where her lover the priest Pierre Clergue had prepared a bed for the two of them for the night. To which the lover replied: "Much harm it will do Saint Peter"

(36). What about a direct connection between loose morals and Catharism, so often suggested in literature (the treatises of Catholic contempories and modern research of Church historians) ? According to Le Roy Ladurie Catharism in the mountains of upper Ariège did not lead to concubinage, adultery, homosexuality or incest, at best it went along with existing social relationships and practices. Catharism did tolerate a high degree of moral freedom.

A well-known fact is also that in early Catharism in southern France women strongly participated in the organization of the movement (37). On the contrary Catharism in Montaillou did not vary from peasant culture in its misogynous stance towards women. The introduction of Catharism in upper Ariège for instance did not spell the end of maltreatment and rape of women. Cathar doctrine in general was in some ways hostile towards women: femininity had often been linked to diabolical activities and female souls were not believed to enter paradise. The women of Montaillou were in a submissive position, also in the religious sphere. Only within the walls of the domus the older woman was able to exercise some authority.

In theory Catharism was also fiercely opposed to marriage and procreation. Reality in Montaillou suggests however, that Cathar families had more children than Catholic ones. Perhaps a special variant of (peasant-)Cathar way of thinking lies at root of this phenomenon. People in the village thought that newly born children received the souls of children who had just died. A lot of other examples could illustrate the popularity of the theme of metempsychosis in the conversations between the villagers. In short, the deeper structure of Cathar thought in Montaillou reflected a basic opposition between metempsychosis and salvation; an opposition which corresponded to the contrast in daily life between the asceticism of the parfaits and the behaviour of their followers which was governed by custom rather than religious ethics.

In one of the last chapters of the book Le Roy Ladurie points out that Catharism in and around Montaillou was mostly of a moderately dualistic character. For example, nature was not regarded as a sheer Santanic creation. Only specific animals (cats, owls, wolves, reptiles) were considered to be possessed by the Devil. Some peasants saw also the hand of the Devil at work in hail, thunder and storms. Others thought it was God himself who made the crops flourish.

In comparison with religion (meditation on the after-life, the concern for salvation etc.) magic as such was not a central element in the mental outlook of the people in Montaillou, according to Le Roy Ladurie. Nevertheless the Fournier register shows clear examples of the use of fertility rites, magical herb as a contraceptive, all sorts of spells, etc. In the upper Ariège magic was mostly connected with popular medicine which was especially a feminine province. Also interesting is that a kind of diabolisation of these practices could already be observed at the time of Fournier. As long as the inquisitors of the official Church had not at their disposal an elaborated demonology and - as Le Roy Ladurie observes in 'Montaillou' - the social distance between men and women was still small, this diabolisation did not lead to witch-hunting on a large scale (38). To summarize: Catharism (of the Authié's) undermined the Catholic monopoly in the village and thus cleared the way for folkloristic ideas already existing before the arrival of 'heresy'. In a way magical representation and superstition dominated life in Montaillou. But hidden behind the attraction of these representations the big and essential question was:

what will happen to my soul ?

As appears from the depositions of the villagers one of the most striking aspects of religious thinking is the enormous diversity of religious convictions. Some people thought that the soul was made of blood, but for others the soul was wind or bread. One could also find different ideas about the destination of the soul after death and various views on the end of times. According to some Catholics and Cathars the souls of the just dead wandered a couple of weeks on earth before their entry into 'heaven', 'paradise', 'the place of rest', etc. During this short time specialized intermediaries, the messengers of soul , could establish and maintain contact with the dead people surrounding the living. Others thought however that the soul of a dead person returned immediately to heaven. To understand this diversity - ranging from ideas based on scepticism or crude materialism to 'real' devotional interpretations - one should realize with Le Roy Ladurie that : "The Catharism of Montaillou was first and foremost a story, a myth. It was told over and over again, with variations, around the fire ". (39).

CONCLUSIONS

In part two of this article we have already shown that Le Roy Ladurie attempted to chart the mental world of a group of illiterate peasants and shepherds via a document from the 'great tradition' of Catholicism. The same applies to his approach to Catharism. Considering the research into Catharism of ecclesiastical historians, theologians, historians of religion etc. (see part 1 of this essay), it is remarkable that Le Roy Ladurie slips in by the back entrance: through the village of Montaillou by way of the 'little, popular tradition' of its inhabitants.

In describing this little tradition, Le Roy Ladurie paints a picture of village life that can be adequately compared to the model of the (peasant-)little community as this was once developed by the American anthropologist Robert Redfield (40). Redfield considered the little community as an integrated whole that could be recognized by four characteristics: 1. the village possesses a quality of distinctiveness that is expressed in group consciousness and collective mentality of its inhabitants; 2. the village is small; 3. the ideas and activities of the villagers are homogeneous; 4. and finally, the community is socially and economically self-sufficient (41). With the exception of the characteristic of homogeneity, the situation in Montaillou largely coincides with Redfield's model. To typify the social structure of a little community, Redfield suggested to develop a holistic concept of this structure. For instance, is there a central organizing idea in terms of which everything else in the life of the villagers is seen ? In the case of Montaillou such a concept does indeed seem demonstrable , namely, the ostal and the sentiments connected therewith. Redfield further stressed that much of the economy and the religious and magical practices in such a community are expressions of social structure. This observation also appears at various times in 'Montaillou'. According to Le Roy Ladurie many of the activities and ideas of the people of Montaillou may be traced back to the ostal-complex. Finally, one could point to the following global similarity between Redfield's model and Le Roy Ladurie's monography. Both researchers stress that small peasant communities are part of a larger whole (a region, a diocese, a county, or a nation-state) and that there are considerable 'outside' influences on village life. In Montaillou this influence was also manifest: materially - the transhumance, the Inquisition, the collecting of church and secular taxes, as well as 'mentally' - the official Catholic doctrine and Catharism.

This last aspect of Redfield's model, and the similarities it shows with Le Roy Ladurie's description of outside influences, explain in a socio-cultural way the attraction of Catharism for many inhabitants of Montaillou and their countrymen. The increasing clerical pressure (the actual collection of taxes) and the repressive rule of the Inquisition assailed the existent local, social and cultural relationships, and threatened the autonomy of peasant communities such as Montaillou. Catharism offered a universal framework of interpretation within which these outside influences could be labeled as evil and demonic (42). The unintended consequence of the spread of Catharism was, however, that it created differences between people of the country and, together with the activities of the Inquisition, brought out the dormant social conflicts in this peasant society.

At first these conflicts were controled by local traditions and by the local authorities. In time, however, the outside influence grew and finally forced the conflicts to be resolved, usually under the pretense of religious difference, and to the benefit of more central authorities and very small minorities of the peasant society. However much Catharism offered a framework of interpretation for changing political and social relationships, its religious component - for example the ethics of non-violence and the emphasis upon individual salvation - prevented its adherents from forming a collective, organized political front against the central authorities.

The comparison between Redfield and Le Roy Ladurie leads us to a more general discussion such as that presently held by historians of religion. This discussion is also recognizable in Le Roy Ladurie's 'Montaillou': how is the great tradition (of Catholicism and, in a way, even Catharism) communicated to common people and how is it incorporated in the little tradition, the popular culture ?

Until recently many researchers only granted the popular culture a passive role of adjustment in its confrontation with the ideas and representatives of the great tradition (the dominant culture, the elite-culture). Partly under the influence of anthropological studies various points of view are now differentiated between. Some authors point out that popular culture is usually too quickly equated with mass-culture - a concept that often does injustice to the existence of different variants of popular culture. Others emphasize the partially persisting autonomy of the popular culture in its contact with the products of the great tradition, or presume that the great and little traditions reciprocally influence each other (43).

Moreover, a research model in which the relationship between great and little tradition is not one-sided, can make us aware of the disadvantages related to misleading, dichtomous interpretations. According to Natalie Davis objections can be brought against the research of some historians of popular culture in Europe (44). She states that by differentiating between beliefs that are 'truly' religious and practices which are 'superstitious' or 'magical', these historians are identifying themselves too strongly with the producers of their sources. In her extensive critique Davis discusses three limitations of their work.

In the first place the result of the conveyance of religious doctrine and sensibility to the laity (especially peasants) by the clergy is , often wrongly, considered as magical distortion of the original message. Davis asserts that laymen and lay women were sometimes active, indeed innovative, in sacred matters. As an example of such an innovation she names the creation of 'heretical' beliefs.

Secondly, Davis determines that the differentation between 'religion' and 'magic' such as it is made by the learned clergy is mostly arbitrary. It is known that a number of the suppositions and practices which the laity were especially prone to, and which can hardly be called anything other than 'magic':- in the sense of the methods to tap supernatural power for solving concrete problems and misfortunes - were for a long time tolerated by the learned clergy. By recognizing the arbitrary character of the above distinction, it is brought to the attention of historians of religion that the relationship between learned clergy and (semi-literate) laity is not only a battle of 'religion' contra 'magic' but simultaneously a struggle between 'central' and 'local' authorities for power over the countryside.

Finally, Davis points out that a premature division between the functions of religion and those of magic, such as they are expressed by the contrast between an extensive theology and a so-called 'ritual method of living', sometimes clouds our historical vision. Rituals are not by definition less rich in meaning than a system of beliefs, and in closer inspection also point to issues such as the nature of the cosmos, social relationships and social duties.

The summary of Le Roy Ladurie's interpretations of the religious life in Montaillou in the second part of this article shows that Davis' critiques are only partially applicable to Le Roy Ladurie's analysis. Although he also distinguishes between religious notions (Cathar and Catholic) and magical practices derived from popular tradition, Le Roy Ladurie simultaneously shows how important the ritual dimension was for the inhabitants of Montaillou and how their magical actions point to cosmological notions. His study also indicates that magical practices need not prevent the formation of a diversity of religious opinions. On the contrary. Magical and religious notions strengthen each other reciprocally and may be considered as a more or less integrated system of ideas that functions as a local variant of Christianity in this peasant society. Without assuming a direct relationship between protestant versions of Christianity and the dominant religion in Montaillou, Le Roy Ladurie draws our attention to the anti-clericalism, the hostile attitude towards the indulgences, the tithes, the good works, and the harboring of the notion of justification by faith, which characterize religious life here and foreshadow the fundamental themes of the Reformation (45).

How does Le Roy Ladurie supplement the existent knowledge on Catharism as a religious and social phenomenon ? More than in other studies on Catharism we were informed about the relationship between beliefs and actions. To what degree do Cathar beliefs influence the day-to-day life of the average believer, the Cathar layman ? The author's description of life in Montaillou seems to suggest that this influence is not significant. In contrast to the parfaits, the laity need not lead an ascetic life. Their religious duties seem at first sight to be no more than participation in a few rituals and the demonstration of loyalty to their foremen. The latter being dependant upon their followers for their subsistence and physical protection. Furthermore it makes sense to view the most crucial religious aspiration of the laity - salvation - as the sublimation of the traditional notions of everyday happiness in a peasant society: a long and peaceful life in good health. Le Roy Ladurie himself affirms these thoughts when he recognizes a transposition of social aspirations and relationships in certain Cathar beliefs (46). In short, the image presents itself of laity who only express their true religious feelings in borderline situations such as sickness and death.

But many passages in Le Roy Ladurie's study also point in another direction. The fact that the topic of salvation is often discussed in daily conversations between simple believers shows that they have developed an internal need to reflect upon their religious status. Important in this respect is also the specific nature of the relationship between believers and their parfaits. The interaction between simple believers and foremen, and the education of the latter directly represents the religious sphere in the daily life of these believers. Surely one can recognize a type of worship in the laity's care for the parfaits, the living symbols of the other world. But it is as important to notice that we are speaking of local heros, people of flesh and blood who remain directly recognizable and approachable to the believers.

In the first part of this essay it was shown that some researchers merely viewed Occitanian Catharism of the 14th century as a 'degeneration', a 'magical' distortion of the 'original', 'real', radical Catharism (47). The opinion that illiterate peasants, in contrast with other social (urban, middle-class) groups, are not able to independently rid themselves of their magical world view, forms the basis of this vision (48). A less prejudiced vision of Catharism among the peasants of upper Ariège, draws our attention to the question whether there is not a more or less independent dynamic incorporated in Cathar doctrine (49). This inherent dynamic may be schematically represented in the contrast between 'withdrawal from this world to obtain extra-mundane salvation' and 'an extension of beliefs and actions which are <u>also</u> aimed at this world'.

The missionary activities of the last Cathar leaders and the active reception by many of a specific set of religious notions show that this development was reflected in - yes, Montaillou (50). That this development, which was necessary for the continuation of Catharism, was only able to achieve partial expression in Montaillou has been discussed above. Stronger still, the combination of social (and religious) conflicts in the village itself and the repressive rule of the central, ecclesiastical authorities brought this development to an abrupt end.

ACKNOWLEDGEMENTS

I want to express my gratitude to Rineke Coumans, Joan Kalideen and Dick Taatgen for their assistance in the translation of the original Dutch version of this article.

NOTES

1. Le Roy Ladurie, E.: Montaillou, village occitan de 1294 à 1324 ,Paris, 1975. I also used Barbara Bray's translation:Montaillou. Cathars and Catholics in a French village, 1294-1324, London, 1978. Considerable differences exist between the French edition and the English translation. The cutting away of many interpretations and literature references reinforces the literary value of the book.

2. See e.g. Thomas, K.: The wizard of Oc. In: New York Review of Books, Oct.12, 1978; Bossy, J.: The smell of human flesh. In: Encounter, 51, 1978 p.69-73; Cobb, R.: Rixende, Condors, Esclarmonde. In: New Statesman, June 9, 1978; Davis, N.: Les conteurs de Montaillou. In: Annales E.S.C.,1,1979 p.61-73.

3. Cf. Hobsbawm, E.: The revival of narrative: Some comments. In: Past and Present, Febr. 1980 p.3-8.

4. In 1965 J. Duvernoy published a complete edition (in three volumes) of the original Latin text of Fournier's Inquisition interrogations: Le register d'Inquisition de Jacques Fournier, évêque de Pamiers, 1318-1325, Toulouse, 1965. Le Roy Ladurie used this edition and he himself translated all testimonies which supported the analysis in his study. D.Herlihy reproaches Le Roy Ladurie for dubious translations: Review of E.L.L.: Montaillou. In: Social History, Oct. 1979 p. 517-520. N. Davis on the other hand thinks L.R.L.'s translations are satisfactory: Les conteurs de Montaillou p. 69. She does argue, however, that the author says too little about the problems which arose by using this source: what was, for instance, the role of the scribes in the final version of the depositions and why did people remember events which sometimes happened more than twenty years ago ?

5. Cf. Dondaine, A.: L'origine de l'hérésie médiévale. In: Rivista di Storia della Chiesa in Italia, 6, 1952 p.47-78.

6. Cfr. Morghen, R.: Problèmes sur l'origine de l'hérésie au moyen âge. In: Revue Historique, CCCXXXVI, 1966; Russell,J.B.: Some interpretations of the origins of Medieval heresy. In: Medieval Studies, XXV, 1963.

7. See Borst, A.: Die Katharer, Stuttgart, 1953; Wakefield, W.L.: Heresy, crusade and Inquisition in Southern France,London 1974

8. See Bru, P.Ch.: Eléments pour une interprétation sociologique du Catharisme occitan. In: Nelli, R. e.a., Spiritualité de l' hérésie: le Catharisme, Paris 1953; Nelli , R.: Les Cathares, Paris 1972 ; idem: La vie quotidienne des Cathares du Languedoc au XIIIe siècle, Paris 1969.

9. For original documents vide Moore, R.I.: The birth of popular heresy (Documents of Medieval history I), London, 1975.

10. The above summary was derived from: Borst : Die Katharer p. 143-151, and Wakefield: Heresy, crusade and Inquisition p. 34-35.

11. Nelli : Les Cathares p. 89.

12. Wakefield: Heresy, crusade and Inquisition p. 27. On the ecclesiastical organization of Catharism cf. Moore: The birth of popular heresy p. 137-138; Borst: Die Katharer p. 231-239.

13. Borst: Die Katharer p. 135-142; Lambert, M.: Medieval heresy, London, 1977 p. 138; Nelli : La vie quotidienne des Cathares p. 257-273.

14. Nelli: Les Cathares p. 128.

15. Borst: Die Katharer p.190-202; Wakefield: Heresy, crusade and Inquisition p. 36-39. See also Duvernoy, J.: Le Catharisme : la religion des Cathares, Toulouse, 1976 p. 203-216.

16. Cf. Nelli: Les Cathares p. 123; Wakefield: Heresy, crusade and Inquisition p. 40-41; Lambert: Medieval heresy p. 138; Borst: Die Katharer p. 137-141.

17. Borst: Die Katharer p. 197.

18. Wakefield: Heresy, crusade and Inquisition p.42.

19. Borst: Die Katharer p. 180-189.

20. Lindeboom, J.: Stiefkinderen van het christendom (Stepchildren of Christianity), 's Gravenhage (The Hague), 1929 p. 57.

21. Borst: Die Katharer p. 199.

22. idem p. 105-142; Nelli: Les Cathares p. 19-37.

23. Hamilton, B.: The Medieval Inquisition, London, 1981 p.57.

24. Borst: Die Katharer p. 138.

25. idem p.139; Nelli: La vie quotidienne des Cathares p. 271-273. It is clear that both authors have pronounced ideas on the essence of Cathar doctrine. Nelli: idem p. 77: "Le Catharisme, religion abstraite et ennemie de la superstition".

26. Cf. Moore: The birth of popular heresy p. 132.

27. Borst: Die Katharer p. 205; Wakefield: Heresy, crusade and Inquisition p. 70.

28. idem p. 205; and idem p. 68-71.

29. On Authié vide Vidal, J.M.: Les derniers ministres de l'albi-

géisme en Languedoc: leurs doctrines. In: Revue des questions historiques, 41, 1909 p. 357-409; 42, 1909 p. 5-48. And Nelli: La vie quotidienne des Cathares p. 266-268.

30.Hamilton: The Medieval Inquisition p. 70.

31.Le Roy Ladurie: Montaillou. Cathars and Catholics p. 356. (idem: Montaillou, village occitan p. 625).

32.Studies of Goubert, Poitrineau, Fourquin, Fossier, Duby and Bloch. Cf. Le Roy Ladurie: Montaillou, village occitan p. 9.

33.Le Roy Ladurie: Montaillou. Cathars and Catholics p. 318 (idem: Montaillou, village occitan p. 523-524).

34.idem p. 297 (idem p. 468-469).

35.idem: Montaillou, village occitan p. 541.

36.idem: Montaillou. Cathars and Catholics p. 309 (idem: Montaillou, village occitan p. 497).

37.Cf. Nelli: La vie quotidienne des Cathares p. 79-94.

38.Cf. Hamilton: The Medieval Inquisition p. 92-99.

39.Le Roy Ladurie: Montaillou. Cathars and Catholics p. 325 (idem: Montaillou, village occitan p. 537).

40.Redfield, R.: The little community, and, Peasant society and culture, Chicago, 1973 (1956).

41.idem: The little community p. 4.

42.Bélibaste, the parfait, once said: "There are four great devils ruling over the world: the lord Pope, the major devil whom I call Satan; the lord King of France is the second devil; the Bishop of Pamiers the third; and the lord Inquisitor of Carcasonne, the fourth"; Le Roy Ladurie: Montaillou. Cathars and Catholics p. 13 (idem: Montaillou, village occitan p. 37).

43.Cf. Muchembled, R.: Culture populaire et culture des élites dans la France moderne (XVe - XVIIIe siècles), Paris, 1978; Burke, P.: Popular culture in early modern Europe, New York, 1978; Ginzburg, C.: The cheese and the worms. The cosmos of a sixteenth-century miller, London, 1980 (Italian edition: 1976).

44.Davis, N: Some tasks and themes in the study of popular religion. In: Trinkaus, C. and Oberman, H. (eds.), The pursuit of Holiness in late Medieval and Renaissance religion, Leiden, 1974 p. 307-336.

45.Le Roy Ladurie: Montailou. Cathars and Catholics p. 335-

336. (idem: Montaillou, village occitan p. 563).

46.idem: Montaillou, village occitan p. 539.

47.Cf. Nelli: La philosophie du Catharisme, Paris, 1975 p. 9.

48.Cf. Borst: Die Katharer p. 135-137.

49.Cf. Weber, M.: Die Wirtschaftsethik der Weltreligionen. In: Gesammelte Aufsätze zur Religionssoziologie, I, Tübingen, 1947 (4. Aufl.) p. 258-259 : "Die rationalen Elemente einer Religion, ihre 'Lehre' ... haben eben auch ihre Eigengesetzlichkeiten, und die aus der Art der Gottesvorstellungen und des 'Weltbildes' folgende rationale religiöse Heilspragmatik hat under Umständen weittragende Folgen für die Gestaltung der praktischen Lebensführung gewonnen ".

50.With relation to the description of this process of active reception there are some fascinating similarities between Le Roy Ladurie's 'Montaillou' and C. Arensberg's The Irish Countryman, Gloucester, Massachusettes, 1937.

Contention and Alliance of Gods: The Nias Case

L. Leertouwer

The motif of rival gods, their contendings and alliances is one of the paramount traits in the religious beliefs of the inhabitants of Nias and the Batu-Islands (Indonesia, opposite Sumatra's West-coast). In a recent survey of Indonesian traditional religions, Waldemar Stöhr pointed out, that this motif dominates the Niasans' idea of God and, consequently, their ritual practice (Stöhr, 1976 p.151). (1)

In his description of this motif and of its influence on the structure of the religious cosmology of Nias, Stöhr follows the well-known analysis of P. Suzuki (1959). According to Suzuki, a threesome of gods represents the nucleus of Niasan culture and religion i.e. Lowalangi, the Lord of the Universe in the Upper World, his brother Lature Danö, Lord of the Nether World, and the goddess Silewe Nazarata, who founded the priesthood. Silewe acts as an intermediary between the two brothers and in this way she embodies their symbolic unity and totality (Suzuki, 1959 cf. Stöhr, 1976).

With this analysis Suzuki's doctoral thesis follows the principles of the Leyden school of structural anthropology: he draws a parallel between the relations within the Niasan pantheon and the structure of social organization in this culture (see for these principles De Josselin de Jong, 1977 p.1-29). His reconstruction can be summarized very briefly in the following way:

The chieftains of the villages and their kin, the Niasan nobility, are connected with Lowalangi by genealogy as well as by sharing in the symbolic values of the Upper World; the common people, separated from the noblemen by clear-cut social boundaries, belong to the Netherworld and are therefore symbolically connected with Lature Danö. The priesthood, having Silewe Nazarata as their tutelary goddess, bridges the gap between the nobility and the commoners by intermediating between the two groups, in the same way as Silewe herself constitutes the link between the two divine brothers.

Slaves have no place in this structure, although in pre-colonial times slave-trade was one of the most important economic activities of the Niasan noblemen. Accordingly, they have no status whatsoever in the social system and are compared to and treated like domestic cattle (Suzuki, 1959 p.39-55).

According to Stöhr, Suzuki's efforts to prove the structural coherence of the social with the religious system, though fascinating, are not completely convincing. After a careful review of the available historical data Stöhr concludes that the social system as described by Suzuki - a territorial division into separate districts, combined with a threefold social hierarchy - is a fairly recent phenomenon. This system could have gradually overruled a much older system, consisting of genealogically structured clans and phratries. With Loeb (1935, p.141) and others he supposes that these changes occurred under external influences of Hindu-Indonesian origin. A complete asymmetry between nobility and commoners does not fit well into the framework of the older social system. So the origin of the nobility becomes a problem which is not solved by Suzuki's model.

Nias is a typical megalithic culture. In this type of culture, an enormous potential of cheap labour had to be available for the establishment of new settlements and the construction of stone monuments, comparable to what the ancient Egyptians needed for the building of their pyramids. As far as can be made out from the facts, Nias culture knew slaves from time immemorial. But these impressive collective performances were not the work of slaves, who were only used for doing household chores and agricultural work outside the villages. The commoners were expected to 'volunteer' for the building tasks; they also had to supply the lion's share of the numerous feasts organised on behalf of the noblemen and at their initiative; they were supposed to make the preparations but also to pay the costs.

It stands to reason - and Stöhr does not deny this - that the exalted status of the nobility in Niasan mythology was probably one of the important factors which enabled the village chiefs to extort such an amount of statute labour from the common people. To acknowledge this, however, is not the same thing as to accept it as historical evidence for an interdependence of the mythological and the social system from olden times.

The later division of the territory into separate districts bears some of the characteristics of the early state: fixed borders, as well organised bureaucracy, responsible for the administration of justice and the inspection of weights and measures. In many respects, the position of the chief in this political system was the same as that of the javanese radjah. The prestige which is attributed to the nobility in the myth, reflects and legitimates their social position (Stöhr, 1976 p.153 and Suzuki, 1973a). But this system is of fairly recent date - so the explanation of the origin of the nobility in Niasan political history must be sought elsewhere. In any case, a mythical genealogy which proclaims a lineal descent from Lowalangi for the chiefs and their families cannot be used to solve the historical problem.

Suzuki's analysis of the position of slaves excites the same kind of historical questions and criticisms. In the seventeenth and eighteenth century, the importance of slaves for Niasan economy was as high as their status in the mythology was low, or, as we have already seen, non-existent. As late as 1848, when British and Dutch colonial governments had been fighting public slave-trade already for decades, Nias exported slaves to the value of no less than D.F.39,600, on a total export amounting to D.Fl.132,110 (Anonymous 1848). In 1693, a contract of the Vereenigde Oostindische Compagnie already points out, that 'business and trade on this island deals mostly with slaves and foods' (Van der Kemp, 1894 p.601). As was the case with all trade activities, the nobility had the monopoly of buying and selling slaves. Only noblemen were allowed to keep slaves on the island itself for their personal use as well as for merchandise. In 1904, the export of slaves had finally stopped, but within the Niasan community slave-trade still existed, in spite of strict prohibitive regulation by the dutch government (Schröder, 1917 p.201).

The fact that slaves are not mentioned in the creation myths, can be explained from the way they were recruited, mainly from two different groups: free men unable to pay their debts and prisoners of war. In the latter category, we find Niasans as well as foreigners from Sumatra's West-coast. For the Niasans, whose world-view was, in this respect, no less ethnocentric than that of any other isolated people, the members of both groups were simply not human beings. Bankrupts lost their human rights as soon as they could no longer fulfill their financial obligations; foreigners, as well as captured prisoners from the island itself, fell into the same category, if their relatives were unable or unwilling to pay ransom money. This fact is strikingly illustrated by one of the Niasan words for slave, <u>sawuju</u>. Steinhart (1937, cf. Suzuki, 1959 p.45) offers the following translation: 'the immature, the minor, one who does not yet count'. Whereas commoners were considered to be the pigs of the divine brothers (in the southern parts of Lowalangi's, in the central and northern parts of Latüre Danö), slaves were in the eyes of their masters equivalent to pigs. Even their quarters were built after the model of a pig-sty (Schröder,1917 p.178).

Nevertheless, all this is not sufficient to explain the total exclusion of slaves from the religious system. With the Ngadju-Dajak (Kalimantan) for instance, whose social system is also based upon a dualism of nobility and commoners, and whose pantheon shows the same dualistic complementarity as the Niasans', slaves play a very important role in the creation myth (Schärer , 1946 49 sq.). According to this myth, slaves were created at the same moment as other human beings; but whereas the latter descended from the Upper World with the aid of golden ropes, the slaves had to come down by ordinary long wooden sticks. Niasan slaves are considered not to possess a soul - Ngadju slaves on the contrary, have a soul, albeit of a lower quality than the souls of free men. Schärer follows Hardeland when he takes the possibility into consideration that the inclusion of slaves in the creation stories could be an interpolation of a later date. With the Ngadju - Dajak, a free person could only become a slave by 'breaking the divine laws and holding in contempt the primeval rules' (Schärer, 1946 p.52). In this view, then, this class of condemned transgressors of the sacred adat was recruited from the lowest ranks of the free people and gradually took over their most humble duties. The crucial role of a slave in the creation myth is also expressed ritually. Slaves, both male and female, functioned as priests and from their midst a victim was chosen for the human sacrifice, demanded from the moiety associated with the Nether World.

Even if one assumes that a similar process took place in Nias, in which process the class of slaves gradually developed out of the group of commoners, the question remains, why a relatively large part of the population, representing a vital economic interest, left no traces at all in the creation myths of the Niasans. Probably, part of the answer is to be found in the specific circumstances already summed up above: slavery being a kind of debt-redemption and the destiny of unransomed prisoners of war (foreigners as well as fellow countrymen) and not a punishment for transgressors of religious law, as with the Ngadju-Dajak; and last but not least, the lucrative possibilities of the slave-trade.

These particular circumstances, though, don't make up an adequate explanation. For the Dajak slave, in spite of his inclusion in the sequence of the creation myth, had no status at all in the daily practice of religion, or at least a very humiliating one. In this ritual respect, he is nearly as insignificant as his opposite number in Nias. For instance, if incidentally he had a dream about the Upper-or Netherworld, and thus committed a sin against the adat, as a slave is not entitled to have dreams on these subjects, he could not take any initiative to expiate his sin. He had to confess to his owner, who could decide to arrange for a ritual of purification - or again could refuse to do so. In the latter case, the unfortunate dreamer virtually became a pariah.

Dajak eschatology offers another striking example of the slave's inferiority in religious matters. After death, he is supposed to journey to the realm of the dead like other human beings. The Niasan slave, on the contrary, is just 'thrown away' and, having no soul, is supposed to vanish into thin air, or, at best, to be reborn as a worm. In actual fact, the Dajak slave is not much better off. Once arrived in the hereafter, he has no alternative but to be the pai lenge (= hands and feet) of his former owner for all eternity. From the religious point of view the fate of the slaves after death is deplorable in both cases. The differences don't counterbalance the decisive similarity: in both cases, the genealogical line which connects man with the gods and guarantees a more or less dignified existence in the hereafter, has been cut off, or has never existed. The Batak on the mainland of Sumatra have similar ideas about 'slave-eschatology': according to the Toba-Batak certain categories of transgressors of the adat will stay for ever in the fifth sphere of heaven, locked in stocks like insolvent debtors on earth (Tobing, 1956 p.96, cf. Leertouwer, 1971 p.258). There is, however, at least one Batak legend that grants to slaves that are buried alive with their deceased masters, a continuing existence in the hereafter in subservience, in the capacity of 'dew-flicker' or 'huntsman' (Ködding, 1888 cf. Leertouwer, 1977 p.51).

In Nias culture, we find none of these conceptions. As slavery appears to have a very long history in the Nias archipelago, we might conjecture a development of mythology dissimilar to the Dajak events as reconstructed by Schärer. When the district-system was introduced and the power of chiefs increased, slaves became just another kind of merchandise. Possibly the Niasans no longer had a valid reason to grant slaves a status, however modest, in the religious cosmology: their existence and status no longer called for a religious explanation. So creation myths could do without them. This is, of course, mere speculation, as we have no records about a change of this kind.

With Waldemar Stöhr, we must come to the conclusion that Suzuki's structural model cannot adequately explain the origin of the nobility and of a class of slaves, as it does not take into account far-reaching changes in Nias' social organization.

Yet, the Nias version of the 'contention between gods'-theme reflects mythologically the asymmetry between the nobility and the commoners. In this case, perhaps, we do better to speak of complementary relations between gods, as the divine brothers never concluded a formal alliance.

When we review Suzuki's mythological data with respect to this theme, the following survey can be given:

A. Northern Nias

Lowalangi and Lature Danö grew like fruits on one of the upper branches of the Tree of Life. Another version of the myth speaks of two trees, a bad and a good one. Lature Danö and all the evil spirits spring from the former, Lowalangi, together with another god, from the latter tree. In both versions, there is a marked rivalry between the brothers: Lature Danö tries his hand at creating a human being, but he fails; Lowalangi on the other hand manages to blow the breath of life into the nostrils of a human body made by another god, and thus he creates man. In the second version, the motif of competition and rivalry between the brothers has taken another form. This version begins with a story about Sirao, the mythical ancestor of all Niasans. He lived in the Upper Worlds and had nine sons. Two of them, Luo Mewöna and Bauwa Danö, may be regarded as the doubles of our divine brothers. In order to decide which of them would stay with Sirao in the Upper World, the father thrusts a spear into the earth. The younger brother Luo Mewöna (= Lowalangi) managed to climb into the spear and to sit on top of it, but the elder brother fell down. So the winner inherited Sirao's office and stayed in the Upper World,

B. Central Nias

In these parts of the archipelago, the creation myths do not mention any kind of competition between the brothers. It is told here, that the gods grew inside the fruits of two life-trees. Luluao, the first-born, split two fruits of the second tree with his chapper and so two pairs of gods, each of them consisting of a brother and a sister, were born. Another version stresses the function of the god Nadsjuwa Danö as the carrier of the Nether World, but nothing is said in this version about a struggle for precedence. This theme does not fit into the framework of the myth, as Luluo (Lowalangi's double) by giving life to all the other gods, could claim precedence in advance.

C. Southern Nias and the Batu Islands.

Here the motif of contention and alliance appears to be very important. The myths tell us about two female ancestors, one succeeding the other, the second of which gave birth to a foursome of children, viz. two pairs of twins. Each pair consisted of a boy and girl; once grown up, the boys married their sisters. The boys bear the names of Latura-Danö and Sabölö Luwõ gõgõgi. According to Schröder's informants quoted by Suzuki in this context, the latter name was Lowalangi's child-name.

In the contendings of the two brothers, neither succession to political power nor the rule over the Upper World is at stake. It is simply stated that both gods chose their domiciles without dispute. A feud between them flares up as soon as Lowalangi, once arrived in the Upper World, at variance with the truth proclaims his seniority. Lature is outraged and starts a war against his younger brothers, a fight of cosmic dimensions. Lowalangi throws huge boulders of rock at his brother, but Lature comes to no harm. In turn, Lature causes a big earthquake, shaking the foundations of Lowalangi's house so violently that the walls collapse. Thereupon Lowalangi surrenders and the cosmic struggle ends. Remarkably enough, this issue does not entail any change in the status of the brothers. *Lowalangi* remains in the Upper Worlds, 'the benevolent God' while *Lature* 'the snake of the Nether World' goes back to his job as carrier of the earth. Other versions of the same myth emphasize the rightness of this division of powers by having *Lowalangi* being born from the 'good' Tree of Life; the bad tree gives birth to an unnamed evil god. *Lature,* in this verion is not mentioned at all;the 'snake of the Nether World' comes into being by a magical trick: *Lowalangi*'s sister and wife, *Silewe Nazarata*, transformed the ring that originally sustained the earth into a snake.

In the myths of Southern Nias, the theme of contention and alliance between gods is expressed in genealogical terms: the elder and the younger brother are fighting for precedence.

In this case, the myth seems to give a direct reflection of social conflict, as Schröder's description of the laws of inheritance, to which we will now turn, clearly shows (Schröder, 1917 p.423).

Formally, on the level of chiefs of districts the senior rightful claimant in the male line of descent should come into office. In practice, however, the line of succession can at least temporarily shift to the brothers of the deceased. Whenever the first rightful claimant is found not to have the wisdom and the strong character demanded for high office, the second claimant in the line of succession is often chosen. The situation reminds us of *Lature Danö*'s unsuccessful attempt to create human beings. *Lowalangi,* though he is the younger brother, is the one who transfers the breath of life into man. This breath, *noso,* is called *eheha* when the souls of people of noble descent are concerned. *Noso/eheha* determines the qualities and creative powers of man; to exercise authority, a man must have powerful eheha. It is the property of Lowalangi and returns to him after death, to be stored in the treasure-chamber of the Upper World like gold-dust in the coffers of the nobility on earth. Before a human being is born, Lowalangi interrogates him about the amount of noso he wishes to carry. No soul receives more than ten grammes. In this way, man is responsible, not only for his character, but also for the social status he will have during his life on earth; that he has chosen for himself. Differences of class and prestige, so vitally important in a society as class-conscious as this one, are thus religiously legitimated.

In the funerary rituals of the nobility, the eheha of the deceased chief is collected in a small cask, which is put upon the coffin. During the funeral, the successor ritually swallows the eheha and with it the qualities required for exercising power. Moreover, eheha as a quality of the soul is identified with the most outstanding quality of a nobleman, his eloquence. Commoners, the Niasans say, stammer and twaddle, but the speech of a nobleman is like a stream of pure gold (Leertouwer, 1977 p.153).

It stands to reason, that the laws of inheritance on the family level, where a proper division of the estate is of more consequence than succession to office, show a less direct link with the primeval events described in the myths. Yet, on this level, there is the same conflict of interest between the eldest son and other heirs and similar exceptions to the rule exist. The law provides for a bigger share for the eldest son. His portion can vary from one-third up to two-thirds of the estate, depending on the number of other children. But, if it is found he lacks the qualities to manage his father's estate, another privileged heir is appointed and the eldest son may get a smaller share or even be disinherited.

In every system of law, in Indonesia as well as elsewhere, we must expect to find this tension between seniority and competence. In Nias, a particular stress is laid upon this tension by its inclusion in the creation myth. Therefore, we have here a striking example of a myth acting, as Clifford Geertz puts it, 'as a model for and a model of society'.

The accumulation of economic power and social prestige of the nobility as a result of the introduction of the district system increased the tensions between members of wealthy families and created an almost unbridgeable gap between the classes of society. In Nias, as in eighteenth-century Germany, 'fängt der Mensch erst an beim Baron.'

Suzuki (1959 p.9) ranks still another genealogical motif among the mythical expressions of class antagonism, viz. the occurence of twins. It is open to doubt, or so it seems to me, whether this phenomenon must be explained as 'another manifestation of antagonism and tension' (Suzuki, 1959 p.9). The argument depends on a rather far-fetched comparison with other cultures outside Indonesia. In the northern and central traditions, the motif is primarily an expression of the complementarity of the divine twins, not of their antagonism, whereas in South Nias the emphasis shifts to the marriages of the brothers with their twin-sisters. Here again,it is not the antagonism, but another theme, viz. the concern for the purity of the primeval dynasty that is stressed.

Suzuki could have strengthened his case by referring to the Niasan custom concerning the birth of twins. Surprisingly he does not use these data. The birth of twins was considered as an anomalous event, which had to be put right by killing one of the newborn babies. The victim was put into a sack and this was hung in a tree. Sometimes both children were killed in this way, but more often only one child was killed; the girl, or when the twins were both of the male sex, the weaker boy was put to death. One report about this custom (Schröder, 1917 p.248) tells, that the father simply hung the sack in the nearest tree of his compound; according to others, a tree on the cemetery was chosen. In a few reports, some food - a handful of rice, a piece of sugar-cane - was put into the sack - in others, no provisions of food are mentioned. A direct reference to the creation myths is nowhere to be found. The most extensive - but also the most emotional - description of the custom by the German missionary Fehr, 'explains' the ritual by a reference to the dogged superstition of the natives and to their fear of evil spirits.

Yet, a clear parallel can be found between the custom and the myth of creation. As we have seen, the Tree(s) of Life is a very prominent symbol in this myth. The divine brothers and many other primeval beings grew like fruits on this tree. When Luluo (Lowalangi) in the version of Central Nias, openend two fruits of the Tora'a tree with his chopper, two pairs of twins, both consisting of a boy and a girl, were born. The boys later on married their sisters. Schröder (1917 p.478) maintains that this episode bears witness to the fairly recent origin of the tradition. According to him the incest-taboo in Nias is not autochthonous; in this episode the people of Central Nias, influenced by contacts with foreigners, solved the problem of the incestuous marriages of the gods of Southern Nias, a part of the country much more isolated from foreign influences. In this part of the country, then, people would have taken no offence at incest, at least not when committed by their gods and ancestors. This view, of course, is utterly unconvincing. In order to be able to share this view, one has to accept two equally improbable conditions. In the first place, in Southern Nias a perfect similarity of human behaviour with the conduct of mythical beings would have existed: quod non licet bovi, non licet Lowalangi. On top of this, we have to believe that all Niasans had no feelings about incest, until Sumatran traders taught them a lesson. This is, in fact, what Schröder thinks, as he supposes explicitly that incestuous marriage was common practice in Nias and just a matter of imitation of the divine example. By calling into the witness-box the famous Arabian voyager Edrisi in this context, Schröder does nothing to strenghten an already very weak case. For Edrisi reported about the Batak of Sumatra and does not write a word about the Niasans, as Schröder adds a wild historical speculation to a misrepresentation of the relation between myth and social practice. In fact, we have to reverse the argument. For in Nias, as in other parts of Indonesia and elsewhere, twins of different sex were suspected of having committed incest when still in their moster's womb, one of the many details of Nias culture we know thanks to Schröder's ethnographic precision. This, I think, is the background of the custom. To explain the killing one has to refer to the creation myth all right. The incestuous marriages of the twins in myth have not been interpreted by the Niasans as an example: if this were true, the custom would become unexplainable. On the contrary, they learned from their mythology that sexual intercourse and marriage of twins was a privilege of the gods. Whenever a pair of twins of different sex were born, people suspected a violation of this privilege. They had to do something to undo this evil transgression, so they performed a symbolic act: by putting one of the babies in a sack and hanging it in a tree, they identified the child with the unchopped fruits of the Tree of Life and in so doing, restored the cosmic order of primeval times.

This article attempts to offer some marginal notes to Suzuki's thesis that the structure of the Niasan mythology and especially of the Niasans' idea of god, is closely interwoven with the social structure. It was not my intention to pass judgement upon the theoretical model adopted by Suzuki from the Leyden school of structuralist anthropology. Yet the Nias case shows clearly what contradictions one has to cope with, when cosmic dualism is used as an explanatory concept for the historical succession of different social systems (Kubitscher, 1969). As Stöhr pointed out (1976 85 sq.), elements of culture of ancient-Indonesian origin have been mixed with younger-Indonesian elements and it is very difficult to explain them all on the basis of the same religious structure.

In the mythology of Nias about contention and alliance of gods, a genealogical principle which implies consanguinity of gods and men, is united with the principle of complementary dualism. These are both ancient-Indonesian principles. When these principles are projected into a social system of much later date, many questions must remain unanswered.

Economic developments entailing an increase of power of the nobility and resulting in a monopoly of foreign trade, appears to have disproportionately enlarged the asymmetry of commoners and nobility to a degree out of proportion.

In the myths, the antagonism between the two classes is only mildly reflected by the contention of Lowalangi and Lature Danö. In these stories, their complementarity is predominant.

BIBLIOGRAPHY

Anon, 1848: Overzicht. In: Tijdschrift voor Nederlands-Indië, jrg. 1848 p. 189-190.

De Jong, J., 1977 (ed.): Structural anthropology in the Netherlands, a reader, with an introduction by the editor, The Hague.

Van der Kemp, P.H., 1894: Een bijdrage tot E.B. Kielstra's 'opstellen over Sumatra's Westkust'. In: Bijdragen tot de taal-, land- en volkenkunde van Nederlands-Indië, XLIV p. 257-320 and p. 525-615.

Ködding, W., 1888: Die Battakker auf Sumatra. In: Globus, illustrierte Zeitschrift für Land- und Völkerkunde, Jhrg. 53, Braunschweig p. 57-59; 75-78; 90-92; 107;111.

Kubitschek, H.D., 1969: Soziale Strukturen in Indonesien. In: Ethnographisch-archaeologische Zeitschrift, 10, Berlin p. 1-13.

Leertouwer, L., 1971: The cannibalism of the Batak. In: Nederlands theologisch tijdschrift, jrg. 26, Wageningen p. 241-260.

Leertouwer, L., 1977: Het beeld van de ziel bij drie Sumatraanse volken, doctoral thesis, Groningen.

Loeb, E.M., 1935: Sumatra, its history and people. Wiener Beiträge zur Kulturgeschichte und Linguistiek, 3, Wien, p. 1-303.

Schärer, H., 1947: Die Gottesidee der Ngadju-Dajak in Süd-Borneo, Leiden.

Schröder, E.W.Gs., 1917: Nias, ethnographische, geographische en historische aantekeningen en studieën, Leiden.

Steinhart, W.L., 1976: Niassche teksten, verhandelingen van het Koninklijk Bataviaansch Genootschap van Kunsten en Wetenschappen, Batavia LXXIII.

Stöhr, W., 1976: Die altindonesischen Religionen, Handbuch der Orientalistik, dritte Abteilung, zweiter Band, Abschnitt 2, Leiden/Köln.

Suzuki, P., 1959: The religious system and culture of Nias, The Hague.

Suzuki, P., 1973: Autochtonous states of Nias: Extinct or extant? Bulletin of the International committee on urgent anthropological and ethnological research, 15 p. 27-49.

Tobing, P.L., 1956: The structure of the Toba-Batak belief in the high-God, Amsterdam.

The War of the Gods in Scandinavian Mythology

J. Oosten

INTRODUCTION

The Indo-European gods were always involved in warfare. Wars were fought in the mythical past as in the present, and wars will be fought in the future. In Indian mythology the Devas and the Asuras had fought ever since the Devas robbed the Asuras of their share in the sacred potion of immortality. In Persian mythology the Devas and Asuras will fight until the end of time, when the Asuras will be victorious and the Devas will be destroyed. In Greek mythology the Titans were defeated by the gods, although many of them retained their divine status for a considerable time. The giants could only be defeated with aid of human being. Herakles assisted the gods and thus the enemies of the gods were destroyed. In Scandinavian mythology the gods killed the first giant and continued to make war upon all giants who were his descendants. Their final battle will be fought at ragnarok when the world will be destroyed and renewed.

Two groups of Scandinavian gods, the Aesir and the Vanir, fought each other in a mythical past. The war was ended by a treaty and both groups were united. A variant of this theme can be found in the myth of the war of the Devas and the Aśvins in Indian mythology. In both cases the gods refused to admit another group of gods into their commensal community, but were finally forced to do so.

In Irish mythology, groups of gods were represented as human beings, who made war upon each other during the mythical conquest of Ireland. Many gods killed in these battles (Nuadu, Ogma, Macha and others), were venerated in Celtic religion.

These Celtic myths represent a transition from tales about gods to tales about human beings, that is very common in Indo-European mythology. In Scandinavian and Roman mythology myths about the gods were often transformed into pseudo-historical tales. The wars between the gods were not only fought by the gods themselves, but also by their human representatives. In the Indian Mahābhārata the main antagonists in the two opposing factions, the Pāṇḍavas and the Kauravas, were sons of the most important Indian gods. They favoured and supported their sons just as the Greek gods did in the Iliad. Some of the Greek gods even participated actively in that war. In Roman mythology the war between the Romans and the Sabines constitutes an important variant in the complex of the myths about the war between the gods. The gods make war when they are in competition for exclusive power or the exclusive possession of land or magical goods. They never share unless they are forced to do so. They cheat and deceive to gain control and if necessary they make war to exclude others.

The nature of these wars is described with especial richness in the Scandinavian myths which have been preserved.

Scandinavian religion was the religion of the peoples of Denmark, Sweden, Norway and Iceland before they were converted to Christianity. There was much cultural variation between these peoples but it is difficult to make a good assessment of the nature of these differences, since our most important literary sources for Scandinavian religion come from Iceland. As a consequence we are much better informed about Icelandic religion than about any other Scandinavian religion.

The most important text is the poetic Edda, a compilation of poems about gods and heroes, that was written in Iceland in the thirteenth century. Another important source, the prose Edda, a survey of mythology was written by Snorri Sturluson

(1179-1241), a famous Icelandic historian. He was also the author of another important book, the Heimskringla, a history of the Norse kings. These three texts contain the most important variants of the myths about the wars of the gods in Scandinavian mythology. An important text for the study of Danish mythology is the Gesta Danorum, a history of the Danish kings written by a monk, Saxo Grammaticus, in the beginning of the thirteenth century. It contains many interesting variants of Icelandic myths, some of the most important of which will be discussed in the course of this book.

THE SCANDINAVIAN PANTHEON IN ICELANDIC SOURCES

The world was ruled by the gods. They consisted of two groups, the Aesir and the Vanir. The most important gods among the Aesir were Odin and Thor. Odin Allfather was the father-god and the highest god of the pantheon. He had killed the primordial giant and created the world from his body with his two brothers, Vili and Ve, who play only a small part in mythology. He was wise and skilled in magic. He was also associated with war and death. When he threw his magical spear, Gungnir, over his enemies they were seized by fear and fled in panic. He led the band of warriors who had been killed in battle, the Einherjar. They would assist him in the last battle of ragnorak. Odin was married to the goddess Frigg and many gods were considered his sons.

Thor also excelled in war. He was the champion of the gods in their wars with the giants, and killed many of them in battle. While Odin was crafty and cunning, Thor preferred open warfare. His weapon was the hammer Mjollnir that caused lightning and thunder. Thor was a great lover of the sacred mead and he was also associated with fertility. His hammer was a symbol of fertility that was probably used in the ritual of marriage. Thor was associated with the farmers, while Odin was a god of the nobility. Thor's wife was the goddess Sif.

Tyr was probably an important god among the Aesir in the past and he may have been Odin's predecessor as lord of the gods. His name Tyr (derived from Tiwaz) testifies to an ancient origin since it is derived from the old Indo-European word deiwos, "luminous, celestial", that can be found in many words for god. Tyr lost his right hand when he put it into the mouth of the wolf Fenrir as a pledge of good faith. The gods were afraid of the strength of this wolf and twice they bound him with ropes and twice the wolf broke them. The third time they contrived magical ropes, that looked thin and fragile. The wolf did not trust the gods and therefore he only allowed himself to be bound if the god Tyr put his hand in his mouth. When the wolf discovered that he could not free himself, he bit off Tyr's hand. This may have caused Tyr's downfall as lord of the gods. In Irish mythology Nuadu, the lord of the Tuatha De Danann, had to give up his kingship, when he lost his hand in the first battle of Mag Tured. Tyr played a part in the myth of the capture of the cauldron of mead from his father, the giant Hymir.

Loki, the trickster played an important part in the creation of magical goods like the hammer Mjollnir, the spear Gungnir, the ring Draupnir, etc., and in the retrieval of magical goods like the hammer of Thor and the apples of Idun that were captured by the giants. He was also responsible for the death of Balder, the son of Odin, and finally he turned into an enemy of the gods. He was chained to a rock and tormented by the poison of a snake, but at ragnarok he would free himself from his fetters and lead the enemies of the gods into the last battle. He was to be killed by Heimdal, the guardian of the rainbow

Bifrost that connected heaven and earth, Asgard and Midgard. It was his task to warn the gods with his great horn when the final onslaught would begin. Balder, the son of Odin, was killed by his brother Hoder in an important myth of the origin of death. The author of this crime, however, was Loki. Hoder was killed in revenge by Vali, another son of Odin, who was begotten for this sole purpose. Balder and Hoder, Vidar and Vali, sons of Odin, and Magni and Modi, sons of Thor, were expected to rule the new world that would arise after ragnarok.

Lodur, Hoenir and Mimir played a part in some creation myths. Lodur may have been another name for Loki. Hoenir was probably related to intelligence, and Mimir to memory and wisdom. Other gods among the Aesir were Ull, Forseti and Bragi, the god of poetry. He was married to Idun, who guarded the apples of youth, but not much is known about these gods.

The most important Vanir were Njord and his children Freyr and Freyja, who were born from an incestuous union between Njord and his sister. Freyr also had an incestuous relation with his sister Freyja. Snorri states explicitly that the Vanir were allowed to marry their own sisters, while this was forbidden to the Aesir (Ynglinga Saga 4), Njord and Freyr both married daughters of the giants. Njord married Skadi, the daughter of the giant Thiazi, and Freyr married Gerd, the daughter of the giant Gymir. Both marriages are explained in important myths. All Vanir were related to wealth, fertility and possibly kingship . Freyja was also explicitly connected with witchcraft and warfare. She received one half of the number of warriors who were killed in battle while Odin took the other half. It was thougth that Freyja introduced witchcraft to the Aesir (seidr) and in the Lokasenna Loki reproaches her for having sexual relations with all Aesir.

After their war the Aesir and the Vanir became one group of gods and lived together in Asgard but at ragnarok Njord and Freyr will return to Vanaheim (the home of the Vanir).

The giants lived in Utgard, outside the ordered world of Midgard and Asgard, that was controlled by the gods. De Vries considers them to be the original inhabitants of the world and the ancestors of the gods (cf. De Vries 1970, 242). Odin was the son of the giantess Bestla, Tyr of the giant Hymir, and Loki of the giant Farbauti. Heimdal was the son of the nine daughters of Aegir, who is sometimes considered as a god and sometimes as a giant (cf. Hymiskvida). In fact, however, there is not always a strict distinction between giants and gods. Loki belonged to the Aesir, but he was also closely associated with the giants (Gylfaginning 46). Mimir is also referred to as a giant. The giantesses Skadi and Gerd were accepted in the pantheon. The relations between the giants and the gods seem to be similar to those between Titans and gods in Greek mythology. The Titans were defeated by the gods, but many of them retained their divine status (cf. Hyperion, Thetys, and others). De Vries' conclusion that the giants were predecessors and ancestors of the gods seems to be well founded with regard to the Aesir, but no such evidence can be found for the Vanir. We simply do not know where the Vanir came from. In some cases the giants originally seem to have been celestial gods like the Asuras in Indian mythology and the Titans in Greek mythology.

Another important group in Scandinavian mythology were the dwarves, artisans par excellence. They were thought to live in the mountains and most magical goods were manufactured by them. Many other groups of divine beings existed (e.g.

different groups of elves), but since they do not play an important part in mythology, we will not discuss them here. A more important part was played by several demoniacal monsters, usually considered to be the offspring of Loki, notably the wolf Fenrir, who was to kill Odin at ragnarok and Jormungand, the midgardsnake, that encircled the world and was to be killed by Thor in that same battle. Thor, however, would not survive his enemy for long. He was to be killed by the poison of his dying enemy.

Such then are the protagonists in the wars of the gods. The wars themselves, in Scandinavian mythology, fall into three main cycles:

1. The war between the gods and the giants,
2. The war between the Aesir and the Vanir,
3. The war of ragnarok

THE WAR BETWEEN THE GIANTS AND THE GODS

The gods and the giants ever had been at war since Odin and his brothers slew the giant Ymir and created the world from his body. All the giants were drowned in Ymir's blood, except for Bergelmir and his wife, who became the ancestors of all later giants (Gylfaginning 7).

The gods were related to the giants by kinship ties, the Aesir by descent, the Vanir by affinity. The Aesir made war with the giants, but relations between the giants and the Vanir were less hostile.

Odin, Vili and Ve were the sons of Bor and the giantess Bestla, daughter of the giant Bolthorn. Since all giants were descended from Ymir, Odin and his brothers apparently killed their maternal ancestor. The killing of a senior maternal kinsman is a recurrent theme in Indo-European mythology (cf.the killing of Balor by Lug in Irish mythology, the killing of Amulius by Romulus and Remus in Roman mythology, the killing of Kaṃsa by Kṛṣṇa in Indian mythology, etc.). But this was not the only relation between Ymir and the sons of Bor. Bor's father, Buri, was licked from the ice by the cow Audumla that fed the giant Ymir. Thus Audumla acted as mother of both Ymir and Buri, feeding the one she had not created and creating the one she did not feed. It seems probable that a notion of brotherhood is expressed in this relation between Ymir and Buri. In that case the myth represents a weak version of the Indo-European mythical theme of the creation of the world through the slaying of the first man by his brother (in this case the killing of a man by the grandsons of his brother; cf. Lincoln 1981 Ch.IV).

The Aesir were matrilineally (Odin,Heimdal) or patrilineally (Tyr, Loki) descended from the giants and it may be that they were thought to be descended bilaterally from the giants as the Greek gods were descended from the Titans. The Aesir made war with their ancestors and they were always victorious. Many myths relate how the giants lost their magical goods to the gods or proved to be unable to keep them once they had captured them. Their daughters were seduced by the gods, they lost their magical goods and, finally, they were killed.

The sacred mead was captured from the giants by Odin. He seduced Gunnlod, the daughter of the giant Suttung, who guarded the mead, to obtain three draughts of the sacred potion. They sufficed for Odin to swallow the whole stock. He transformed himself into an eagle and escaped to Asgard. The furious giant, who pursued him was killed by the gods (Skåldskaparmål 2).

The cauldron of mead was captured from the giant Hymir by Thor and Tyr. Hymir and his giants were killed by Thor and so Tyr became an accomplice to the killing of his own father (Hymiskvida).

The giant Thrym once captured Thor's hammer and said he would only return it when he received the goddess Freyja as his wife. Heimdal counseled Thor to disguise himself as Freyja. Accompanied by Loki he went to the land of the giants, recovered the hammer and killed all giants with it (Thrymskvida).

The apples of youth and the goddess Idun were once delivered up to the giant Thiazi by Loki, but the gods obliged Loki to regain them. The giant pursued him, and was killed by the gods (Skáldskaparmál 1.)

In the Snorri Edda it is related that once a giant offered to build the stronghold of Asgard for the Aesir in exchange for marriage to Freyja, and the sun and the moon. On Loki's advice the gods consented, but they set a time limit for the completion of the construction. When it became clear that the giant would succeed in time, Loki turned himself into a mare and seduced the stallion that the giant needed for his work. The giant failed in his task and he was killed by Thor (Gylfaginning 42).

Thus the giants either lost the goods they possessed or failed to retain them once they had captured them, and were killed by the gods. The giants repeatedly attempted to marry the goddess Freyja, but never succeeded. At the same time their daughters were seduced by the Aesir, but no marriages were made. Gunnlod was seduced by Odin to capture the mead. Another giantess, Rind, was also seduced or raped by Odin in order to beget the god Vali who would avenge the death of Balder. The daughters of the giants did, however, marry the Vanir, even if they sometimes preferred the Aesir.

When the giant Thiazi had been killed by the gods, his

daughter Skadi came to Asgard to avenge her father. The gods offered compensation. She could choose a husband from among the gods. When she had to make her choice , she was only shown their feet. Skadi wanted to marry the god Balder, and she chose the most beautiful feet she saw since she assumed that they belonged to him. They turned out to be the feet of Njord, and Skadi stipulated that she would only marry him, if the gods could make her laugh. Loki bound a rope around his own testicles and connected it to the beard of a goat. He then started to pull the rope and he made such funny grimaces that the giantess could not restrain herself and burst out laughing. The marriage, however, proved an unhappy one. Njord wanted to stay near the sea and Skadi wanted to reside in the mountains. Odin further compensated Skadi by placing the eyes of Thiazi as stars in the sky (Skåldskaparmål 1).

The god Freyr fell in love with Gerd, the daughter of Gymir, when he saw her entering the house of her father. He gave his servant Skirnir his own sword, that could fight of its own accord, and his horse that could pass through the wall of flames that surrounded Gerd's residence, and sent him as his representative to the giantess. Skirnir went to Gerd and the text suggests that he killed Gerd's brother, probably because he attempted to prevent him from entering (Skīrnismāl 16). At first Gerd refused the match, although Skirnir offered her eleven apples of gold and the ring Draupnir. He threatened to cut off her head with the magical sword, that was to kill her father too, but Gerd still refused to accept Freyr as her husband. Finally Skirnir threatened her with a magical branch that would send her to the gate of Hel and condemn her to eternal infertility and she consented. Thus Freyr married Gerd, but from that time on Freyr no longer possessed the magical sword (Skīrnismāl).

Thus both Vanir were married to giantesses. In the first case the marriage was explicitly related to the institution of wergild. Skadi was offered a husband in compensation for her father. In the second case compensation may have played a part since Gerd's brother was killed by Freyr's representative. Certainly in both cases the marriage was related to the killing of a close male relative of the giantess. In the first case Odin compensated Skadi by placing Thiazi's eyes as stars in the sky, in the second case, Freyr may have delivered up his sword as compensation. In any case he gave gold to marry the giantess (Lokasenna 42).

The relations between Vanir and the giants were therefore marked by marriage and compensation for killings. Although in both cases giants were killed, they were not killed by the Vanir themselves. (Skirnir was not one of the Vanir - Skirnismâl 18).

The Aesir were descended from the giants and marriages with the daughters of the giants would therefore have had incestuous connotations. The Vanir were free to marry the daughters of the giants. Thus the Aesir and Vanir were related through the marriages of the daughters of the giants, as wife-givers and wife-takers. Yet in the myths of the war between these groups we do not find an exchange of women, but an exchange of men.

THE WAR BETWEEN THE AESIR AND THE VANIR

The most important accounts of the war between the Aesir and the Vanir can be found in the Voluspá, the Skáldskaparmál and the Ynglingasaga.

According to the Voluspá (14) a woman named Gullveig (Gold-drunk) was killed by the Aesir. She was three times burnt and three times reborn. She practiced sorcery and corrupted minds (16). De Vries suggests that she may also have induced the gods to unlawful sexual behaviour (De Vries 1970, 217). Dumézil thinks that she was sent by the Vanir in order to corrupt the Aesir (1959, 37). The sequel of the myths makes it probable that the woman did indeed come from the Vanir. She may have been associated with Freyja who brought witchcraft (seidr) among the Aesir. The fact that Gullveig was three times reborn recalls the name Tritogeneia of the greek goddess Athena, like Freyja a goddess of war, who played an important part in the wars with the Titans and giants. The crime of the gods had to be expiated and the main problem seems to have been whether the Aesir should admit the Vanir into their commensal community and give them a share in the offerings that were made to the gods. The Aesir refused to do so. Odin threw his magical spear over the Vanir, but the Vanir proved to be a match for the Aesir and they entered the stronghold of Asgard (Voluspâ 17-18). Other sources carry the story further.

In the Skâldskaparmâl it is related that peace was made and confirmed by a ritual. All gods spat into a vessel. From this liquid was born Kvasir, the embodiment of wisdom (the name refers to an alcoholic drink; cf . Norw. kvase). He was killed by two dwarfs, who made the sacred mead from his blood and informed the gods that Kvasir had choked in his own wisdom. The dwarfs were forced to give up the mead as wergild to the giant Suttung after they had killed his parents. Suttung guarded the mead jealously and allowed no one to touch it, but it was captured by Odin. Then it became the drink of the gods, who thus consumed the offspring of their union (Skâldskaparmâl 2).

Another version of the treaty between the Aesir and the

Vanir can be found in the Ynglingasaga. The Aesir and the Vanir made peace and exchanged hostages. The leaders of the Vanir, Njord and Freyr, were exchanged for Hoenir and Mimir, who were considered as chiefs of the Aesir by the Vanir. Kvasir was also sent to the Aesir by the Vanir. Hoenir never gave an independent decision, and always consulted Mimir or left others to decide. The Vanir thought they had been cheated by the Aesir. They cut off Mimir's head and sent it to Odin, who preserved it and consulted it about secret matters, thus profiting from Mimir's wisdom. The name Mimir is etymologically related to memory (Lat. memor) and Mimir is always associated with wisdom. The Voluspâ indicates that Odin exchanged one of his eyes for the wisdom that was provided by Mimir's source (Voluspâ 28; cf. De Vries 1970,270). Hoenir was the god who gave mankind odr ,'mind', 'feeling', in the myths of creation. De Vries considers Hoenir and Mimir to be a complementary pair: Hoenir the silent one and Mimir the speaking one (De Vries 1970, 270). It seems also possible to interpret the consultation of Mimir by Hoenir as the consultation of wisdom and memory by mind and intelligence.

The first variant of the treaty explains the creation of wisdom, at first embodied in the man Kvasir, then in the sacred mead. The second variant explains the loss of wisdom by the Vanir. Although they acquired it at first in the person of Mimir they lost it by killing him and returning his head to Odin. Thus the Vanir cheated themselves and became the losers in the exchange. In both variants, wisdom was finally controlled by Odin.

Aesir and Vanir thus became one group of gods and their unity would last until ragnarok when the Vanir would return to Vanaheim. Although the Vanir were victorious at first, and won the war they lost in the exchange Freyr, Freyja and

Njord were accepted among the Aesir, and the Vanir lost their significance as a distinct group.

If we consider the alliance relations between the Aesir and Vanir we see that these relations were not symmetrical. The Vanir married the daughters of the giants, but they did not return their own women to the Aesir or the giants. Freyja had a mysterious husband Od, who is identified with Odin by some researchers (cf. De Vries 1970, 87), but hardly anything is known about this god and Frigg is generally considered to be Odin's wife. Acoording to the Voluspâ, Od's wife was once delivered up to the giants, but no marriage was concluded. The giants always wanted to marry Freyja, but they seem not to have been interested in the women of the Aesir. Even when Idun was captured by Thiazi, marriage was not discussed. An interesting problem is posed by Gullveig who may have played a part similar to that of Tarpeia in Roman mythology (cf.Dumézil 1947).

Livy relates that the Romans and the Sabines made war because the Romans had captured the daughters of Sabines. The Sabines then besieged Rome. Tarpeia, the daughter of the Roman commander of the Capitol desired the golden bracelets that the Sabines had on their arms, and she proposed to betray the Roman stronghold in exchange for what the Sabines had on their arms. The Sabines entered the Capitol, but instead of giving her the gold she craved for, they crushed her with the shields that they also wore on their arms. The war then continued until the Sabine wives of the Romans intervened and asked their husband, brothers and fathers to make peace with each other. Both groups were then united and the Roman king Romulus and the Sabine king Titus Tatius jointly ruled over both peoples (Livy, 1.9-1.14).

The parallels between the Roman and the Scandinavian wars are striking:

A. The Romans were wife-takers and the Sabines were wife-givers	A. The Aesir were wife-givers the Vanir were wife-takers
B. The Sabines did not marry a Roman woman, who craved for gold, but killed her instead	B. The Aesir did not marry a woman sent by the Vanir, and called Golddrunk, but killed her instead.
C. Both groups were united	C. Both groups were united.

In both myths the relation between wife-givers and wife-takers are symmetrical. The wife-givers do not accept women from the wife-takers. On the contrary, they kill them. An interesting problem is posed by the inversion of the relation between wife-givers and wife-takers in the two cycles. In the Roman myth the wife-takers possess the stronghold of the Capitol, in the Scandinavian myth the wife-givers inhabit the stronghold of Asgard. In both instances their enemies enter the stronghold at first, but the inhabitants of the stronghold are victorious in the long run.

In the Roman myth the victors were the wife-takers, who were concerned with the continuity of Rome: they needed wives and children. The continuity of life is stressed. In the Scandinavian myths the victors are the wife-givers. The result of the war is the creation of the cultural good: wisdom embodied in the sacred mead. The opposition between wife-takers and wife-givers is therefore related to an opposition of nature and culture.

The Romans and the Sabine women had offspring and thus assured the continuity of Rome. Although the Aesir and Vanir did not exchange women in the myth of their war, they still had offspring, generated by spitting in a vessel. The union of these two groups, who exchanged men instead of women and copulated symbolically by spitting in the same vessel resulted in the creation of a cultural good. It did not result from birth, but from death, since the mead was created from Kvasir's blood.

The Aesir were not allowed to marry their sisters, while the Vanir could do so. Internal relations between the Aesir were not marked by incest, but by fratricide. The killing of brother by brother is most clearly expressed in the myth of Balder and Hoder.

Snorri presents an extensive version of this myth in the Gylfaginning. Balder, the son of Odin had dreams that foreboded his death. He informed the gods and they took council. Frigg, his mother, took an oath from all beings that they would not harm Balder, but she omitted the mistletoe since she thought it was too young. The gods assumed that Balder was now out of danger and they enjoyed themselves by throwing all kinds of weapons at him, none of which did him any harm. This annoyed Loki. He went to Frigg in the disguise of a woman and he heard from her that the mistletoe had not sworn an oath. Loki took the mistletoe and brought it to Hoder, the blind brother of Balder, and encouraged him to throw it at his brother. Hoder did so, but in its flight the mistletoe changed into a weapon and killed Balder. The gods were greatly upset and Odin sent Hermod on the eightlegged horse Sleipnir to Hel in order to obtain Balder's release from her realm. In the meantime the gods organized Balder's funeral. Odin placed the ring Draupnir on the pyre. Balder's wife Nanna, who died of a broken heart, was also carried on the pyre. Thereafter eight rings of equal value dropped from Draupnir every ninth night.

Hel granted Hermod's request provided that all beings should weep for Balder's death. Balder gave Hermod the ring

Draupnir and some other gifts and Hermod returned to the world with his message. All beings wept for Balder's sake, except the giantess Thökk, but that was enough to confine Balder to the realm of death. Snorri adds that Thökk was thought to be Loki. Odin begot a new son, Vali, to avenge Balder and to kill Hoder, a new killing of brother by brother, and potentially the start of infinite regression (Gylfaginning 49).

We have not outlined some of the most important features of the relations between the giants, Aesir and Vanir. They can be represented in a simple scheme:

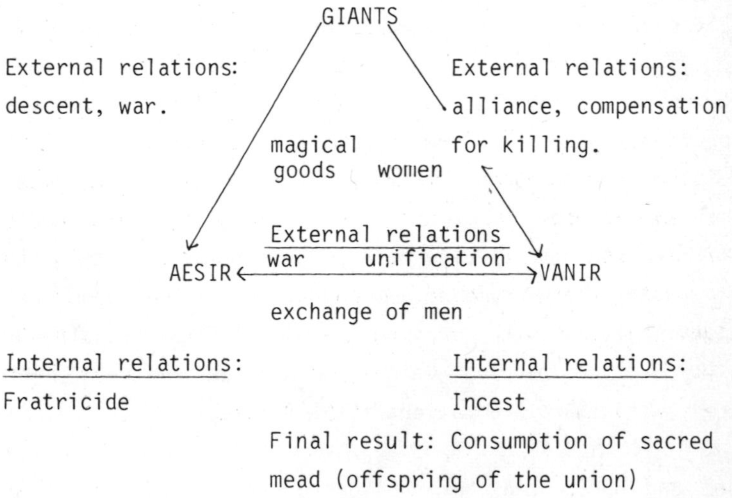

This scheme is not derived from one particular myth, but from Icelandic mythology as a whole. It expresses the basic structure of the relations between the most important groups of the Scandinavian pantheon. The Aesir receive magical goods and kill the giants, the Vanir receive women and have no direct part in the killings. Relations between Aesir and giants are not reciprocal while those between giants and Vanir are.

The scheme suggests that war and fratricide, associated with the Aesir, and alliance and incest, associated with the Vanir, were contrary principles in Scandinavian mythology. This can be confirmed by an examination of some variants of the Balder myth.

Saxo Grammaticus gives a very complex variant of the myth and I will only present the most relevant points here.

Hotherus, the son of king Hothbrod, became the fosterson of king Gevarus when his own father was killed. He fell in love with his fostersister Nanna, and she responded to his love. Balderus, the son of Othinus (Odin), also fell in love with Nanna when he saw her bathing, but she rejected him.

Hotherus is described as a great hero. All the virtues that Snorri ascribed to Balder (wisdom, eloquence, etc.) are now attributed to Hotherus by Saxo. He even acquired a magical ring, that guaranteed wealth and a magical sword, that could kill Balderus, who was invulnerable, in a hazardous trip to a distant country that resembled the underworld. The opponents fought many battles with varying results. Finally Hotherus was victorious. He married Nanna and killed Balderus with his magical sword (Saxo Grammaticus 1979,69-75).

Balder and Hoder can be considered as the Scandinavian variant of the Indo-European pair of the divine twins. Usually one is human, the other one divine (cf. Kastor and Polydeukes in Greek mythology) or becomes divine (cf. Romulus and Remus in Roman mythology). Snorri's version retains the notion of brotherhood while Saxo's version retains the notion of one human and one divine member of the pair. As a rule the two brothers have only enough life for one person and therefore one of them has to die. They can share life and death (as Kastor and Polydeukes do), or one brother can kill the other one and become the only divine being (as Romulus killed Remus), or both can die and return at the end of time (like Balder and Hoder after ragnarok), etc. Other famous variants of these divine twins are the Aśvins in Indian mythology, and Hengist and Horsa, Uther and Pendragon in Anglo-Saxon myhtology.

Although the central theme of the killing of Balder by Hoder is retained in Saxo's variant, everything else seems to be inverted. Hotherus is not a brother of Balder, but a foster-brother of Nanna. Nanna is not married to Balder, but she marries Hotherus instead. Virtues and magical goods (like the magical ring) that belonged to Balder in Snorri's version are now attributed to Hotherus, etc. The transformation of a myth of fratricide into a myth of alliance thus implies an inversion of a number of important features.

The relation between these variants becomes even more striking when we consider a third variant of the Balder myth: the marriage of Gerd an Freyr as it is described in the Skīrnismāl 2. Freyr became infatuated at the sight of Gerd and many authors have stressed the resemblance between Balderus and Freyr in this respect. Freyr used a representative, supplying him with his horse and his sword, like Odin did when he sent Hermod as his representative to Hel in order to save Balder's life. In the Balder myth the god never returned to the world, but the gold did and it had acquired a new life giving force. In the Skīrnismāl Skirnir offered apples of gold and the ring Draupnir. They were refused at first, but from the Lokasenna we can infer that they were finally accepted and the giantess came to Freyr. In the Balder myth, the god was killed and sent to Hel by a magical branch that turned into a weapon.

In the Skīrnismāl, Gerd was threatened with a magical branch that would send her to the gate of Hel and condemn her to eternal infertility is she refused the marriage (Skīrnismāl 27-34). The mission to Hel is unsuccessful. The gold returns, but Balder does not. The mission to Gerd is successful. The gold and the magical sword do not return, but the woman comes to Freyr as his wife.

Even the theme of brotherhood is present in the Skīrnismāl, since Gerd's brother is killed by Freyr's representative (Skīr-nismāl 16).

The three myths present problems of brotherhood and alliance in different ways. The relations between the most important protagonists, who are related by brotherhood and alliance, can be represented in three simple schemes:

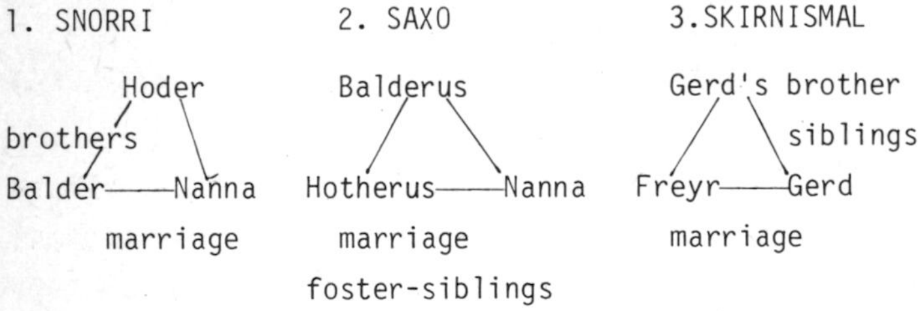

All schemes deal with a married couple and a second man who attempts to prevent or dissolve a marriage. From the male standpoint we have the killing of a brother (1), a rival (2) and a brother-in-law (3). From the perspective of the woman we have the killing of a husband (1), the killing of a suitor (2) and the killing of a brother (3).

In the first scheme the death of Balder is followed by that of Nanna and finally by that of Hoder, who is killed by Vali. All protagonists are members of the same group (the Aesir) and the myth deals with the self-destruction of that group.

In the second scheme the killing of Balderus is followed by the killing of Hotherus by Bo, Odin's son, but Hotherus had a son and his patriline continues to exist. Balderus belongs to another group (he is semi-divine) while Nanna and Hotherus are not only human beings but also foster-siblings. The combination of marriage and foster-siblingship is only partially successful. The patriline is saved, but Hotherus still has to die because of blood revenge.

In the last scheme the death of Gerd's brother will be followed by that of her father. Thus we have destruction of Gerd's male paternal relatives, but the ensuing marriage seems to be successful. We find no traces of blood revenge in this case. Only the third scheme represents a real alliance in the sense that two different groups are allied by marriage.

Scheme 2 constitutes a transition from self-destruction of a patriline to alliance with another patriline and the killing of its male members . While Snorri is mainly concerned with internal problems of the royal patrilines in the Ynglinga-saga, Saxo is mainly concerned with problems of alliance in the first chapters of the Gesta Danorum.

The opposition between alliance and war, marriage and death is also expressed in the relations between the myth of Balder and the myth of the marriage of Njord and Skadi.

Skadi wanted to marry Balder but chose Njord instead. Her condition, that the gods should make her laugh is in direct opposition to the condition in the myth of Balder, that all beings should weep. Weeping and laughing express contrary emotions, but the expression of emotions itself can be considered as an expression of life, while the refusal of emotions can be considered as a denial of life. Marriage establishes a social relation between two groups in order to create new life.

In both myths of the marriages of the Vanir, the substitution of a god of the Vanir for Balder implied a transformation from death to life. The subject of the myth is changed from death to marriage, and whereas the gods fail in the case of Balder they succeed in the case of the Vanir. Marriage rather than the return from the realm of death is the answer to death in Scandinavian mythology, and this notion is clearly expressed in the struture of the myths. Balder feared death and died; Gerd feared not death, but infertility and so she married.

The Aesir are connected with war (externally, against their ancestors; internally, between brothers) and the Vanir are connected with alliance (externally: with the giants and internally between brothers and sisters). Fratricide and incest preceded ragnarok (Voluspâ 38) and the Scandinavian myths make quite clear that these deeds are committed by the gods themselves.

RAGNAROK

The word ragnarok means deeds of the gods. Another term ragnarokr means twilight of the gods, and this had become the most wellknown phrase for the destruction of the world (cf. Van Holten 1977, 19-22). Extensive descriptions of this war are given in both the Voluspâ and the Gylfaginning, while many other texts refer to it.

At the end of time all social and physical bonds will be destroyed. The tree of the world, the giant ash Ygdrasil that maintains and connects the worlds, will fall down and the bridge Bifrost that connects Asgard and Midgard will be broken. Monsters and demons will break their fetters. The huge wolf Fenrir, the wolf Garm that guards the entrance to Hel and Loki will free themselves and attack the gods. The giants of the North and the Muspelsons of the South will all join in that battle. Then Odin will be killed by Fenrir, but Vidar will avenge his father and kill the wolf. Thor will kill the midgard snake but he will die of the lethal effects of its poison, and he will walk only nine paces from his dead enemy. Freyr will fight with Surt, the fire demon and leader of the Muspelsons, Tyr with Garm, and Loki and Heimdall will kill each other in battle. Finally the Muspelsons will burn the world. The great dragon Nidhogg will come and carry away the dead. Then a new world will arise that will be ruled by the sons of the great Aesir (Balder and Hoder, now reconciled, Vidar and Vali, the sons of Odin, and Magni and Modi the sons of Thor). Of the old gods only Hoenir is mentioned in the Voluspā.

In the battle of ragnarok the old world is destroyed. Both the gods and their enemies die. It is significant, however, that the gods do not fight their age-old enemies, the giants. Although the giants participate in the war they no longer play a significant part. Rather the great monsters and the fire demons are the main enemies of the gods in the battle of ragnarok. The most important Aesir fight Loki and his offspring Jormungand and Fenrir. Not much is known about Garm. He may have been a double of Fenrir. Freyr fights Surt, probably, because he has no quarrel with Loki and his sons.

The significance of the battle with the monsters is difficult to assess but the slaying of the snake or dragon by the thundergod is a well-known theme in Indo-European mythology. It is usually placed in a mythical past. Thus Indra killed the snake Vṛtra long ago. Ivanov and Toporov have suggested that originally the snake was not a monster, but a divine being that controlled the forces of water, thunder, and lightning. As a consequence the killing of the snake may originally have been a crime. Traces of this notion can probably still be found in the guilt of brahmanicide that fell on Indra when he killed his halfbrother Vṛtra. Ivanov and Toporov stress the cosmic significance of the snake and its well attested connection with the tree of the world (cf. Ivanov and Toporov 120-121).

Wolves also played an important part in ragnarok. A wolf devoured the sun and the moon and both Odin and Tyr were killed by wolves. Originally the wolf may also have been a more positive mythic figure. Kretchmar has demonstrated that the notion of a dog or a wolf as first ancestor and guardian of the underworld is spread over a wide area in America, Asia and Europe, and we have to acknowledge that traces of these notions are clearly present in Indo-European mythology. Garm and Kerberos are guardians of the underworld in Scandinavian and Greek mythology. The myths of Romulus and Remus and of the origin of the Lykians suggest descent from a wolf. It may be significant that neither the snake nor the wolf commits an offense against the gods before ragnarok. Fenrir is tricked by the gods with magical ropes because they fear him and not because he gives offense. However that may be, more research is needed to assess the original significance of these monsters and here we will confine ourselves to their sifnificance in the battle of ragnarok

Jormungand and Fenrir are considered to be the sons of Loki. Hel is thought to be his daughter. They all side against the gods, and Loki seems to be the leader of the enemies of the gods in the great battle of ragnarok.

The problem of the significance of Loki has intriged many researchers. Both De Vries and Dumézil have devoted important studies to this dark and complex figure. Why was Loki transformed from a god into an enemy of the gods and why was he chained to a rock? Snorri explains Loki's punishment by his part in the killing of Balder. Loki tried to escape the revenge of the gods. During the day he hid himself as a salmon in a waterfall. He tried to anticipate how the gods would try to catch him and invented a net. When the gods approached his hiding-place, he quickly burnt it and jumped into the stream. The god Kvasir saw the pattern of the net in the burnt ash and understood its purpose. The gods made a net and caught Loki. Then Loki's sons Narfi and Vali were captured. The Aesir changed Vali into a wolf, and he tore his brother Narfi apart. From Narfi's entrails they made the ropes that bound Loki. Then a poisoned snake was fastened over Loki so that its poison would drip onto his face. Loki's wife Sigyn protected his face with a basin, but each time she had to empty it the poisonous drops tormented him and his convulsions made the earth shake. This was thought to be the cause of earthquakes (Gylfaginning 50).

Loki's fate reminds us of that of Prometheus, the clever son of Iapetos, who created man. He tricked Zeus in the institution of sacrifice, when he gave Zeus the choice between two bags, one filled with meat, covered with the stomach of the sacrificial animal, the other containing bones hidden beneath a rich layer of fat. Zeus chose the bag with bones and thus the meat of the sacrificial animal was preserved for human beings. Zeus was outraged and wanted to avenge himself by withholding fire from mankind so that men would have to eat their meat raw. Prometheus stole the fire from the sun and thus defied Zeus. The father-god punished Prometheus by chaining him to a rock. Each day his liver was eaten by an eagle and at night it healed again. Finally Prometheus was freed by

Herakles, the son of Zeus. Prometheus was Zeus' paternal cousin and a brother of Atlas and Menoetios, two Titans who chose Kronos' side in the war against the gods. Prometheus was thus associated with sacrifice and the origin of fire. Another instance of enmity between a god of fire and Zeus can be found in the relation between Zeus and Hephaistos, who was thrown from the Olympus by the angry father-god, and lamed.

The gods of sacrifice, fire and light often have an ambiguous position in Indo-European mythology. The Indian god of fire, Agni, hid himself in the water from the other gods under the leadership of Indra. He became hoṭr, sacrificial priest, and was thus associated with both fire and sacrifice. He was the mediator between gods and human beings.

In the Mahābhārata a central issue is the conflict between Karna, the eldest of the Pāṇḍava brothers, and the son of the god of the sun, Sūrya, and Arjuna, the greatest hero of the Pāṇḍavas, the son of Indra, the god of warfare, thunder and lightning.

In Celtic mythology the god Lug was also associated with the sun and light. His name probably means light (cf. Greek leukos). He was the great rival of the Celtic Allfather, Eochu Ollathair, the great Dagda, and there was lasting enmity between their patrilines.

The gods of fire were usually considered to be clever and often they outwitted the father-god. Loki has a similar position in Scandinavian mythology. His name is associated with logi, 'fire'. In the Gylfaginning he lost a contest with a man called Logi. Both ate as much as possible, but Logi devoured the bones and the trencher and thus won the contest (Gylfaginning 46).

Loki also played an important part in a myth that probably discusses the origin of cooking. Once Odin, Loki and Hoenir attempted to roast an ox, but each time they scattered the fire the animal was still uncooked. An eagle sitting in a tree promised them that the meat would be done soon if the gods gave him a share of the meat. The gods agreed and when the meat was done the eagle sailed down and took two thighs and the shoulders. Loki was outraged and drove a stick into the feathers of the bird. It flew away and Loki was dragged along because he clung to the stick. The eagle, who was the giant Thiazi, was only prepared to release Loki when he promised to deliver to him the goddess Idun and her apples of youth. Loki agreed and duly fulfilled his promise. We have already seen that the gods forced him to bring Idun and her apples back to Asgard. Thiazi, who pursued him, was killed and his daughter Skadi was compensated for her loss by the gods (Skālds-kaparmāl 1).

Thiazi clearly controlled the preparation of food, but how ? Was he master of cooking or a master of time, or both? the gods could have their food cooked in exchange for the best parts of the meat. When Loki begrudged him his share, he had to give Thiazi the apples of youth in exchange. This exchange suggests that Thiazi controlled time. The gods gave up eternal time, that did not permit the process of cooking to be finished, in exchange for the passing of time that implies that food can be cooked, but also that all living beings age. Eternal time seems to be incompatible with the apples of youth that imply rejuvenation and the passing of time. The exchange therefore seems to be logical, but the gods got the best of the deal. They acquired the passing of time, that enabled them to finish the things they wanted to and escaped its consequences through the apples of youth. The preparation of food is often an important measure of time (cf. also the baking of bread in the epic of Gilgamesh).

Loki thus seems to be associated with fire and possibly

also with the art of cooking. In the battle of ragnarok the world is burnt and this may be another indication of Loki's close association with fire.

Both Odin and Thor, who share important characteristics of the Indo-European father-god are Loki's enemies. The original significance of this ancient conflict between the father-god and the gods of fire and/of light is not clear, but probably the fire and light gods were somehow deprived of their rights by the father-gods.

Karṇa and Arjanu were brothers, Prometheus and Zeus were paternal cousins, and according to the Lokasenna Loki and Odin were blood-brothers. Although they were therefore related as brothers, enmity between their patrilines is strong. Molenaar has pointed out that Loki made Odin's sons kill each other, while the Aesir made Loki's sons Vali and Narfi kill each other (Molenaar 1981). In the battle of ragnarok Loki's son Fenrir will kill Odin and then Fenrir will be killed by Odin's son Vidar in return. Loki's other son Jormungand will kill Thor, who drove Loki from Aegir's feast in the Lokasenna. Thus Loki's main enemies will be killed by his sons. Odin's mother was a giantess, Loki's father was a giant. The status of Odin's father and Loki's mother is not clear. It may be that the antagonism between both gods is related to a conflict between patrilineal and matrilineal descent as was suggested by Molenaar (Molenaar 1981).

We have already seen that Odin may have been related to Ymir by matrilineal descent and by a symbolic brotherhood between Ymir and Buri. A similar combination of elements may have existed between Odin and Loki. While Odin was descended through his mother from the giants, Loki was descended from them through his father. At the same time they were blood-brothers and thus a cultural bond was established between the two gods that seems to be an inversion of the natural bond that connected Ymir and Buri. The natural bond was negated and a maternal kinsman was killed (Ymir). The result was the creation of the world. When the cultural bond between Odin and Loki was negated it meant the destruction of the world.

Thus the war between Loki and Odin expresses internal strife and self-destruction of the descendants of the giants and the result is cosmic catastrophy. A new world arises that is ruled by the sons of the Aesir. While their fathers made war upon their fathers and brothers, and killed their ancestor Ymir, the sons of the Aesir avenge their fathers in battle. Balder and Hoder are reconciled. The new gods inherit a new world as rightful successors of their fathers and not as usurpers. We do not hear anything of the Vanir. Hoenir is mentioned once, but the general conclusion is that the Aesir will be succeeded by their sons.

The three great wars of Scandinavian mythology all deal with wars between kinsmen. The wars of the gods among the Scandinavians can be considered as variants of two standard themes in Indo-European mythology: the wars between allied groups (Rāmāyaṇa, Iliad, Romans, versus Sabines, Tuatha De Danann versus Fomorians etc.) and the wars between brothers (Mahābhārata, Seven against Thebes, Romans versus Alba Longans, Tuatha De Danann versus Firbolg, etc.). Moreover, we have a structural conflict between matrilineal and patrilineal principles of descent that can also be traced in other mythical cycles (the Roman kings, the Celtic mythical cycle of the Conquest of Ireland, etc.).

BIBLIOGRAPHY

Dumézil, G., 1947: Tarpeia: cinq essais de philologie comparative indo-européenne. Collection "Les mythes Romains", vol.3, Gallimard, Paris.
Dumézil, G., 1948: Loki, Paris.
Dumézil, G., 1952: Les dieux des indo-européens, P.U.F., Paris.
Dumézil, G., 1959: Les dieux des Germains, P.U.F., Paris.
Dumézil, G., 1966: La religion romaine archaique, Payot, Paris.
Dumézil, G., 1968: Mythe et épopée 1, Gallimard, Paris.
Dumézil, G., 1971: Mythe et épopée 2, Gallimard, Paris.
Dumézil, G., 1973: From myth to fiction, Chicago and London.
Edda, 1962: Die Lieder des Codex Regius nebst verwandten Denkmälern I Text. Herausgegeben von G. Naeckel, Heidelberg
Edda, 1968: Die Lieder des Codex Regius nebst verwandten Denkmälern II. Kurzes Wörterbuch von Hans Kuhn, Heidelberg.
Edda, 1952: Klassieke Galerij, nr. 67868. Vert. J. de Vries, Antwerpen.
Ellis Davidson, H.W., 1977: Gods and myths of Northern Europe, Harmondsworth.
Farwerck, F.E., 1978: Noordeuropese mysterieën en hun sporen tot heden, Ankh. Hermes, Deventer.
Gilgamesh, 1972: The epic of Gilgamesh. Sandars, N.K. (ed.), Harmondsworth.
Gurjewitsch, A.J., 1978: Das Weltbild des Mittelalterlichen Menschen, Dresden.
Hesiod, 1968: Theogony. Transl. H.G. Evelyn-White, London/Cambridge (Mass.).
Van Holten, A.T., 1977: De dood van de goden, Wolters-Noordhoff, Groningen.
Ivanov, V. and Toporov, V., 1970: Le mythe Indo-Europèen du dieu de l'orage poursuivant le serpent: Reconstruction du schéma. In: Echanges et communications, melanges offert à Claude Lévi-Strauss à l'occasion de son 60ème anniversaire réunis par Jean Pouillon et Pierre Maranda, Mouton, The Hague/Paris.
Lincoln, B., 1981: Priests, warriors and cattle, Berkeley, Los Angeles/London.
Livy, 1976: Books I and II. Transl. B.O. Foster, Cambridge, Mass./London.
Mahābhārata, The Vol.I and II. Transl and Edited by J.A.B. van Buitenen, Chicago and London, Vol. I, 1950; vol.II, 1975.
Meletinsky, E., 1973: Scandinavian mythology as a system. In: Journal of symbolic anthropology 1 and 2 (July / September1973), Mouton, The Hague.
Molenaar, H.A., 1981: De sterfelijke god, Ica Publication no.44, Leiden.

Oosten, J.G., 1977: De godenstrijd in de Germaanse mythology, Ica Publicatie no. 24, Leiden.
Oosten, J.G., 1981: De Germaanse koningen. In:Hagesteijn, R. R. and Van der Vliet, E.Ch.K. (eds.), legitimiteit of leugen; achtergronden van macht en gezag in de vroege staat, Ica Publicatie no.41, Leiden.
Saxo Grammaticus, 1979: History of the Danes. Transl. by Peter Fisher, D.S. Brewer-Rowman and Littlefield, Cambridge.
Scott Littleton, C., 1973: The new comparative mythology, Berkeley, Los Angeles/London.
Snorri Sturluson, 1968: Edda, Gylfaginning og prosafortellingene av skāldskaparmāl. Utgitt av anna Holtsmark og Jōn Helgason, Kobenhavn/Oslo/Stockholm.
Snorri Sturluson, 1954: The prose Edda. Transl. by Jean J. Young, Cambridge.
Snorri Sturluson, 1974-1978: Heimskringla I, the Olafsaga's, vol.I (1978) and II (1974), London/New York.
Snorri Sturluson, 1975: Heimskringla II, Sagas of the Norse king, London/New York.
Tacitus, 1980: Agricola. Transl. by M. Hutton and R.M. Ogilvie; Germania. Transl. by M. Hutton and E.H. Warmington; Dialogus. Transl. by Sir W. Peterson and M. Winterbottom, Cambridge, Mass./London.
Thompson, E.A., 1965: The early Germans, Clarendon Press, Oxford.
De Vries, J., 1933: The problem of Loki, F.F. Communications no. 110, Helsinki.
De Vries, J., 1956-1970: Altgermanische Religionsgeschichte I (1956) and II (1979), Walter de Gruyter, Berlin.

Inanna/Ishtar as a Figure of Controversy

H. L. J. Vanstiphout

1. The Mesopotamian goddess Inanna or Ishtar is known to us from a plentiful variety of mainly literary sources as an exceedingly complex figure. Indeed, the number of references to her, or texts about her, is so great that even the sketching of the outlines of a complete treatment would far exceed the framework of a normal paper. Instead, we will concentrate in this contribution on a few aspects, that are perhaps salient, and in any case are deemed to be relevant, even central, to the subject of these essays. In Mesopotamia proper she is known from very early on under her Sumerian name *Inanna*, which may have been originally *IR.NIN (=*victoria*) and later etymologized as *(n)in-an-a(k) 'Lady of Heaven' (1). Her Akkadian name *Ishtar* (2) is also attested from early times, and this name is obviously cognate to divine names in other Semitic languages, both female (Syria: ^{c}aṯtart-; ^{c}aštart-) (3) and male (Syria and South Arabia: ^{c}aṯtar) (4). In Mesopotamia, the plural form is used as a generic term for goddesses (*ištarātu*)(5).

Apart from the references to her cult as a city goddess, in which character she does not appreciably differ from other gods, and a number of rituals invoking her together with Dumuzi, (6) and usually connected with potency, the vast majority of texts mentioning her are at least partially literary in character (hymns, myths, epics)(7) so that the references to her specific cult are secondary at best. Her relationship to the rest of the pantheon is far from clear. The main tradition has it that she is either a daughter of the Sky god An, or of the Moon god Nanna - both relationships obviously referring to her celestial symbol, which is the Evening Star. But one might well ask whether these relationships may not ultimately depend on popular etymologies. There is also a tradition which makes her a daughter of the god ENLIL, executive head of the pantheon (8). This point however is not elaborated, and might perhaps be understood through her membership of the committee of seven gods: most of them are understood to be children or grandchildren of ENLIL.

2. Her membership of this executive committee, which rules the universe, provides an interesting starting point: In this committee, INANNA has no clear-cut function, this in contrast to most of the others (UTU/SHAMASH is responsible for justice, NINURTA is the champion of the gods, and is besides responsible for agriculture, ENKI/EA stands for wisdom, cunning, magic and technology, NISABA rules over education, scribal craft, literature and bureaucracy...) (9). Nor is this an interpretation *e silentio*: one of the relevant texts specifically mentions that she has *no* special domain and this point is doubly relevant, since the text in question is precisely about the Ordering of the Universe by ENKI (10). This ordering takes the form of apportioning parts of the Universe as domains of the several gods; Inanna is advisedly ommitted.

Nevertheless, this must not lead us to a purely negative conclusion. JACOBSEN (11) pointed out that, though she may not have a specific task or domain, this may well be her special feature: she is the goddess of *infinite variety*, a variety illustrated by the fact that she seems to possess a far greater number of personal traits than the other gods. To list only the most frequently mentioned ones, she stands for:

- sexual love (*not* fertility as such, although the fertility idea must be present in some way) (12);

- battle and slaughter (battle is called the 'Dance of Inanna', and the Assyrian army carried Ishtar of Arbela with them into battle);
- destruction (she destroys Mount Ebiḫ, a monster-mountain standing for the modern Jebel Ḫamrin; this feat is mentioned rather circumstantially in three major poems) (14).
- rival rulership (she is said to be the goddess dwelling in the rival cities of URUK and ARATTA, thus in a way giving rise to the epic cycle treating this rivalry; she appears explicitly in the poems as *at the same time* the object, the origin and the spoils of the contest between the rivals)(15);
- gathering, c.q. stealing, of the ME's (these ME's are a central concept in Mesopotamian religious or philosophical thought; they can best be understood as'quintessences' of all that exists, whether concrete or abstract; they are thus related, perhaps, to Platonic ideas, but they are nevertheless also concrete objects, at least in the divine world, for they can be taken in the hand, stolen, carried by boat - sometimes even mounted and ridden. Nothing can exist without its ME, since an important feature seems also to be that they somehow are related to the primal, first material out of which everything was made. It should be pointed out that INANNA gathers the ME's by trickery: they are not hers by right) (16);
- jealous concupiscence (already illustrated in her adventure concerning the ME's, but far more general throughout her whole career: she tricks her way into the Underworld sacrificing her husband DUMUZI in the process; she wheedles AN into exalting her far above her station;

she constantly seeks out new lovers and sheds them as quickly - while she rages uncontrollably when Gilgamesh refuses her) (17).

3. This rough and ready, and very incomplete, list of features is meant to carry three interrelated points. Firstly, her unique complexity may well be seen as implying her lack of a special, exclusive domain. Secondly, she is never content with the manifold 'possessions', of one kind or another, she has gathered - often by trickery, and which in a sense make up her complexity. To the contrary, as with lovers, she is constantly trying to get greater, one presumes ultimately supreme, power. Thirdly, she never quite succeeds, neither subjectively (i.e. she will always be jealous for more things), nor objectively (she does not attain full supreme power). In other words, and again this is unique, she can be said to have a career - a career which does not quite work out. Now the rest of the great gods are rather static figures, and not much is supposed to change in their status or dominations. Her case is almost the exact opposite: she is always and ever moving from one conquest to another.

4. Inanna's variety of features, her constant movement, her unabating struggle for domination, her lack of a central and dominating domain, her not having a specific competence in the worlds divine and human - all of these have been explained in various ways. These may be brought under the headings of either syncretism (meaning that the Inanna/Ishtar we know has gradually grown as a conglomerate of originally unconnected and quite separate divine figures) or of intrusion (meaning that she is a Semitic goddess catapulted into the already structured Sumerian pantheon; in this case her career would

illustrate the gradual taking over of Sumerian culture by the Semitic inhabitants of Mesopotamia), or, perhaps, a combination of both (18).

While either of these explanations, or perhaps both, may well have been 'true' in a historical sense, it is important to observe that we do not possess any evidence whatsoever for either theory. There is no indication of a gradual fusing of originally distinct personalities, nor is there the slightest trace of bands of Inannites invading Mesopotamia and adding Inanna to the Pantheon in the process. Indeed, the problem with this approach, and incidentally also the problem with Inanna, is highlighted by a curious attempt to arrange some (literary) evidence in this manner - with completely contradictory results (19). But even if there could be shown some traces of events such as these, I doubt very much whether they would have any relevance. For it is a matter of fact that the sources throughout the whole Mesopotamian civilization present us an Inanna with all her characteristics. The different accentuations are clearly a matter of literary genre; not of Inanna's personality. Since Inanna is consistently presented in the way indicated above, it is a reasonable inference that, even granted some degree of external influence, an acceptable explanation of Inanna can be found within the system.

5. It should be clearly stated at this point that my intention is not to provide a unitary explanation of Inanna. This would violate her essential variety. Nor do I intend to give even the outline of a complete interpretation: every Assyriologist knows that even a preliminary listing and description of the source material would result in a fair sized monograph. I do claim, however, that we should try to understand Inanna as a distinct personality, albeit with many different features.

Nor is this a requirement that we are forcing upon the evidence: the high literary level, and the constant way in which Inanna is presented with all these features, presuppose an acquaintance on the part of scribes, composers and public with a distinct and clearly recognizable personage. And perhaps there is something in the make-up of Inanna's personality which might explain in some way the principle of variety as well as some of her various characteristic features, without causing the variety to disappear. Moreover, such a basic structural element in her character might well be very relevant to the *interpretatio mesopotamica* of the theme treated in these essays, viz. divine conflict.

6. There is one very important text eminently suitable for our purpose. This poem, known variously as the *Agušaya Hymn* or *Ea and Ṣaltu* runs as follows:

> After a hymnal introduction in which Ištar is praised presented in her aspects of inscrutability, love of war and aggression, loud clamour etc...., the god Ea calls together the assembly and puts it to them that her behaviour can no longer be tolerated. He suggests that he create a suitable opponent. Upon the gods'approval he proceeds to create (with the dirt of his fingernails) a personage called *Ṣaltu*. She is to provoke Inanna by violating, with loud clamour, her privacy, and challenging her. However, in explaining to *Ṣaltu* how she will recognize Istar, he waxes so eloquent that *Ṣaltu* becomes furiously jealous. The climax is lost in that we do not have the text describing the meeting of the two, but at the end so much is clear that we know that Inanna stops her irritating behaviour, very probably because she has seen, from *Ṣaltu*, what it is like. Ea then causes *Ṣaltu* to disappear (20).

Apart from the very interesting psychological angle (Ištar is pacified as soon as she sees how ridiculous her behaviour is), it is rather obvious that to the people who knew this composition, this was as near as anything to a 'basic' characteristic of Ištar. _Ṣaltu_ is Ištar, albeit viewed only in the negative. Therefore she disappears when Ištar stops acting in this way. And the important point is that _Ṣaltu_ means 'strife, contention, quarrel, litigation'.

7. The not altogether unexpected observation from this text, viz. that basically Ištar is strife, is born out by quite some other important texts. There are many hymns to the goddess ascribing different features of human life to her, and many of these have to do with contention or jealousy. But perhaps the best corroborration comes from the mythical story, already alluded to, about Enki and the World Order (21). Here it is told how Enki orders the universe by apportioning its main parts to the several gods. Inanna is omitted, and, when she complains about this Enki replies that she has no cause to complain since, although she has no sphere of domination as her own, she has strife. An important implication seems to be that in this view strife is not one of the constructive portions to be allotted, but something apart - and at the same time it seems to belong to the complete structure.

8. A further point needs to be made. The above should not be read as implying that Inanna is deified Strife, or any other abstract principle. On the contrary, although the Mesopotamians, not being different from any other civilizations in this respect, did work and work well with abstract ideas (22), they chose from the very beginning to regard their gods as real figures in the round, behaving much like ordinary humans if on another plane and on an altogether bigger scale.

Yet the great gods _do_ stand for certain principles, so that (some of) their actions and (part of) their character become predictable to a certain degree. In the case of Inanna, at least the literary tradition has therefore integrated the Strife principle into a real though perhaps not always lovable personage: Inanna is consistently presented as a very wilful and headstrong young girl (23). She never takes no for an answer, she constantly tries to get her own way, not hesitating to use tricks or flattery; she is ever being difficult since she thinks she is being neglected; fickleness and jealousy sometimes erupt into violence. An yet she never enters into open conflict with the other gods: indeed, often her antics seem to be viewed with good-humoured if somewhat uncertain tolerance. In this way one might perhaps say that controversy or strife have been incorporated into the family of the gods.

9. And this brings us back to the matter underlying all these essays in one form or another: that of conflict among the gods. Somewhat hesitatingly I would propose that this controversy aspect of Inanna, and perhaps even more the way in which Strife has been locked into a 'real' personality, goes some way towards understanding why divine contention is relatively absent from the structure of Mesopotamian theology. Mesopotamian gods do not fight each other. When they do fight, the battle is against external enemies: the forces of evil and chaos - in other words, disorder (24). The gods stand for order, and so Inanna's battle against Mount Ebih must also be understood as a battle against a monstrous representant of chaos (25). Only in the creation Epic, <u>Enuma eliš</u>, do we find a generation conflict. But even in this text we see the earlier generations only as very vague and abstract entities; a good point could even be made against the divine character of the opponents of the great gods (26). And surely the point hardly needs stressing that the 'creation' consists of the ordering of

the universe in all its aspects - most importantly the setting up of a well structured pantheon in this instance taking the form of a monarchy under Marduk. At this point it may be useful to keep in mind a basic distinction. On the one hand we have the opposition between Order and Chaos; Chaos is a foreign, external element (27), and although in individual instances singular chaos monsters can be overcome, the danger is always there (28). This is the sphere of the battles of the gods (29). On the other hand we have the internal opposition between order and disorder, or harmony and conflict within the structure of the pantheon. Unlike as in other religious systems, this divine conflict has not been incorporated as such in Mesopotamian thought. On the contrary, divine government is itself well-ordered, and a guarantee for the orderliness and well-being of the universe. And yet, in all human society, and certainly in Mesopotamia, there is controversy or strife. It is my contention that Mesopotamian theologians (or literati - they may have been partly the same), tried to solve this problem in two complementary ways. Firstly, they presented the divine world, and therefore the Universe, in such a well-ordered way that most if not all reasons for strife were absent. Secondly they so to speak eliminated Strife as an abstract principle by incorporating it into the psychology of Inanna. There it is understandable, almost to be expected, and therefore controllable. Still, they were well aware of the ever present and dangerous opposition between order and strife: this may be argued from the fact that Inanna seldom appears in connection with other great gods (30). When she does so appear, however, it is in connection with Enki, the god of order.

NOTES

1. See Gelb, I.J.: The name of the goddess Innin. In: Journal of Near Eastern studies, 19 (1960) p. 74 ff. For a slightly different Akkadian etymology (inin= PIRS formation of anānum 'to skirmish') see Roberts, J.M.: The earliest semitic pantheon, Baltimore, 1972 p.36.
2. See in general Roberts, J.M.: The earliest semitic pantheon, Baltimore, 1972 sub Eštar.
3. See Pope, M.H. and Röllig, W. apud Haussig, H.W.: Götter und Mythen im vorderen Orient = Wörterbuch der Mythologie, Bd I, Stuttgart, 1965 p. 249-252 and Gese, H.: Die Religionen Altsyriens, Altarabiens und der Mandäer (= Schröder, Ch.M. (ed.), Die Religionen der Menschheit Bd. 10,2), Stuttgart, 1970 p. 137-139 and 161-164.
4. See fn.3 and Höfner, M. in Schröder, Ch.M. (ed.): Die Religionen der Menschheit, Bd.10,2, Stuttgart, 1970 p. 268-272.
5. See CAD(= The assyrian dictionary of the oriental institute of the university of Chicago), vol. 7 (I and J), Chicago, 1970 p. 271-274.
6. For the potency incantations, where Ishtar is often invoked, see in general Biggs, R.D.: Ša.zi.ga. Ancient Mesopotamian potency incantations, Locust Valley, 1967 and now the splendid edition by Farber, W.: Beschwörungsrituale an Ištar und Dumuzi, Wiesbaden, 1977.
7. For an overview, see Edzard, D.O. apud Haussig, H.W.: Götter und Mythen im vorderen Orient (see fn.3), p. 81-89.
8. See Edzard, D.O.: fn. 7 p.82.
9. See Edzard, D.O.: fn.7 under the different headings.
10. See Falkenstein, A.: Enki und die Weltordnung. In: Zeitschrift für Assyriologie, Bd. 56 (1956) p. 45-129; also, for the first presentation of this very important composition, Bernardt, I and Kramer, S.N.: Enki und die Weltordnung. In: Wissenschaftliches Zeitschrift der Friedrich Schiller-Universität zu Jena, 9 (1959-1960) p. 231-256. More complete as to the text material, but less careful than the older studies, is Benito, C.: Enki and Ninmah and Enki and the world order, (un. of Penn, dissertation), Ann Arbor,1969.
11. Jacobsen, Th.: The treasures of darkness, New Haven, 1976 p. 135-143.
12. See especially Kramer, S.N.: The sacred marriage rite, Bloomington, 1969; Kramer, S.N.: Cuneiform studies and the history of literature. The sumerian sacred marriage

texts. In: Proceedings of the American philosophical society, vol.107, no.6 (1963) p. 485-527; Kramer, S.N.: From the poetry of Sumer, Berkeley, 1979, especially p. 71 ff. It is of interest to note that there has been a recent attempt to relate Ištar even to the negative side of fertility, Fauth, W.: Ištar als Löwengöttin und die löwenköpfige Lamaštu. In: Die Welt des Orients, Bd. XII (1981) p. 21-36. This remains to be seen.

14.The main text has not yet been edited. See provisionally Limet, H.: Le poème épique 'Innina et Ebih', une version des lignes 123 à 182. In: Orientalia, NS 40 (1971) p. 11-28. The other two poems however make explicit allusions or references to this battle. See Hallo, W.W. and Van Dijk, J.J.A.: The exaltation of Inanna, New Haven, 1968; Sjöberg, A.W.: In-nin Šà-gur-ra: a hymn to the goddess Inanna by the en-priestess Enheduanna. In: Zeitschrift für Assyriologie, Bd. 65 (1975) p. 161-253. A partial interpretation of the Ebih story has been presented by Kinnier Wilson, J.V.: The rebel lands, Cambridge, 1979 p. 1-11.

15.See my paper: Some problems in the matter of Aratta, to be published in Iraq, vol. XLV (1983) (= comptes-rendus of the 29th rencontre assyriologique internationale, London 1982).(Iraq, vol. XLV, 1983 p. 35-42).

16.A very good edition of the text has been given by Farber-Flügge, G.: Der Mythos 'Inanna und Enki' unter besonderer Berücksichtigung der Liste der ME, Rome, 1973, where also much information about the ME's and related concepts can be found. But also the extensive review-article by Alster, B.: On the interpretation of the Sumerian myth 'Inanna and Enki'. In: Zeitschrift für Assyriologie, Bd.66 (1976) p. 20-34, is very important.

17.See in general the studies by S.N. Kramer, cited in fn.12 and add Kramer, S.N.: A blood-plague motif in Sumerian mythology. In: Archiv Orientalni, vol. 17 (1949) p. 399-405; for the exaltation text see Hruška, B.: Das spätbabylonische Lehrgedicht 'Inannas Erhöhung'. In: Archiv Orientalni 37 (1969) p. 473-522; for the Gilgamesh episode see now most conveniently Labat, R. (et.al.): Les religions du Proche-Orient asiatique, Paris, 1970 p. 181-187.

18.For both explanations - not very carefully kept apart - see mainly Van Dijk, J.J.A.: Les contacts ethniques dans la Mesopotamie et les syncrétismes de la religion sumérienne. In: Scripta instituti Donneriani Aboensis, vol. 3 (1969) p. 171-206; further Roberts, J.M. (see fn.1): The earliest semitic pantheon, Baltimore, 1972 p. 145-155.

Also Edzard, D.O. (ed.): Inanna/Ištar (entry). In: Reallexikon der Assyriologie, Bd.5 (1976-1980) p. 74-89 is important.

19. See Wilcke, C.: Politische Opposition nach sumerischen Quellen. In: Finet, A. (ed.), La voix de l'opposition en Mésopotamie, Brussel, 1974 p. 37-65. The Sumero-akkadian opposition which underlies this study and in which Inanna takes opposite sides (!) was already denied by Jacobson, Th. (1939): The assumed conflict between the Sumerians and Semites in early Mesopotamian history. In: Journal of the American oriental society, vol.59 (1939) p. 485-495. Much more material for the terminological aspects of this matter can now be found in Kraus, F.R.: Sumerer und Akkader. Ein Problem der altmesopotamischen Geschichte, Amsterdam, 1970; also Cooper, J.S.: Sumerian and Akkadian in Sumer and Akkad. In: Orientalia NS 42 (1973) p. 239-246 is very important.

20. We possess only two broken tablets belonging to this composition, and one of these has been lost since its publication (as a bad photograph) in 1918. For the text see Groneberg, B.: Philologische Bearbeitung des Agušaya-Hymnus. In: Revue d'assyriologie, vol. 75 (1981) p. 107-134. The interpretation of the aspect which is most relevant for us in this paper, is based upon Foster, B.R.: Ea and Ṣaltu. In: Ellis, M.Dej. (ed.): Essays on the ancient Near East in memory of J.J. Finkelstein (= memoirs of the connecticut academy of arts & sciences, vol. XIX), Hamden, Conn., 1977 p. 79-84, although with a slightly different emphasis.

21. See fn.10.

22. The proposition, still sometimes met with, that a. the semitic languages possess no abstract nouns, and b.consequently the Semites (whoever they may have been) are weak in abstract reasoning, probably goes back to E. Renan. It has never been substantiated or even illustrated.

23. The fullest presentation of Inanna under this aspect is by Kramer, S.N.: From the poetry of Sumer, Berkeley, 1979, especially the last chapter.

24. See e.g. the fights against Azag, Anzu and also Tiamat.

25. See fn.14.

26. That is, Tiamat to all purposes should be put into a class with Azag and Anzu, especially the former. Even so, it should be noted that Th. Jacobsen has repeatedly drawn attention to the possibility that the Tiamat figure and motif may have been occidental in origin (Jacobsen, Th.:

The battle between Marduk and Tiamat. In: Journal of the American oriental society, vol. 88 (1968) p. 104-108; Jacobson, Th.: The treasures of darkness, New Haven, 1976 p. 167 ff.)

27. See previous footnotes.

28. This point may be thought to be reinforced by the fact that Chaos is represented by a number of individual figures: Tiamat, Azag, Ebih, Anzu .. each of whom is duly slain. Note also that at least in the Ninurta myths reference is made to a number of otherwise unknown but very probably cognate monsters. Should one care for a 'natural' interpretation perhaps the ever present threat of attacks from the eastern mountains might qualify.

29. This should be qualified: there is a very slender thread of evidence pointing to a tradition wherein Marduk frees his generation from Enmešarra (see Reallexikon fn.18, sub voce). But the chances are that this is just another version of something like the Marduk story as told in Enuma eliš. Secondly, there is the epic of the Plague god Erra. But even this god, for whom see Edzard, D.O.: fn.7 sub voce, does not enter into battle with the other gods.

30. Naturally , an exception must be made for the complex of Dumuzi/Inanna traditions. But here the point is almost always the sexual aspect of Inanna, and perhaps this too could be brought into line with the interpretation offered in these pages, for, quite apart from the identical character features of Inanna in both complexes, one might see in her sexual role also something like Strife leading into and out of harmony.

ADDENDUM

Almost immediately after the manuscript was completed two short but highly important papers have been published. They are:

1. Buccellati, G.: The descent of Inanna as a ritual journey to Kutha ? In: Syro-Mesopotamian studies, vol. 4, Issue 3 (1982) p. 3-7.
2. Heimpel, W.: A catalog of near eastern Venus deities. In: Syro-Mesopotamian studies, vol.4, Issue 3 (1982) p. 9-22.

In (1) it is proposed that in the literary text describing Inanna's descent the Inanna personage is not only viewed as a divinity, but also and at the same time as a statue journeying from Uruk to Kutha. Without exploring this in any detail, one may safely accept this proposition: it tallies with the evidence from other literary texts describing divine journeys, and also with what one presumes to be one level of meaning of the Temple Hymns.

(2) is much more than a catalog. It contains many interesting observations and clarifies Inanna/Ištar's character as Venus, while also discussing her relationship to cognate divine figures, and, most importantly, her sexual nature and the implications thereof. Since a strong point is made of her (resulting) ambivalence one might well think that my totally different approach finds at least some reinforcement in Heimpel's observations.

Relations and Conflicts between Egyptian Gods, particularly in the Divine Ennead of Heliopolis

H. te Velde

1. RELATIONS BETWEEN GODS AND POLYTHEISM

The Egyptian religion was a polytheistic religion. Participants in a polytheistic religion assume that their gods have mutual relationships, of a positive or negative nature, that they form a constellation to use a term of Assmann. Such a constellation may be strongly developed or prove to be rudimentary. In the course of history all kind of alterations may take place in the constellation. Old established gods with many relationships may fade away to a name or even disappear entirely. Newcomers will often have a rather isolated position. When one can follow the historical course of a culture's religion over thousands of years, as we can in Egypt, the pantheon of its central authority, i.e. the royal court, proves to consist of a permanent nucleus of gods and goddesses but also of many divinities who are but sojourners there; in any case we can see that there may be a good deal of change in the mutual relations of the gods. The way the gods are related is indeed essential in the polytheistic Egyptian religion.

Sometimes, especially when gods are concerned of no more than local significance, the relation may be no more than a vague colleagueship. Since many gods were not recognized over the whole country it was presumably not considered necessary to determine and specify their relationships with all manner of gods with whom they did not come into direct contact through festivals or other occasions. But when, after having lived in retirement for centuries, a god begins to be active on occasions reaching beyond his own locality, as for instance by taking part in the national Sed festival, then he suddenly proves to be a manifestation (ba) or son of the sun-god or of some other god or goddess. In the documents, which naturally reflect the situation of a particular moment, it may happen that a great deal is said about one particular god without a full account being given of his relations with other gods. Working out the relationships between gods, however, was an important and favourite task of Egyptian priests. Prominent gods Ptah, Sokaris and Osiris can be conjoined to form a single god Ptah-Sokaris-Osiris, while at the same time these gods continue to exist individually with their specific traits of handicraft and arising life. One of the aspects of the originally abscure god Amon proves to be of the nature of the sun and the name Re is then added to his name as a determinative. Amen-Re then takes up the very important place of king of the gods, with many relationships with numerous gods and particularly goddesses. The Asiatic goddess Astarte can be given citizenship or godhood in Egypt and be adopted as daughter of Ptah. In spite of her nationalization and adoption, exotic peculiarities, such as riding naked upon a horse, a thing hardly done by Egyptian goddesses, are not denied her.

The god Amon of Karnak has at first a rather vague and undefined relationship with the goddess Amaunet 'who dwells in Karnak'. To judge by this name, however, the relationship must surely have been of ancient date and very close; quite recently it has been characterized as that of 'Muttergattin'. In the course of the 16th. century B.C. the cult of the goddess Mut, who had already been worshipped for centuries in the little provincial town of Megen, was introduced into the capital.

She is then called a daughter of Amon and soon forms an established triad with Amon and Khonsu after the model: father-mother-son. Amaunet maintains her place in the Theban constellation of gods as 'the who dwells in Karnak', but Amon and Mut remain a permanent pair within and without Karnak until the end of the Egyptian religion.

Relationships between gods develop and are lasting, especially on a local level. Some divine relationships, e.g. those of the ennead of Heliopolis, attain to and maintain national importance quite transcending their local beginnings. For that matter, interlocal relations were not precluded. The god Horus of Edfu and the goddess Hathor of Denderah, whose temples were many hundreds of kilometres apart, maintained a relationship (of Living-Apart-Together) by bringing each other an annual visit, which was most exuberantly celebrated.

Often we do not have sufficient data to be able to make out the nature or even the existence of relations between gods. Also, the participants in the Egyptian religion have never fully mapped out the network of divine relationships. They continued working upon it until the Egyptian religion perished.

In the scope of the present article it is not possible to give even a rough sketch of the whole panorama of relations between the gods in the Egyptian religion. Even the old question whether there was a single Egyptian religion, or a plurality of Egyptian religions with separate networks of divine relationships, must remain unaswered here.

2. ALLIANCES BETWEEN GODS AND ENNEADS

When one sets out to seek for alliances between gods in the Egyptian religion, one automatically comes to those groupings of gods that are called enneads. When Van Baaren (Mensen tussen Nijl en Zon, p.43) proposes to introduce the reader to the principal Egyptian gods, he writes: 'I begin with the sun-god and with the ennead of Heliopolis to which Osiris belongs, and after that will treat a number of gods in alphabetical order'.

The ennead of Heliopolis consists of nine gods. This would seem self-evident, since the word psḏ.t (ennead) signifies a nonary. It is not superfluous to note this, however, as quite a number of groups of gods are known that consist of more and fewer than nine, and are still called enneads. As a rule, the names of the gods and goddesses of the ennead of Heliopolis are: Atum, Shu and Tefnut, Geb and Nut, Osiris and Isis, Seth and Nephthys. Already in the Pyramid texts the retiring figure of the goddess Nephthys is sometimes replaced by the goddess Neith, while in later times the god Seth, not because of inconspiciousness but rather on account of his controversial behaviour, tends to be replaced by some other god, e.g. Horus or Thoth. On the other hand Horus is sometimes called the tenth god, while Thoth usually fills the part of scribe of the ennead, a kind of officially allocated secretary. This function, subordinate in form, should however be regarded in the light of the Egyptian society in which the state official and scribe had an influential position. Already in the Pyramid Texts, but especially in later times we repeatedly see the afore-mentioned names added to or even replaced by the names of other gods and personifications.

Thus the names of the members of the ennead and even their number are not definitely fixed . This variation in names and number is already found in texts of more than local, of national significance such as Pyramid texts and Coffin Texts and Book of the Dead, but is very marked indeed in temple texts of various places. The great ennead of Karnak numbered fifteen gods: Month, the nine Heliopolitan gods named above, and in addition Horus, Hathor (not though of Denderah, but of Gebelein), Sobek, Tjenenet and Iunet. Apart from the Heliopolitan set, these gods had temples in the Theban nome. Thoth's divine status was clearly not of sufficient degree to give him an entry into this great ennead. He was, though, accounted no. one of the small ennead of Karnak which also included Harendotes, Wepwawet of the south, Wepwawet of the north, Sobek lord of the Iuntiu, Ptah-upon-his-great throne, Anubis lord of Ta-djeser, Ptah-at-the-head-of-the-gods, Dedwen-at-the-head-of-Nubia, Dewenawi, Merimutef and the four children of Horus. Amon of Karnak presided the greater and the small ennead. At first it seems peculiar that the two other members of the triad of Karnak, Mut and Khonsu, are not named, whereas even the Nubian god Dedwen has been given a place, be it in the small ennead. Presumably these two, who like Montu had important temples in Karnak, could not be simply ranged in these groupings. As part of Amon's immediate family they already occupied a place of exception. In Abydos, however, Amon,Mut and Khonsu are placed before Re, Shu, Tefnut, Geb, Nut and Wepwawet in an ennead of nine gods, in which the name of Osiris is lacking. Other documents show the ennead of Abydos to be composed of seven gods (two Khnum-gods, Thoth, Horus, Harendotes and two Wepwawet-gods) or of twelve gods (Osiris, Harendotes, Isis Nephthys, Min, Iunmutef, Re-Harachte, Onuris, Tefnut, Get, Thoth and Hathor). We can understand that the name of Seth, the murderer of Osiris, never appears in the ennead of Abydos, the sacred city of Osiris. After all there were limits, however much the number and the names of the members of the ennead of Abydos might vary.

The examples given above are only a comparatively arbitrary sample from the data concerning enneads, in which there is even a much greater variation as to names and number of the members than summarily indicated here. Further information is to be found in the book by W. Barta, 'Untersuchungen zum Götterkreis der Neunheit', Berlin 1973, which contains a list of 84 enneads.

The complicated information to be found about the enneads in textual and visual material led to a controversy quite in the beginning of the investigation, around the middle of last century, which has not yet been overcome. Brugsch and others regarded an ennead as a 'Neungötterkreis' (a squared plural: 3x3). The word controversy is not exaggerated. Not long ago J.G. Griffiths, 'The Origins of Osiris, Leiden 1980 (2), 121, n.135, repeated the opinion he had formerly set forth: 'Kees (Götterglaube, 158) misleads therefore,when he suggests that the number three is the basic unit of the Ennead in the sense of undetermined plurality (unbegrenzte Vielheit)'. His historical-genetic view is, that in origin the ennead meant a certain group of nine gods, and that the word was then used in a derivative sense in referring to other groups of gods whose number might be more or less than nine.

Nevertheless, every ennead is an alliance of gods, and so is the ennead of Heliopolis. How and when, historically speaking, this ennead came into being cannot be ascertained. The earliest data showing the existence of the ennead of Heliopolis compared with other enneads is that it is set forth as a family group and in order of seniority. It is a reasonable assuption that the term of ennead for an alliance of gods was borrowed from the Heliopolitan theology by the priests of other temples. Evidently priests of other temples interpreted the term ennead not as a circle of nine gods, but as a circle of a plurality of gods. This was possible because the ennead of Heliopolis did not merely function as nine personifications in the creational doctrine of Heliopolis, like the ennead of Karnak, also functioned as the retinue of the council of the god, who was regarded as the principal god. As we shall see below, the ennead of Heliopolis also functioned as a court of justice, e.g. in the judging of the dead.

3. RELATIONSHIPS AND CONFLICTS BETWEEN GODS IN THE ENNEAD OF HELIOPOLIS.

A. FAMILY RELATIONSHIPS

It was already remarked that the special thing about the ennead of Heliopolis is that the gods and goddesses are ordered according to their ages and as a family group. They constitute a genealogy for Horus the tenth god: the pharaoh is a Horus and was traditionally crowned in Heliopolis. It is possible to regard the mythology of Heliopolis as a mythology of creation. Here we shall mainly take notice of the relations and conflicts in this family of gods consisting of four generations. Atum belongs to the first, Shu and Tefnut to the second, Geb and Nut to the third and Osiris and Isis and Seth and Nephthys to the fourth generation. As members of the ennead these gods constitute an alliance which remains directed upon the actuality of human affaires and sees to it, for instance, that Egypt gets the right pharaoh in the form of Horus.

Special relations and conflicts are hardly seen at all between grandparents and grandchildren, between Atum and Geb and Nut, between Shu and Tefnut and Osiris, Isis, Seth and Nephthys, if we except the situation of conflict between Seth and the Ennead. The Egyptian language has no special words for grandfather, grandmother, grandson and granddaughter, unless one were to recognize father's father and similar terms as such, expressions that are, however, never used in connection with the ennead. Special relations and conflicts do occur between members of the same generation (brothers and sisters) or, to a far less extent, between successive generations (father, mother, son, daughter).

The Egyptian language is in general poorly provided with terms of kinship , which is not surprising in an urban culture, where the family group consisted of parents and children and perhaps unrelated persons also belonging to the household. Hardly any other terms of kinship are known than those mentioned above. Only recently has it been established that a certain rather rare word must signify mother-in-law. In the Egyptian language indeed things, e.g. parts of the body, are often not indicated by specific terms, but by paraphrases. This is also the case with terms of relationship: uncle was paraphrased as brother of the mother. The Egyptian word that is translated as brother is also a paraphrase: sn is the number two. It can be used to indicate the opponent in a lawsuit without conveying the meaning that claimant and defendant are blood-relations. Furthermore brother (sn) and sister (sn.t) are also terms that can signify a marital relationship. We can conclude from the above that the apparent contradiction that Seth is called both brother (sn) of Osiris and brother of the mother, i.e. Isis (sn n mwt) and also brother (sn) of Horus, the son of Isis and Osiris, a matter that has been so much discussed and which has often been explained as the confusing of two originally separate traditions, is really no more than a problem of translation. When it is to be stressed that Horus is not inferior to Seth but is his equal, then the gods are called the two brothers (sn.wy), but when Horus is regarded as still a little child or a minor, then Seth is his mother's brother.

B. THE ONENESS OF ATUM

In the beginning there were no gods, no relations and no conflicts. Then there was a god all alone: Atum, whose name is connected with an Egyptian word (tm) that can mean everthing and nothing. He came forth from the primaeval waters (Nun). Nun is sometimes called the father of the gods, but there is no question of a relation between Nun and Atum, for Nun is not real. It is expressly stated that Atum originated by himself (ḫpr ḏsf). Atum has problems with himself, and indulges in solosex:

> I am he who came into being as Khepri. When I had come into being, being(itself) came into being, and all beings came into being, and all beings came into being after I came into being. Many were the beings which came into being, before the ground and creeping things had been created in this place. I put together (some) of them in Nun as weary ones, before I could find a place in which I might stand. It (seemed) advantageous to me in my heart; I planned with my face; and I made (in concept) every form when I was alone, before I had spat out what was Shu, before I had sputtered out what was Tefnut, and before (any) other had come into being who could act with me.
>
> I planned in my own heart, and there came into being a multitude of forms of beings, the forms of children and the forms of their children. I was the one who copulated with my fist, I masturbated with my hand. Then I spewed with my own mouth: I spat out what was

> Shu, and I sputtered out what was Tefnut.
>
> Pap.Bremner-Rhind 26, 21 ff.
> Translation J.A.Wilson in: J.B. Pritchard, Ancient Near Eastern Texts, Princeton 1955, 6f.

The problem is loneliness, for Atum has no partner as the gods of the subsequent generations have. As was mentioned before, Amon too appears as president of the great and the small ennead of Karnak without a partner, without Amaunet of Mut and Khonsu. In Heliopolis Atum too could form a triad with the goddesses Hathor-Nebet-Hetepet and Saosis, who were venerated in temples there. Their names indicate the female and male sexual organs (ḥtpt 'bliss', etc., iw.s-^{c}3 .s 'she comes while she grows large'). These two goddesses could also be conjoined in a single figure: the hand; a word also used in the above quotation. The word mouth, too, from which Shu and Tefnut emerge, can indicate the vulva in erotic Egyptian literature. In this quotation however and in many other texts the goddesses remain reduced to part of the body of Atum, who is alone. Nor does the goddess Temet obtain an independent place in the ennead as companion or daughter of Atum.

One might wonder in how far this lonely place of the creator-god corresponds to the monarchial state in a culture that has an otherwise polytheistic religion. The pharaoh, however, is king of Upper-Egypt and king of Lower-Egypts. It is a dual kingship. In the Egyptian culture solitude was pitiable and even suspect and reprehensible. The dissolute Sethian man is an 'Einzelgänger'. The Man who is weary of life is at the point of despair because there is no one he can talk to. The motif of loneliness returns in the mythology of the ennead as a result of the grave situation of conflict caused by Seth: Isis bears Horus in the solitude of the marshes of Khemnis.

Osiris is killed by Seth in the desert according to some versions but loneliness is localized in the marshes or in the Nun, where Atum was alone. Frankfort (Ancient Egyptian Religion, paperback ed. 154) says in another connection: 'The waters of chaos and the primeval hill formed a sort of landscape of 'the first time' which played as great a part in the religious imagination of the Egyptians as did the Judaean hills with the Garden of Gethsemane and the Mount of Golgotha in that of Christians'. A god all alone is balanced between being and non-being. 'Hier stossen wir auf den gedanklichen Grund des ägyptischen Polytheismus: Göttliches muss, sofern es seiend ist, differenziert sein' (Hornung, Der Eine und die Vielen,171).

The transition from a single divine being to an alliance of gods with all the relational problems involved, was considered necessary and natural. Thus the one god becomes three gods: Atum, Shu and Tefnut. In hieroglyphic writing three equals the plural. Shu and Tefnut are the first pair differentiated as man and woman. Thus the problem of the loneliness of the androgynous creator-god, who has problems with himself, is moved on to the problem of the relation between man and woman.

C. THE TWO-IN-ONENESS OF SHU AND TEFNUT

Shu and Tefnut are the twins. These two gods, almost inseparable in the texts, are the double lion or the pair of lions, or the pair of eyes or the pair who procreated the gods. The first female being was already prefigured by parts of Atum's body: not Atum's rib, but Atum's hand, penis of Atum and Eye of Re. These female aspects of Re or Atum, for the names of these two gods can be used interchangeable, are now carried over to Tefnut, whose epitheton is often not only daughter of Re, but also eye of Re, as with many Egyptian goddesses who are regarded as an Eve .

In the tangle of multitudinous allusions to the myth of the sun's eye in Egyptian texts it is not always easy to find one's way: it is stated that when Re's one eye returns from searching for Shu and Tefnut, as they had been spewed out, it becomes angry because its (in Egyptian her) place has been taken by another eye. Egyptian texts, that so often speak of the loneliness of Atum, sometimes also refer to the primeval time before there was any duality. This implies that at that time Atum did not yet have two eyes, but was one-eyed. The myth of the half-man that is current in some cultures, does not lie at the surface though in Egyptian texts. As far as I know it has never been written about in Egyptological literature. Shu and Tefnut, as we saw, are the pair of eyes. Tefnut does not accept her partner and goes off as the furious eye of the sun to more southern parts where she retires to the solitude of the dessert as a growling and sulky lioness.

Shu then sets out to fetch her back, seconded by Thoth, the professional secretary of the ennead, who is always there when he is needed. After almost endless attempts at conciliation by Thoth, the ape, the male and the female deity are reconciled, and the furious lioness changes into a charming pussy-cat. The lability of the relationship between that inseparable pair, Shu and Tefnut, clearly shows when we see that at the slightest provocation Tefnut, the Nubian cat, can change into a malevolent lioness.

A variant of the myth of the angry eye is to be found in the tale of the destruction of mankind or of the deluge Re sends forth his eye, his daughter, there called the goddess Hathor, as the terrible lion goddess Sakhmet to defeat the people, who had rebelled against him. Re himself then brings peace by pouring out red beer over the world, which the bloodthirsty goddess takes for blood and begins to drink, so that she becomes drunk, stops slaughtering the people and loses her evil humours.

The triumphant return from Nubia and the calming of the raging eye of the sun was exuberantly celebrated in and around the temples of many Egyptian goddesses. A not unimportant and often mentioned title of a male functionary in the temple of Mut in Karnak was that of Embracer of the Eye.

D. THE TWO-NESS OF GEB AND NUT.

The oneness of Atum, which was transformed into the two-in-ness of Geb and Nut. The begetting and birth of Geb and Nut may very well have been regarded as so normal that it was not thought necessary to pay special attention to it. Tefnut is not a celebrated mother goddess like Isis or Nut, she is the inseparable companion of Shu. Judging by the texts, it is not the birth but the separation of Geb and Nut that is the important mythological point. The reason is sometimes given that in their alliance, which as we may indirectly conclude from the iconography consisted of an endless coition, Geb and Nut quarrelled because like a sow that eats up her own litter, Nut swallowed up her children the sun, moon and stars. The result of the separation of the earth-god Geb and the sky-goddess Nut was the forming of the course along the sky which sun, moon and stars could pass along to fill the world with light and life. In contrast with divine pairs of heaven and earth in many other countries, the earth-god in Egypt is male and the sky-goddess female. In Egypt water did not rain down from the sky, which elsewhere could be regarded as the semen of the sky-god impregnating the earth-goddess, but came from the inundation of the Nile, that is to say from the earth, which thus was to be regarded as male.

Naturally heaven and earth continue to form a unity, but then it must be expressly added that this unity was looked upon as differentiated. Heaven and earth are concepts that belong together, but that in the Egyptian language cannot be replaced by any single word such as cosmos or world, neither in the singular nor in the pural. Geb and Nut are not considered to be twins like Shu and Tefnut. There is no textual or iconographical material to be found which could confirm the supposition that the Egyptians assumed that heaven and earth, Geb and Nut, conjoined each night. A conjunction of heaven and earth,i.e. the collapse of the sky, was not thought impossible but it was looked upon as a cosmic catastrophe, a threat that gods and magicians might use, but that could not take place unless perhaps at the end of time. The differentiation of Geb and Nut was deeper than that of Shu and Tefnut.

E THE CONFUSION AND ORDERING OF PLURALITY IN THE FOURTH GENERATION

After the oneness of Atum, the two-in-oneness of Shu and Tefnut, the two-ness of Geb and Nut one would finally expect a triad. The triad is the ideal divine formation in Egypt. This triad does indeed appear in its familiar form: Osiris, Isis and Horus with the variant Isis, Nephthys and Horus, but before getting so far a complicating factor was worked into the structure of the ennead. This was the coming of the god Seth that according to an Egyptian text was the beginning of confusion (ẖnnw). Though Seth is the symbol of confusion, he is all the same included in the ennead. The ennead represents a higher order, higher than the order of duality of the triad, and in this order the element of disorder and confusion is integrated. This would seem to be the chief raison d'être of the ennead. Not only is chaotic plurality ordered, but also that which pre-eminently symbolizes confusion is admitted and ordered in the perfect number nine.

The order of one divine pair (Shu and Tefnut) generating a following divine pair (Geb and Nut), is now broken: in fourth generation of gods we see not the one divine pair Osiris and Isis, but also Seth and Nephthys.

Nephthys is a rather colourless figure in the Egyptian world of gods. Within the ennead she seems to be a double of Isis, except that she does not represent all the aspects of Isis. Her name means mistress of the palace, yet she is not like Isis the model of conjugal fidelity and motherhood. Neither, however, is Nephthys a sex symbol like Hathor for instance, whereas the immoderate, disorderly sexual energy of Seth directed both hetero- and homosexually is well-known. There is a variant according to which Nephthys, who is sometimes said to lack a vulva, did not remain childless. Her child Anubis though was not supposed to have been begotten by her official partner but by Osiris. For the rest, Nephthys plays those parts in mythology that women without a husband filled in the Egyptian society, i.e. as wailing-woman and nursemaid. She helps Isis to lament Osiris and to bring up Horus. Isis and Nephthys are called the two sisters and the two women, as Horus and Seth are called the two men and the two brothers.

In so far as Seth and Nephthys are really accounted a pair, they form the anti-pair of Osiris and Isis. The relation between the pairs Osiris-Isis and Seth-Nephthys was not symmetrical, for Seth was the 'trickster', the 'god of confusion', who brought death into the world by murdering Osiris. Isis, famous as a woman of magic, cares for the dead body of Osiris, conceives by him his heir Horus, and through her astuteness manages to escape the assaults of Seth and bears and brings up her child in solitude. Sometimes Isis is said to have been assisted in her lonely position by Nephthys. When Isis thinks Horus is old enough, the law-suit begins for the office of Osiris, that is to rule over the world as king, and then the conflicts between Horus and Seth arise.

When the two gods, the two lords, the two men (rḥwy), the two combatants are mentioned by name, Horus as the prototype of the Egyptian gentleman-king always comes first and Seth as the spirit of disorder comes second, for Horus has the more central and Seth the more peripheral position. Together they rule over the world through the pharaoh whom they purify and crown, but each has his own half of the world, Lower Egypt and Upper Egypt or the Black Land (home country) and the Red Land (foreign country). Not only the bipartition of the world, but also many other contrasts could be connected with Horus and Seth: north and south, heaven and earth, earth and underworld, right and left, black and red, being born and being conceived , rulership and strength, life and dominion. Horus and Seth not only oppose each other in sporting contests, using all kinds of legitimate means of clever tricks, they also commit various acts of violence, so that Horus lost the light of his eye and Seth the semen of his testicles. Seth even induced his nephew Horus to take part in paederastic acts. The fruit of this homosexual relation was the moon or Thoth,the 'son of the two lords'. Helped by his mother Isis Horus gains the upper hand of Seth, but Seth is not totally destroyed. The juridical proceedings do not invariably result in Horus being proclaimed the victor and Seth being condemned as the looser even though Horus is pronounced to be justified with regard to Seth. The two gods are separated and the quarrel is settled. When offerings are made it is said that Horus is given his eye, but sometimes also that Seth is given his testicles. The justification of Horus certainly already had an exclusive tendency and led to some, chiefly later, exclusive variants of the myth. Horus and Seth, who are reconciled, unite the two lands, so that the pharaoh can rule over a country of order, unity and peace. Yet this fair cosmos was preceded by a chaos of disorder, dissension and strife. The pharaoh is a Horus reconciled to Seth or a gentleman in whom the spirit of disorder has been integrated.

FINAL REMARKS.

The pharaoh is the representative of the cosmic order. The ennead is his family tree. This does not mean, however, that the ennead itself belongs to primaeval times and is no longer of present importance for the world of men. It continues to function as a kind of council of elders. When the people rebel against the sun-god, the latter convokes his Eye, Shu and Tefnut, Geb and Nut and the fathers and mothers who are in Nun to consult with them what must be done. The ennead, that as a court of Justice has judged the case of Horus and Seth or of Osiris and Seth, continues to function as a body of judges that justifies a man who has died against possible enemies at the judgment of the dead. Also a man living upon earth who feels he has been wronged by someone who has died, can try to obtain redress from this high court. In accordance with this judicial function the ennead may function as a less strict commission of reception in the realm of the dead and welcome a defunct person like a king. An extension of this is the lifegiving function of the ennead that is so often mentioned.

The ennead also continues to play a contemporary part

as retinue and council of prominent gods, as appears e.g. in various hymns to the gods. The official presidency of the ennead may be assigned to others of its male members and is not automatically exercized by the eldest god Atum-Re. Important gods from outside such as Amon-Re are sometimes also named as president of the ennead of Heliopolis, which is then no more than a retinue.

The secretariate of the ennead is not exercized by the members in turn, but is the permanent task of the officially adjudicated secretary Thoth, the scribe of the ennead and the lord of the divine words (hieroglyphs). It is just because of this technical-administrative function that Thoth is important as mediator. As moon-god Thoth can provide light in the absence of the sun-god, whose substitute he is said to be. We have already mentioned Thoth's intercession in the conflict between Shu and Tefnut. In illustrations representing the separation of Geb and Nut by Shu, Thoth is also often depicted standing beside them. Thoth also played an important part during the confusion of the fourth generation. His official task as functionary secretary required impartiality, but reproach that the functional secretary was manipulating affairs is not far to seek. The Pyramid Texts already transmit that not only Seth but also Thoth failed to lament for Osiris after his murder. In this connection it has been remarked (H. Jacobsohn, 'Das Gegensatzproblem im altägyptischen Mythos, in:Studien zur analytischen Psychologie C.G. Jungs II, Zürich 1955, 191) that 'Seth, eine prahlerische Kraftnatur und notorischer Tölpel und Rüpel, war zu einer solchen Gewalttat leicht zu verführen. Thoth aber war der Gott, der genau wusste was er wollte. Er hatte offenbar das ganze göttliche Drama in Gang gesetzt'. Thoth was also deeply involved in the contentions of Horus and Seth, so that he can even be called 'the son of the two lords', that is to say a creature resulting from their paederastic relations. In cases where besides the ennead as a whole or one of its changing presidents Thoth is also named as the one who separates and reconciles the warring gods Horus and Seth, this should rather be understood as a measure of technical administration than as the act of statesmenship itself. Yet in a civilization with an extensive bureaucracy of officials and where so much had to be put down in writing, the position of this divine scribe can hardly be overestimated, and it must be admitted that Thoth filled a key position in the ennead.

Finally it can be pointed out that in the world of men the ennead remained known as a group of gods venerated especially in Heliopolis. As hardly anything remains of the town and temples of Heliopolis, very little indeed is known of this. Since Heliopolis was of old, in any case from the time of origin of the Pyramid texts until the breaking up of the Egyptian religion, one of the most important religious centres of Egypt, the ennead of XXXX,Heliopolis had a more than local importance and was the alliance of gods whose mutual relations and conflicts were known everywhere.

I express my thanks to mrs. G. van Baaren-Pape, who translated the Dutch text of this paper into English.

Changes of Belief in Spiritual Beings, Prophethood, and the Rise of Islam

J. Waardenburg

Quite a few studies about religion in ancient Arabia,in particular Central Arabia including the Hejāz, concentrate on the religious situation before Islam and aim to discover what continuities and differences there were between the ancient religion and Islam. Our problem here is slightly different, namely: what changes in the relationships between groups of spiritual beings - including both deities and spirits - of the ancient religion may have taken place before the rise of Islam ? To what extent do these changes foreshadow the new kind of classification of spiritual beings which would be proclaimed in the Koran and become accepted and curring in Islam ?

In these changes of relationship between spiritual beings there is not only a conflict between gods (in which Allah wins), but also a conflict between the high god (Allah) and those spiritual beings called jinn (1) (where Allah is not the unqualified winner). Our focus here is especially on the latter conflict and we shall have to look at the significance which Allah and the lower intermediary spiritual beings had before, during and also after the process of Islamization in Arabia.

The conflict between Allah, the other deities and the jinn must have represented a struggle between various groups and parties in Arabia in the course of time in which Muhammad's claim to prophethood and the movement resulting from it played a decisive role. On the one hand, the religious and ideological development can hardly be understood without references to an earthly history at the end of which the early Muslim community emerged as victor. On the other hand, this historical ending itself cannot be understood adequately without taking into account those changes which occurred in the world of spiritual beings, changes which gave a religious and ideological significance to the earthly course of events. The changes in the function, classification and meaning of spiritual beings took place at the same time as major economic, social and political changes occurred in the societies whose members gave their loyalty to these beings in one way or another.

1 SPIRITUAL BEINGS BEFORE ISLAM

Religious developments among the nomadic Beduin were different from those in the settled areas, oases and towns, among which Mecca deserves special attention here.

A THE BEDUIN

Among the Beduin, according to J. Henninger (Henninger 1959b, 128/9), belief in jinn may have been present since ancient times, although it was probably more developed among the settled people than the nomads, as has been the case more recently. More typical of the Beduin were certain forms of reverence paid to ancestors, on whose graves stones were erected and simple sacrifices made, or to certain heroes from the past who were venerated as founders of tribes and tribal federations, or as bringers of culture. In certain cases a transition from tribal ancestor to tribal god (jadd) may be assumed.

There was also a belief in local deities, who may have evolved out of ancestors or jinn, or may simply have personified the powers of nature, like the storm-god Quzah. They may also have been taken over from settled people in some cases. Later they were called asnām shurakā' etc., but not much is known about the Beduin religious beliefs about them. Of astral gods, which were much worshipped in South Arabia, only Venus had among the Beduin an attested cult. The sun (and the moon?) may have been worshipped, but this deserves further investigation. A god of the earth was unknown among the Beduin. Cults were concentrated at certain places where cult stones (anṣāb) were erected or cult trees grew. White animals (camels, sheep and goats) and milk libations were characteristic of Beduin religion, as well as spring festivals in the month of Rajab with sacrifices of first-born animals. The consecration without bloodshed of animals - living in sacred territory (ḥimā) - is typical of Beduin religious practice. Pilgrimages seem to have developed late and among the sedentary people, not the Beduin.

The veneration of Allāh, whom Henninger holds to be autochthonous in Arabia and of nomadic origin, remained in the background. Allah was venerated before all else as the sky god and the bestower of rain, but he was also seen as the creator of the world even then. Allah was venerated in the whole of Arabia, with sacrifices, oaths and calls on him in times of danger; in South Arabia Raḥīm was a similar supreme high god. Allah (al-ilāhu, the godhead) corresponds with El throughout the Semitic world.

B OASES AND TOWNS

In the oases and towns the situation was different, and various spiritual beings should be distinguished.

a. deities

In the settled areas one of the most striking shifts away from Beduin religion was the increase in the number of deities and a movement toward polytheism which is connected in the Arab tradition with the name of ᶜAmr ibn Luḥayy, who is supposed to have lived in the third century A.D. This development may have had to do not only with the natural requirements of life in an agricultural or urban setting, but also with Hellenistic religious influences from the North. This rise and differentiation of the gods must have occurred parallel to the movement of Beduin to the towns with their social, economic and political differentiation.

Maria Höfner (Höfner 1970, 361-7) assigns the deities venerated in Arabia in the centuries before Muhammad's appearance to the following categories:

1. the high god Allāh, together with
2. the three 'daughters of Allāh' (Manāt, Allāt and al-^{c}Uzza, e.g. Sura 53:19, 20) venerated all over Arabia (al-^{c}Uzza especially by the Meccan Quraysh);
3. the five deities of Noah's contemporaries (Wadd, Suwā^{c}, Yaghūth, Ya^{c}ūq, Nasr);
4. some thirty-five other deities often called by their surnames or titles (*al-*, *dhū-*) of which Hubal is the best known thanks to the fact that his image in human form stood in the Meccan Ka^{c}ba.

Prominent Meccan families had their own house-gods represented by images at home.

All deities had their own creative power and were more active in the course of earthly events than the distant Allāh. In Mecca itself Manāt (destiny), Quzaḥ (thunderstorm) and Hubal (chance and luck) were prominent, besides Allah who may have been the protecting deity of the town, just as other towns had their own tutelary god (2).

These different deities were not brought together in one hierarchically ordered pantheon, nor were they of a very celestial nature; in fact, there does not seem to have been a very great distance between them and the *jinn* as spirits or semi-deities. Ernst Zbinden has observed that *jinn* were often venerated at the same place as these deities, which would imply that they were felt to belong together (Zbinden 1953, 79/80).

b *jinn*

Different etymologies have been given of the word *jinn*, varying from the Arabic root *janna* (so that the meaning would be 'those who are hidden, mysterious' or specifically 'covered' or 'covering') to a derivation from the latin *genius*, or a borrowing from an Aramaic word used by Christians to indicate pagan gods degraded to demons. In the latter case *jinn* would originally have referred to degraded deities.

Different theories have been evolved to interpret or explain the belief in *jinn* among the ancient Arabs (Henninger 1963, 280-2; Henninger 1959b, 121-4). The animistic theory, for instance, of which Wellhausen was an exponent, has enjoyed some popularity; this assumes a more or less linear evolution from polydemonism as represented by the belief in *jinn* to polytheism and finally monotheism. The high gods, including Allah, would thus represent the final stage of a long development starting from the *jinn*. W. Robertson Smith (3) held that the *jinn* were a survival from an earlier, totemic stage of the Beduins' development; the different *jinn*-clans would in this case represent original animal species, each having a special relationship with a given clan or tribe. J. Henninger rightly takes a critical stand towards such general theories of the origin and development of religion as have been applied to Arabian data (Henninger 1963, 282).

Jinn in ancient Arabia are spirits, basically nature spirits, and not ghosts. They are immaterial in the sense that they consist of the elements of fire, smoke and dust, but they can take different forms, notably those of animals. A snake, for instance, can always be a disguised *jinni*. *Jinn* can also take the form of birds and in special cases they appear as human beings. *Jinn* are supposed to reside mostly in deserted places, near trees or ruins, or on particular pieces of land, which means that they have to be placated before Beduin pitch their tents there. Jinn work against the ordinary course of events, mostly causing people different kinds of mishaps, including madness (junūn, lit. 'possession by a jinni'; majnūn, lit. 'possessed by a jinni', means madman). Consequently the ancient Arabs developed a whole series of possible measures which could be taken against such evil spirits, including the wearing of amulets and the pronouncing of exorcisms.

It must be assumed that in ancient Arabia both deities and jinn were venerated in cults; in the case of the former the cult must have been open and public, whereas the cult of jinn may have been largely a private affair of the people concerned. A few Koranic verses testify directly to this ancient cult of jinn. In S. 72:6 it is said that certain men repeatedly sought aid of the jinn, and S. 6:100 states in so many words that the unbelievers made the jinn companions of Allah. S. 37:158 adds that the unbelievers constructed a kinship (nasab) between Allah and the jinn. In S. 34:41 the angels are said to affirm that the unbelievers had worshipped the jinn and had put their faith in them, whereas S. 6:28 is sometimes interpreted as referring to the practice of making sacrifices to the jinn. Certain ancient deities may have arisen from jinn, while some jinn may stand for degraded deities of older times; there are insufficient data to warrant either hypothesis (compare Henninger 1963, 315/6).

J. Chelhod speaks of a continuous rise of the jinn as chthonic powers from the lower to the higher world, a rise which would have been halted by the coming of Islam (Chelhod 1964, 77-80, 93-95). This is connected with Chelhod's theory of a fundamental dualism which he assumes to have characterized the sphere of the invisible, the 'supernatural'. On the one hand, according to him, there was the notion of a higher world which was ordered, close to heaven and inhabited by the celestial powers, and, on the other hand, the lower world which was chaotic, beneath the earth and inhabited by the chthonic powers. Since, according to this theory, both the higher and the lower world, as religious realities, share the sacred quality, the pure-impure polarity characteristic of the sacred itself runs parallel to the opposition between higher and lower world, the former being charaterized by purity, the latter by impurity. The high god Allah (El) represents the hidden energy which is the very source of the sacred sphere. The sun goddess would represent a link between both religious worlds, and the jinn are permanently seeking to rise from the lower to the higher world in order to obtain deity status in a movement of purification. Somewhat imprecisely (4) Chelhod refers to remnants of an ancient myth according to which the jinn gave their daughters as wives to Allah; out of these unions were born the angels (represented by the stars), the children of Allah and the jinn. In this myth the elements of the higher and the lower world are combined into a unified whole.

The upward movement of the jinn follows from Cheldhod's structural scheme of interpretation. Toufic Fahd, who does not accept this scheme, remarks (Fahd 1971, 190) on the one hand that it is hard to imagine how spirits without individuality or personality and of a profoundly anonymous nature, could ever be assimilated to deities which at least to a considerable extent were individualized and personified. On the other hand, Fahd does not exclude the possiblity that in certain cases jinn represents degraded deities of older times or from elsewhere. The jinn can act positively towards mankind and, even though they are not themselves individualized or personified, they can very well stand in a permanent relationship to individuals or groups of people. They do not need for that matter to be considered necessarily as gods; their superiority in the eyes of men is given anyhow with the fact that they have weightless bodies and that they are able to perform actions far beyond human powers.

In some cases, particular jinn can acquire a degree of individuality, especially through having access to sources of knowledge inaccessible to mankind. Thus the inspiration of a diviner (kāhin or ᶜarrāf) and of a poet (shāᶜir) was ascribed in ancient times and also in the Koran to a being 'covered' by a particular jinni, who communicated to the human being possessed in this way powerful utterances concerning reality and the future. All 'supernatural' knowledge, indeed, was ascribed by the ancient Arabs to jinn. S. 72:9 mentions that jinn could listen at the heavenly gates and learn what divine plans and intentions were elaborated in heaven; then they could report this knowledge to particular human beings. Ernst Zbinden is right when he characterizes jinn as 'mediators of revelation' (Offenbarungsvermittler) in Arabian religion before Islam (Zbinden 1953,12).

c angels

It is certain that, among the ancient Arabs, the Meccans at least believed in angels, whether as jinn-like beings without divine qualities, or as 'daughters of Allah' and thus nearer to the high god. In the Koran, S. 6:8, 11:12 and 17:95 mention that Muhammad's Meccan opponents asked him to make them acquainted with his 'angel' in order to prove his prophethood to them. Consequently, they must have known that angels are sent to certain chosen individuals like prophets. On the other hand, S. 17:40, 43:19 and 53:27 state explicitly that the Meccans had made the angels 'female beings' who would then be companions or daughters of Allah, and S. 53:26 shows that these angels were thought to be able to intercede for man before Allah. Chelhod believes that the concept of 'angel' indicates a stage in the rise of jinn to the heavenly spheres, and he tries to show that the angels always remain in communication with the jinn and the lower world. He stresses in this connection the mythical view that the angels are the children of unions between Allah and daughters of the jinn (Chelhod 1964, 79/80).

'd shayṭāns

In ancient Arabia, shayṭāns were thought to be serpents and, like jinni's, they could attach themselves to a human being in order to inspire him. They had no demonic character in the current sense of the world, and their role was negligible compared to that of the jinn.

e Allāh

Several arguments have been adduced to establish that already before Muhammad's birth polytheism was on the wane and there was a movement toward monotheism in and around Mecca. One argument is that the economic expansion of the Quraysh and the Meccan confederation brought with it the need for a broader kind of religion to which any Arab could adhere. Chelhod (Chelhod 1964, 104) even speaks of the birth of a 'national' religion and sees a broadening and growth in the role of Allah which would be reflected in his taking over the prerogatives of Qamar, the moon-god and old Lord of Heaven (Chelhod 1964, 96 and 104). He also observes before the rise of Islam the spread of a common religious terminology throughout Arabia, at the same time that power is centralized in Allah in the heavenly sphere.

Toufic Fahd, in his interpretation of Allah as al-Ilāh, with an impersonal character ('the godhead'), holds that before

Islam Allah was '... un appellatif applicable à toute divinité supérieure du panthéon arabe' (Fahd 1968, 44). The Arabs, in his view, always invoked Allah as '... le dénominateur commun entre toutes les divinités du panthéon' (Fahd 1968, 253). Behind the different symbols, names and attributes of a divine nature which were used, the Arabs were essentially conscious of the working of one unique godhead, al-Ilāh. There was a long monotheistic tradition; only those who were called mushrikūn substituted for the cult of the godhead that of his names and attributes.

The foregoing remarks suggest that religion in Central Arabia up to the seventh century of our era was neither everywhere the same, nor fixed in its forms or free from internal conflicts. Different religious traditions existed among the Beduin and the settled people; there was a great proliferation of gods and goddesses with cults some of which rose while others fell; deities and jinn could move towards or away from each other; finally there was a tension between the veneration of the high god Allah on the one hand and that of 'his daughters', other deities and jinn on the other hand.

Such shifts and changes in the spiritual world must have been directly or indirectly connected with the sedentarisation of nomads, new religious needs in the oases and towns in the course of their development, and the rise of Mecca's hegemony in the sixth century A.D. in particular. For such social, economic and political developments changed the context in which people lived, which in turn had important repercussions for morality and religion. The Arab awareness of having one religious tradition in common notwithstanding the development of local traditions - with common forms of ritual behaviour, a common pilgrimage in the month Rajab and a common veneration of Allah and his 'daughters' - is bound up with common patterns of trade, political allegiances and the deep awareness of constituting one people notwithstanding the constant strife and struggle between tribes and clans, and notwithstanding the political ambitions of cities like Mecca under the Quraysh.

This is not to speak of influences from South Arabia and indirectly Ethiopia, the Northern fringe of Arabia and indirectly Byzantium and Persia on the Central Arabian scene, or to take into account the presence of certain Christian and Jewish communities in Arabia. There is reason to suppose that by the end of the sixth century A.D. the belief in a multitude of deities was on the downturn but that their worship was retained as a public ritual, at least in Mecca. There is also reason to suppose that the belief both in a distant high god Allah and in the working of <u>jinn</u> - not only as disturbing elements but also as inspirers of divination, poetry and music - had not diminished. Our contention then is that the transition to Islam should be seen historically as part of a total internal development process which had been under way for centuries. In the course of this process Jewish and Christian elements were assimilated to the ideological structure, and there arose a tendency towards universality over against the existing local cults. This tendency assumed an ultimate religious character in the revelatory events which overtook Muhammad. His role in this overall process, with all its religious, ideological, social, economic and, of course, political aspects was vital. The radical changes introduced by the Koran into the relations between Allah on the one hand, and the deities and <u>jinn</u> on the other testify to the way in which Allah was now seen as playing a more active role on earth. But we shall first look at some data brought to light North of Arabia proper: in Palmyra.

2 A SIDELIGHT FROM PALMYRA

Since most of the data advanced until now have reached us through Muslim sources which had an interest in playing down the role of the jinn, we should see whether sources from elsewhere can throw some light on the classification of spiritual beings in Arabia before Islam and on the jinn in particular(5).

Already in 1949 Jean Starcky wrote (Henri Seyrig et Jean Starcky 1949, 248-257) that the term GNY' found in inscriptions around Palmyra was derived from Arabic, the Arabic janā or janiy (to stretch) being related to the verb ganan, GN standing in all Semitic languages for 'to cover, to protect' (p.255). Starcky held that the first inscriptions about jinn were Safaitic ones in North Arabia and that later inscriptions found in the Syrian desert were a result of Arab invasions during the second half of the first millennium B.C. The Palmyrene inscription of GNY' date from the second and third century. They speak of a ginnayā (pl. ginnayē), of which Starcky stressed the tutelary function and in which he saw one deity. Starcky also pursued an earlier observation by Henri Lammens (6) about an ancient masjid al-jinn which existed in Mecca and W.Albright's hypothesis (7) that the jinn could have been deities from elsewhere which were accepted relatively late by the Arabs. Starcky submitted that before Islam the jinn might very well have been considered by the Arabs as gods '.. quoique leur rôle bienfaisant ne soit guère marqué' (p. 256). Some twenty years later, in 1970/1, Daniel Schlumberger, while refuting Starcky's idea that ginnayā was a proper name, also stressed that the word GNY' (meaning 'divinity' in Palmyrene) was of Arabic origin (Schlumberger 1970/1). This term was used in the arabised Syrian steppe and desert, whereas its equivalent 'LH' was used in towns like Palmyra where Aramaic was the culture language. Both Starcky and Schlumberger stressed the importance of the Arabic concept of jinn in the Palmyran region and pointed out that the concept referred not to spirits but to deities.

The discussion about the relationship between monotheism and spiritual beings in the Near East during the Hellenistic period took a new turn with Javier Teixidor's investigations into the relevant inscriptions in the Northern Arabian area. In his study of 1977 (Teixidor 1977), the author was able to show trends in popular piety in the first centuries B.C. which were quite distinct from Hellenistic religious patterns more current among the intellectual classes. Teixidor maintains that monotheism has always been latent among the Semites (p.13), but that the Near Eastern inscriptions from about 500 B.C. onward show a clear trend toward a practical monotheism (p.161), with a fidelity simultaneously to a supreme god and to more specialized 'deputy' gods and angels with specific functions in the world (p. 15-17). As a general pattern the worship of a supreme god simply coexisted with that of other minor gods, and in North Arabia worship was probably directed towards a unique god who was believed to manifest himself in a plurality of ways (p.75/6). Basically, according to this view, there was no Arabian 'pantheon' with an undiscriminated plurality of gods, as commonly represented, but rather the belief in one supreme god with whom other divine beings were associated (p.76). This supreme god was indicated by proto-Semitic il(u) which developed to el in Northwest Semitic, ilah in Nabataean (p.83) - and, we may add, allāh in Arabic.

Among Semitic peoples the gods were named after the places where they were worshipped (p. 91). The cult was directed not only to a particular idol but also to a particular altar (Nab. mesgida, p.85). Like the altars, the stones erected for the gods (Nab. baetils, p.87) could themselves become objects of worship. As far as the idols were concerned, Teixidor maintains that in North Arabia in an early period they probably consisted of stones of various forms and that only later - under foreign influence - statues were adopted as representations of the gods (p.73). This corresponds with the statement in later Arabic sources that before Islam the Arabs had changed their original cult of stones for that of statues with the appearance of a person. Teixidor affirms that the image (ṣalm) was believed to be the tutelary numen of a given locality, just as the ginnayē (equated to jinn) were known as supernatural protectors in the Palmyrene region: as tutelary deities of villages, settlements, encampments, tribes and so on (p.75). The ancestral gods stood for the uniqueness or idiosyncrasy of a particular group or tribe (p.162). They were not in conflict with the supreme god; one may point here to the religion of the Hebrews.

At the time when a practical monotheism became manifest and a supreme god - often a weather god to whom heaven belonged - was held to retain all power in the last centuries of the first millennium B.C., myths must have lost their relevance. This corresponds with the fact that hardly any mythology is known to us from the Arabian peninsula, except for the South in an earlier period.

Of particular interest for the problem of the jinn is Teixidor's study of Palmyra (Teixidor 1979). After discussing the cult of the supreme god, the sun and the moon, and Allat (al-Ilāt) as the female deity of heaven whose temple in Palmyra must have been the cultic centre of North Arabian tribes in the region (Drijvers 1976), the author treats the ginnayē (gny') which he sees as Arab gods with the function of tutelary deities (Ch.IV). These ginnayē were comparable to the Roman genii: they were deities who were tutelaries of persons and places, who were believed to manifest themselves as human beings and to take care of human lives and enterprises, and who were frequently invoked in pairs (p.77). They protected flocks and caravans, and also those who had settled or were in process of sedentarisation (p.78). Shrines erected for such ginnayē occur especially in the semi-nomadic surroundings of Palmyra in places which were centres of settled life and halts for passing caravans. Teixidor holds the ginnayē to be '... a specific class of divine beings whose function was to be guardians, a task that fully equates them to the Judeo-Christian angels' (p.89). Their Aramaic equivalent were the gad (8). One might conclude that the ginnayē were venerated but not on the same level as the ancestral gods, let alone the supreme god.

These data from Northern Arabia and in particular the Palmyran scene undoubtedly shed new light on the problem of the relations between Allah, the deities and the jinn in Central and especially West Arabia. Even if the conclusion is not warranted that before Muhammad's activities jinn were venerated as full deities in Mecca - in Palmyra they are considered by Teixidor sometimes as deities, sometimes as equivalent to angels -, they should be seen at least as angelic beings, most probably with a tutelary function. In any case the jinn were at the time much closer to Allah's divine 'associates' than later Islamic tradition was willing and able to admit.

Another inference to be drawn from the Palmyrene data is that there may be structural parallels between the rise of a pantheon in Northern trade centres like Palmyra on the one hand and in a commercial town like Mecca on the other. All commercial centres attracted Beduin to settle, and as a consequence the Beduin's religion would encounter the religion of the townspeople, which could take Hellenistic forms. So jinn and deities could come together, being as they were both under the authority of the supreme god. In the urban context the cult of the supreme deity with his associates would proliferate, with tutelary spiritual beings taking care of the daily needs of the people. Under Hellenistic influence stone idols were transformed into statues.

A third conclusion equally confirms what we said earlier. For more than a thousand years before the rise of Islam a latent 'Semitic' monotheism had affirmed itself in the Near East. This monotheism could, however, take various forms in connection with ancestral gods and should not be supposed to exhibit one homogeneous structure at all times and places; its variations and different forms should be studied in detail. All available evidence contests the idea '.. that monotheism is an exclusive patrimony of the Judeo-Christian tradition' (pp.156), though within this tradition it has been represented apologetically in this way.

This and other parallel developments in the Northern, Central and also Southern Arabian region in different periods between 1000 B.C. and 1000A.D. need to be studied in teamwork by historians of religion of the Near East. Finally it was to be the Islamic stamp which for a long time to come would mark the definite 'monotheisation' of the Near East, though some other earlier forms of monotheism were to survive until the present day.

3 A NEW ORDERING OF THE SPIRITUAL BEINGS IN THE KORAN

What does the Koran say about classes of spiritual beings and their mutual relations ?

a Allāh

The revelations received by Muhammad proclaim Allah to

be the sole and supreme god, omnipotent over his creation both in its present contingent existence and at the Day of Judgment. Not only the unbelievers but also the deities, jinn and shayṭāns will be judged (S. 26:94/5).

In terms of the overall process which we described in the first sections, Allah appropriates the attributes of the other deities as his 'beautiful names'. This not only puts an end to the association of companions with him, but it also stops the presumed rise of chthonic powers to the heavenly spheres where they might acquire divine knowledge or even become deities themselves. Heaven and earth as well as the world beneath are now kept separate from each other, except for initiatives which Allah is thought to take in his communicating directives to mankind through prophets, and in his providential steering of the universe either directly or through his angels. These new views are articulated in the Koran with the help of elements which were derived mainly from existing Arabian, Jewish and Christian traditions, but which gain a fresh significance derived from the new views.

Numerous scholars (9) have stressed the essentially 'Arabian' character of the deity Allah proclaimed in the Koran. Some scholars (10) have drawn attention to striking parallels between the Allah described in the Koran and the Jahweh described in the Old Testament. Allah is a god of struggle and combat, and he has the qualities of a leader and general. His care for his believers is expressed in terms of the care which a patriarch takes of his kin. His power on the one hand and his benevolence on the other are stressed in his maintenance of justice. There are no names and attributes suggesting pluriformity of the divine or 'polytheism' (shirk) and he is held to be essentially one and unique. He has certain astral features and can manifest himself through natural phenomena.

Consequently, Islam as proclaimed by Muhammad is much more in line with nomadic and perhaps general Semitic religious feeling than the religious institutions of the Quraysh in Mecca. It has been correctly observed by J. Chelhod that, when attacking the mushrikūn, the Koran attacks less paganism and polytheism as such than what may be called the 'deviationism' of the Meccans (Chelhod 1964, 111). In others words, Muhammad's work was largely that of a reformer working in an urban context with references to basic religious notions which dated from before the establishment of towns, while discarding or at least reinterpreting all religious notions which had appeared in the meantime. This corresponds with T.Fahd's thesis that Allah had always remained the common denominator of all deities venerated by the Arabs and that Allah was an appellatif, rather than one deity beside the others. It was the deviant believers or mushrikūn who had substituted for the cult of the supreme god particular cults of his names and attributes as independent entities, as 'daughters of Allah' or as other deities. In fact, the rapid acceptance of the seemingly 'new' Islamic religion by the Arabs and its further acceptance - after the Arab conquest - throughout the Middle East, become somewhat easier to understand if we accept not only that those participating in the Islamic venture had common political and economic interests, but also that there was nothing strange or new in calling on a primordial deity who was basically known to all and in whose name Arabs - by becoming Muslims - could unite. Muhammad himself, moreover, was the first to stress the continuity between the Urreligion of Adam, the revelations of the prophets, and Islam.

b the jinn

How, further, are the jinn described in the Koran ? The

word itself only occurs in the Meccan revelations, and here the existence of the jinn is unambiguously affirmed. The jinn were created by Allah (S.15:27, 55:15). Both jinn and human beings were created to worship Allah (S. 51:56); messengers from Allah had been chosen among both the jinn and mankind to convey to their fellow beings Allah's revelation (S. 6:130), and this happened from generation to generation (S. 7:38,etc.). Like human beings, jinn too were converted on hearing sūras of the Koran (S. 72:1-3, 46:29-32). In fact, there is a striking parallelism between human beings on the one hand and jinn on the other, the two categories of creation being called together al-thaqalānī, probably meaning 'the two weighty ones' (S.55:31). Both categories have the same kind of social organization and both consist of 'believers' and 'unbelievers' in the message of the Koran. Idolatry consists in putting on the same level the great works of Allah and those of the jinn and shayāṭīn, who have superhuman powers but can only be considered as companions or kin of Allah by unbelievers.

It is clear that Muhammad shares the belief in jinn current in his time; Sūra 72 (of the second Meccan period) is even called after them. Beside the word jinn, jānn occurs, for instance in S. 15:27 and in S. 55:14,39,56,74; it also occurs in S. 27:10 and 28:31 in connection with Moses'staff in the presence of Pharaoh. S. 27:39 mentions 'one of the jinn, an ᶜifrīt'. According to the Koran, the jinn can harm human beings, are uncontrollable, have seductive powers just like human beings (S.114:6). They can occur in the form of a snake (the jānn of Moses; it has been suggested that Muhammad would have considered all snakes as potential jinn (11)); they possess supernatural powers and capacities. These views of the jinn were already in existence, but there are some new elements which cannot have been derived from ancient Arab beliefs and which Muhammad cannot have thought out himself.

Jinn want to listen at the gate of heaven in order to acquire supernatural knowledge and the angels expel them, once the Koran has been revealed, with stones or stars (S. 72:8/9; perhaps falling stars ?). Some of the *jinn* served Solomon who had power over the *jinn* (S. 34:12-14 and 27:38-44). The *jinn* were created from smokeless flame (S. 55:14); some of them are converted, the others will be judged at the Last Day. These particular views must have been derived from Jewish and perhaps also Christian demonology of a popular kind.

More important, however, than such elements considered in themselves, is the total view of the *jinn* developed in the Koran, or rather the two successive views by which the *jinn* are first 'de-demonized' and later 're-demonized'.(12). The earliest preaching of Muhammad affirms that *jinn* have no power of their own, as had generally been believed. Muhammad proclaims that *jinn* have been created like men and should serve and worship Allah; they too have had prophets (S.6:130) and the Koran is also meant for them (S.46:29-32 and 72:1/2). Muhammad preaches to both men and *jinn* (S. 55:33,39) who constitute together *al-thaqalānī*. *Jinn*, consequently, are a group parallel to mankind, they can convert, they will be judged at the Last Day as they were judged in the past (S.46:18). Most important, perhaps, they no longer dispose of special supernatural knowledge. Whereas before they could listen at the gate of heaven and communicate the special knowledge which they had acquired in this way to *kāhins* and *shā^{c}irs*, they are now expelled by the angels (S. 72:8/9, etc.). In other words, people can believe in *jinn* but should not worship them, should not seek aid of them, and should not seek special knowledge from them.

The jinn have been radically 'de-demonized' through being proclaimed creatures of Allah, but we shall see shortly that they are subsequently 're-demonized' through being largely identified with the shayāṭīn. First they could move between earth and heaven; then they became a species parallel to mankind; finally they almost become demons or shayāṭīn themselves, and the distinction between believing and unbelieving jinn disappears. As J. Chelhod formulates it nicely: '...ils oscillent en effet entre les hommes et les démons qui finissent pourtant par les absorber' (Chelhod 1964, 85). In Medina there is no longer mention of jinn, only of Iblīs and his shayāṭīn. In order to appreciate fully, however, the dimensions of the jinn within the world of spiritual beings as the Koran describes them, we should consider first the way in which the Koran views the other spiritual beings: the deities, the angels and the demons.

c the deities

The fact that Allah was proclaimed the sole deity in the revelation to Muhammad implied that no spiritual companions (shurakā') could be associated with him, and that the existing concept of God should be purified. The Koran does not deny the existence of such beings but declares them to be angels only, just as it denounces any association of the jinn with Allah. It is only in later Islam that these deities, including the 'daughters of Allah', are degraded to jinn and shayāṭīn. In the Koran their divine quality is simply denied and their cult forbidden.

d the angels

Parallel to the downgrading of the deities there is an upgrading of the angels who can now no longer be considered as jinn-like beings as they were before Muhammad. The angels, living according to the will of Allah and ever being in his presence, are distinguished by their inherent goodness from men and jinn, who can be good or bad, and are subject to moral judgment and, of course, must face the Last Judgement. Among the angels only Hārut and Mārut (S. 2:102), because of their action in Babel, are bad; this is an incidental borrowing from Jewish tradition. The fundamental mistake of the unbelievers is that they consider the angels, who are only servants of Allah, as 'female beings', i.e. as 'daughters of Allah' (S.43:19 and 53:27). It is interesting to see that in the Koran angels and jinn are radically distinct categories of beings. Nowhere are angels and jinn mentioned together, and jinn are nowhere considered as angels. On the contrary, the angels are essentially adversaries of the shayāṭīn and the evil jinn. We can see the occurrence of a fundamental polarization of the 'intermediaries' at this stage in the Koran. In earlier times, the frontiers were more fluid and there was no radical opposition between good and bad as identified with particular classes of beings.

The angels, then, were created out of light in order to restore order again (iṣlāḥ) in the works of Allah and to inhabit his heavens. They have a variety of tasks. As far as the demons (shayāṭīn and evil jinn) are concerned, they must suppress their revolts and guard the gates of heaven against their curiosity and possible attack. As far as mankind is concerned, the angels are the messengers of Allah to the prophets (S.53:1). They appeal to men to obey Allah's commands, they protect the believers and support them in their struggle against Iblīs and the *shayāṭīn* who want to deflect them from the straight path. As for the universe, the creation of Allah, they supervise and direct its movements. A distinction among the angels is already made in the Koran, when it is said that *al-ḥafaẓa* (S. 6:61) or *al-ḥafiẓ* (S.86:4 and 82:10) keep the record of man's actions, or that *al-mu^{c}aqqibāt* take care of man (S.13:11). In the early Meccan period Iblīs is considered a degraded or fallen angel, not a *jinnī* as in later revelations.

e the demons and *Iblīs*

The existence of demons, like that of *jinn* and angels, is positively affirmed in the Koran. Significantly, the word *shayāṭīn* is used synonymously with *jinn* in a number of cases, referring for instance to the servants of Solomon, the listeners at the gate of heaven, the abducers of human beings. The deities of the unbelievers are sometimes considered to be in fact *shayāṭīn* (S.2:14, and 4:76,177,199/20, etc.), just as they are elsewhere seen as *jinn* (S. 6:100 and 34:41). The status of the *shayāṭīn* in the Koran is, however, closely connected with the position of Iblīs.

According to S.15: 28-42, Iblīs was the only angel who refused to bow down before Adam, in disobedience to Allah's command,presumably because Adam had been created out of lowlier matter (clay) than the angels who had been created out of light. As a result, Iblīs has become man's rival, and even enemy, because man is the privileged creature of Allah. Iblīs, however, cannot oppose Allah but acts within his plans. Later texts say that Iblīs was not an angel originally but a *jinnī* (S.18:50); he was created out of fire (S.7:12). What is important, however, is the fact that Iblīs' disobedience to Allah's command made him the supreme *shaytān,* with an enormous descendence of male and female *shayāṭīn* who are at his service, together with those jinn who disobey Allah's commands and so become shayāṭīn too .

Consequently, the good order of creation is constantly threatened by the actions of Iblīs and his shayāṭīn, which are however checked by the angels. The greatest seduction shayāṭīn can achieve is to have themselves be worshipped as gods. The unbelievers'deities are called the work of shayṭān (S.4:117,119-120, etc.), or even considered to be shayāṭīn themselves (S. 2:41). There are armies of shayāṭīn. Shayāṭīn can perform superhuman deeds like the jinn. They are intensely ugly. Shayāṭīn are at work both among jinn and among mankind as seducers (S.6:112,comp. 41:2). Evil as such is identical with a personified shayṭān (S.34:20-21, 2:34-36, 20:115-120). Shayṭān in the Qur'ān is called mārid ('rebellious'); the same is said of the shayāṭīn (S.37:8-9, 15:16-18). Moreover, the latter transmit lies to the poets (S.26:210, 221,223-224; 6:121).

In this connection the question has been raised as to the difference between evil jinn and shayāṭīn, and why both words occur in the Meccan periods. E. Zbinden (1953, p.88) takes it that the expression 'jinn' is an Arabic concept arising out of ancient Arabian religious beliefs, while the word shayṭān was introduced and used as a loanword for demon. Muhammad would have identified disobedient, unbelieving and demonic jinn with shayāṭīn and vice versa. T.Fahd (1971, p.186) also thinks that the use of both shayāṭīn and jinn would result from super-imposing one demonology on another, each of a different origin, from ancient Arabia and the Jewish-Christian tradition respectively. Once shayāṭīn had been accepted as designating evil beings or demons, and once Muhammad had started to ascribe all evil actions directed against the cause of Islam to Iblīs and his shayāṭīn, he tended to denounce the *shayāṭīn* on all occasions, assuming that, apart from some believers, the *jinn* were evil spirits identical to the *shayāṭīn*. This is what we have called the later 're-demonization' of the *jinn* by Muhammad. The absence of the word *jinn* in the Medinan period can probably best be explained by the identification of *jinn* with *shayāṭīn* and the dropping of the first, still ambiguous term in favor of the second, unambiguous one. The polarization of spiritual beings has thereby been accomplished, with Allah and the angels on the good side, Iblīs and his *shayāṭīn* on the bad side. As we have said, however, Iblīs is not the 'enemy' of Allah, as would be the case in a dualistic system; he acts within Allah's plans.

Whereas a *shayṭān* in earlier times was simply a source of inspiration for *kāhins* and *shāʿirs*, in Islam he became a demon and was made subordinate to Iblīs. After the condemnation of Iblīs, this fallen angel (or *jinnī*) became the protagonist of the evil forces confronting mankind. Both *jinn* and *shayāṭīn* are confounded in a synthesis of the Arabian and the Judeo-Christian concept: whereas Iblīs had been an angel, Muhammad makes a *jinnī* of him. The spiritual beings, probably under Judeo-Christian influences, are now clearly distinguished from one another: the angels, as messengers of heaven, aid mankind, whereas the *jinn* and *shayāṭīn*, messengers of Iblīs, attack mankind.

Even though all divine power comes to be concentrated in Allah as a result of Muhammad's preaching, two interesting points are to be noted. In the first place, particular actions and in part even the ultimate destiny of man come to depend on intermediary forces which remain indispensable and even decisive for the affairs of the world. In the second place, it is not between God and Satan but in the world of intermediary beings that a polarization has taken place between the forces of good and evil, of pure and impure, as the two poles of the sacred.

4 SPIRITUAL BEINGS AND THE DOCTRINE OF REVELATION

The changes in the spiritual beings' classification and rank proclaimed in the prophet's qur'āns are related to changes which took place on earth during and in the nature of Muhammad's activity, and they would have important practical consequences. For instance, his 're-demonization' of the jinn and unmasking of the frightful forces of the shayāṭīn is not unconnected with his own claim to be inspired by an angel who passes on messages from Allah. This claim is related again to the reproach addressed to Muhammad by his Meccan enemies that he was merely a man, perhaps a poet (shā^{c}ir), possessed by a jinnī (S.81:22 and 37:36). In fact, Muhammad's appearance challenged traditional concepts of inspiration which were current in Mecca, and his preaching legitimated itself through a new doctrine of inspiration which traced its source not to jinn but to Allah by way of an angel.

In ancient Arabia the true order of things, including the order of the universe, could be communicated in different ways (Chelhod 1964,113). It could be communicated by a 'hêros civilisateur' or an 'ancêtre éponyme' in ancient, indeed mythical times. It could also be communicated in the present by a jinnī or shayṭān who served as a messenger from heaven. Or it could be communicated through prophetical revelation to some chosen people. For the ancient Arabs the lower spiritual beings like jinn and shayāṭīn took care of communicating to mankind the rules for the social order and the universe through the medium of poets and kāhins who had extended divinatory activities. Muhammad, however, and subsequently Islam only recognized communication through prophetical revelation as valid and rejected any inspiration by heavenly forces lower than angels. This stand brought about the claim of a near infallibility of Muhammad both as a prophet and as a statesman, and it degraded all claims of rival pretenders, poets and kāhins as the work of demons, shayāṭīn. Where the kahin was supposed to be inspired by a jinnī, Muhammad interpreted this in malam partem, equating the jinnī with a shayṭān, just as the poet too in the Koran is said to be inspired by a shayṭān.

For his part, Muhammad claims to be a prophet who has received his qur'āns not from a jinnī but from the 'Spirit of Holiness' (rūḥ al-qudus, S.16:10); over and against this, S.26:220-226 gives a pitiless verdict on the demonic origin of poetic inspiration. In short, Muhammad's claim to prophethood at the same time appropriates all 'supernatural' knowledge, degrades any other inspiration - religious or otherwise - and presupposes a particular view of spiritual beings in the widest sense of the word. At the beginning of Muhammad's career, the jinn were held to be Allah's creatures, accepting or rejecting the prophet's message. But when Muhammad's legitimacy is at stake and he is reproached with being inspired by a jinnī, the jinn are demonized and their works are practically identified with those of the shayāṭīn. T. Fahd correctly observes how rudimentary the angelology and demonology of early Islam were and how anthropomorphic the thinking about the spiritual beings was. The doctrine of revelation in Islam carries the traces of it: 'La conception de l'inspiration et de la révélation s'en est inexorablement ressentie' (Fahd 1966, 75/6).

We may conclude that more knowledge of the belief in spiritual beings and intermediaries current before and during Muhammad's lifetime and of Muhammad's own views about them and their mutual relations is needed in order to understand what Muhammad and his contemporaries, adherents and enemies, considered to be 'revelation'. This is all the more important, since in Islam prophecy and revelation are identified with each other, on the basis of the assumptions just mentioned. According to the Koran, the *nabī* and the *kāhin* are diametrically opposed to each other. Whereas the prophet is devoted to the supreme god and represents monotheism, the diviner serves lower deities and evil spirits and represents polytheism, *ishrāk*. T.Fahd adds that the whole *sunna* literature is at one in giving a negative judgement on the value of messages transmitted by *jinn* and *shayāṭīn*. There is no longer any religious knowledge to be obtained in the ancient way once Muhammad has appeared: *lā kihāna ba^{c}d nubuwwa*. And he observes in conclusion that Muhammad as a *nabī* could not cultivate personal relations with the god whom he proclaimed. In his claim to be inspired by an intermediary angel, Gabriel, he remained tributary to the restrictive concept of revelation existing in Arabia in his lifetime (13).

The new order imposed on the spiritual beings in the Koranic view thus had direct consequences for the historical role of the prophet himself. It had consequences for the history of the early Muslim community as well. Muhammad's experience with his enemies in the late Meccan and early Medinan period must have sharpened his awareness of the workings of *shayāṭīn*. The victory at Badr ascribed to the assistance of angels, the building of the Medinan community and state under the guidance of prophecy, the institutionalization of the new *dīn*, and the *jihād* for the sake of Allah, may all have enhanced the community's awareness of Allah's support for his prophet and his community. This support was effected by means of heavenly intermediaries which at the time were considered to mix freely with human beings.

NOTES

1. 'Djinn, according to the Muslim conception bodies (adjsām) composed of vapour or flame, intelligent, imperceptible to our senses, capable of appearing under different forms and of carrying out heavy labours (al-Baydāwī, Tafsīr, S. 72:1; al-Damīrī, Ḥayawān, s.v. djinn)'. In: The Encyclopaedia of Islam, new edition, vol. II, London: Luzac & Co.; Leiden: E.J. Brill, 1965 p. 546-547. The word is a plural indicating a collective; the singular is djinnī, fem. djinnīya The form djānn is also used as the equivalent of the form djinn, sometimes also used for the singular. Compare J. Henninger, 1963 p. 309-311; A.J. Wensinck, 1920 ; E. Zbinden ,1953 p. 79-80.

2. For the interpretation of Allāh as a high god, and as the town god of Mecca, see W.M. Watt, 1970 and 1981 .

3. Smith, W.R., 1927/1969 p. 126-139, with notes by S.A. Cook on p. 538-541. A refutation of this theory was given, for instance, by Westermarck, E., 1899 p. 264-268.

4. Chelhod, J., 1964 p. 79 N.1 refers to page 42 of vol. 5 of Jawād ᶜAlī's Tārīkh al-ᶜarab qabl al-islām without indicating or discussing Jawād Alī's source.

5. We are grateful to our colleague Prof. H.J.W. Drijvers, of the university of Groningen, for having drawn our attention to North Arabian materials and for having given relevant bibliographical data.

6. Lammens, H., 1926 p. 63 and 69, quoted by Starcky (Seyrig, H. et Starcky, J., 1949) p. 256.

7. Albright, W.F., quoted by Starcky (Seyrig, H. et Starcky, J., 1949) p. 256 .

8. Compare the ancient Arabian jadd or tribal god mentioned at the beginning of this paper.

9. See the literature mentioned by Henninger, J., 1959b p. 134 and in note 79 of his study. Compare Chelhod, J., 1964 p. 105.

10. For instance Chelhod, J., 1964 p. 105-106.

11. Zbinden, E., 1953 p. 93, with a reference to some ḥadīths (al-Bukhārī 59:14; Muslim 39:139-141).

12. Zbinden, E., 1953 p. 85 and 88-89 respectively. Compare Chelhod, J., 1964 p. 83-84.

13. Fahd, T., 1966 p. 522: 'Ces intermédiaires occupent une place dominante dans la divination arabe... La conception de l'inspiration prophétique dans l'Islam primitif en est

fortement imprégnée, puisque le Prophète arabe n'a pas réussi à avoir des relation directes et personnelles avec Allāh.'

BIBLIOGRAPHY

Albright, W.F., 1940: Islam and the religions of the ancient Orient. In: Journal of the American society, 60 p. 283-301.

Chelhod, J., 1958: Introduction à la sociologie de l'Islam: De l'animisme à l'universalisme. (Islam d'hier et d'aujourd'hui, XII), Paris: Maisonneuve, G.P., Besson-Chantemerle.

Chelhod, J., 1964: Les structures du sacré chez les Arabes (Islam d'hier et d'aujourd'hui, XIII), Paris: Maisonneuve, G.P., et Larose.

Drijvers, H.J.W., 1976: Das Heiligtum der arabischen Göttin Allât im westlichen Stadtteil von Palmyra. In: Antike Welt, VII p. 28-38.

Eichler, P.A., 1928: Die Dschinn, Teufel und Engel im Koran. Inaugural-Dissertation, Leipzig.

Fahd, T., 1966: La divination arabe: Etudes religieuses, sociologiques et folkloriques sur le milieu natif de l'Islam, Leiden: E.J. Brill.

Fahd, T., 1968: Le panthéon de l'Arabie centrale à la veille de l'hégire. (Institut français d'Archéologie de Beyrouth, bibliothèque archéologique et historique, T. 88), Paris: P. Geuthner.

Fahd, T., 1971: Anges, démons et djinns en Islam. In: Génies, anges et démons (sources orientales, VIII), Paris: Seuil.

Goldziher, I., 1891: Die Ǧinnen der Dichter. In: Zeitschrift der Deutschen Morgenländischen Gesellschaft, 45 p. 685-690.

Henninger, J.,1959a: La société bédouine ancienne. In: L'antica società beduina... Studi ... raccolti da Francesco Gabrieli. (Università di Roma, Centro di Studi Semitici; Studi Semitici 2), Roma: Centro di Studi Semitici, Istituto di Studi Orientali, Università p. 69-93.

Henninger, J., 1959b: La religion bédouine préislamique. In: the same p. 115-140. Also in the author's Arabia Sacra, 1981 p. 11-33.

Henninger, J., 1963: Geisterglaube bei den vorislamischen Arabern. In: Festschrift Paul Schebesta zum 75. Geburtstag....(Studia Instituti Anthropos, 18), Wien/Mödling: St. Gabriel-Verlag p. 279-316. Also in the author's Arabia Sacra, 1981 p. 118-169.

Henninger, J., 1968: Über Lebensraum und Lebensformen der Frühsemiten (Arbeitsgemeinschaft für Forschung des Landes Nordrhein-Westfalen, Geisteswissenschaften, Heft 151), Köln/Opladen: Westdeutscher Verlag.

Henninger, J., 1969: Zum frühsemitischen Nomadentum. In: Viehwirtschaft und Hirtenkultur (Studia Ethnographica 3), Budapest: Akadémiai Kiadó p. 33-68.

Henninger, J., 1981: Arabia Sacra. Aufsätze zur Religionsgeschichte Arabiens und seiner Randgebiete (Contributions à l'histoire religieuse de l'Arabie et de ses régions limitrophes). (Orbis biblicus et orientalis 40), Freiburg, Schweiz: Universitätsverlag; Göttingen: Vandenhoeck & Ruprecht. See in particular (besides 1959b and 1963): 'Über religiöse Strukturen nomadischer Gruppen' p. 34-57, and 'Einiges über Ahnenkult bei arabischen Beduinen' p. 170-188.

Höfner, M., 1970: Die vorislamischen Religionen Arabiens. In: Die Religionen Altsyriens, Altarabiens und der Mandäer, von Hartmut Gese, Maria Höfner, Kurt Rudolph. (Religionen der Menschheit 10, 2), Stuttgart, etc.: W. Kohlhammer p. 233-402.

Lammens, H., 1926: Les sanctuaires préislamites dans l'Arabie occidentale. In: Mélanges de l'université Saint-Joseph, XI p. 39-173.

Macdonald, D.B. c.s., 1965: Djinn. In: The Encyclopaedia of Islam, new edition, vol. II, Leiden: E.J. Brill; London: Luzac & Co., II p. 546-550.

Schlumberger, D., 1970-1971: Le prétendu dieu Gennéas. In: Mélanges de l'université Saint-Joseph, 46 p. 209:222.

Seyrig, H. and Starcky, J., 1949: Gennéas. In: Syria, 26 p. 231-257. The part written by Jean Starcky has the title: 'B:-L'inscription' p. 248-257.

Smith, W.R., 1927/1969: Lectures on the religion of the Semites: The fundamental institutions (first published 1927), third edition, with an introduction and additional notes by Stanley A. Cook. Prolegomenon by Muilenberg, J. (The library of biblical studies), New York: Ktav, 1969.

Teixidor, J., 1977: The Pagan god: Popular religion in the Greco-Roman Near East, Princeton: Princeton University Press.

Teixidor, J., 1979: The pantheon of Palmyra, (E.P.R.O.E.R.,79), Leiden: E.J. Brill.

Watt, W.M., 1970: Belief in a 'High God' in pre-Islamic Mecca. In: Actes , 5th congress of the union européenne d'Arabisants et d'Islamisants, Brussel; p. 499-505.

Watt, W.M., 1981: The Qur'ān and belief in a 'High God'. In: Proceedings, 9th congress of the union européenne d'Arabisants et d'Islamisants, Leiden: E.J. Brill p.327-333.

Wellhausen, J., 1897: Reste Arabischen Heidentums gesammelt und erläutert, zweite Ausgabe, Berlin: Georg Reimer.

Wensinck, A.J., 1920: The etymology of the Arabic Djinn (spirits). In: Verslagen en mededeelingen der Koninklijke akademie, afdeling letterkunde, 5.IV (1920) p. 506-514. Also: Supplementary notes on the etymology of the Arabic Djinn (spirits). In: the same p. 514a-514c.

Westermarck, E., 1899: The nature of the Arab Ǧinn, illustrated by the present beliefs of the people of Morocco. In: The journal of the anthropological institute of Great Britain and Ireland, 29 (New series 2) p. 252-269.

Zbinden, E., 1953: Die Djinn des Islam und der altorientalische Geisterglaube, Bern/Stuttgart: Paul Haupt.

Index